Giving

Rembrandt van Rijn, *Beggars Receiving Alms at the Door of a House.* Reproduced, by permission, from the National Gallery of Art, Washington, Rosenwald Collection

Giving

CHARITY AND PHILANTHROPY IN HISTORY

Robert H. Bremner

With a new afterword by the author

Transaction Publishers
New Brunswick (U.S.A.) and London (U.K.)

Second paperback printing 2000

New material this edition copyright © 1996 by Transaction Publishers, New Brunswick, New Jersey 08903. Copyright © 1994 by Transaction Publishers, New Brunswick, New Jersey 08903.

This book is printed on acid-free paper that meets the American National Standard for Permanence of Paper for Printed Library Materials.

Library of Congress Catalog Number: 93-14165
ISBN: 1-56000-137-2 (cloth); 1-56000-884-9 (paper)
Printed in the United States of America

Library of Congress Cataloging-in-Publication Data

Bremner, Robert Hamlett, 1917-
    Giving : charity and philanthropy in history / Robert H. Bremner.
        p. cm.
    Includes bibliographical references and index.
    ISBN 1-56000-137-2
    1. Charities—History. I. Title.
HV16.B74   1993
361.7'09—dc20   93-14165
                                                            CIP

Contents

Acknowledgments

My chief debt, gratefully acknowledged, is to the authors, dead and alive, whose words I have quoted and stories retold. I wish to thank the National Urban League, Inc. for permission to quote "How Thin a Blanket" by Langston Hughes.

During preparation of the volume Merle Curti, Richard Magat, Thomas R. Buckman, Irving Louis Horowitz, and Paul A. Varg offered encouragement and welcome advice. Frank Annunziata thoughtfully furnished clippings about charity and philanthropy from a wide variety of magazines and newspapers.

Professor Joseph Lynch shared his knowledge of church history and hagiography with me. He and his successor as chair of the Department of History at the Ohio State University, Michael J. Hogan, kindly made office space and secretarial help available. I wish to thank the office staff of the Department of History for cordial assistance. I am also grateful to members of the reference, circulation, and interlibrary loan departments of the Ohio State University Library for services rendered over many years. I am especially appreciative of Stephen W. Rogers's aid in locating hard-to-find materials and helping solve bibliographical problems.

Clayton Roberts, Ann Bremner, and Michael Spicer went out of their way to provide information on the current state of centuries-old English charitable foundations. Sue Bremner made valuable editorial and stylistic suggestions. I am particularly grateful to Maria Mazon for her skill and patience in typing the manuscript, and to Catherine Marting Bremner for unstinting assistance at every stage of the work.

Introduction

Giving, like love, is an element of both charity and philanthropy; love sometimes is left out, but giving is essential. Getting is important, too, but giving comes first. We can scarcely open our mail, answer the telephone, or walk down a city street without encountering opportunities to give. In addition to tangible things, we give — or withhold — love, trust, friendship, encouragement, sympathy, help, and advice. What we give to alleviate the need, suffering, and sorrow of others, whether we know them or not, is charity. What we give to prevent and correct social and environmental problems and improve life and living conditions for people and creatures we don't know and who have no claim on us is philanthropy.

The following pages survey attitudes toward charity and philanthropy in various periods from antiquity to the present. Histories of charity and philanthropy deal with what benevolent individuals and organizations have attempted to do, how they have proceeded, and whether or not their efforts have proved effective. This study, based on literary sources — stories, poems and ballads, scripture and sermons, novels, biographies, essays, and plays — examines and comments on what writers and characters in their works have had to say about giving in general and giving to the poor, beggars, and good causes. The advice and caveats they offer touch on altruism, self-interest, and gentility; they express opinions on religion, politics, social class, tolerance, and censoriousness; among the topics often discussed are sacrifice, pride, display, luxury, work, and laziness. Their testimony is rendered more valuable by the speakers' vehemence, opposing points of view, and frequent disagreements. Their pointed observations help the account avoid bland benignity.

Charity and philanthropy have so much in common (mainly giving) that the words are often used interchangeably. One respect in which they differ is in their degree of interest in the poor. Charity, a religious obligation to followers of Judaism, Christianity, and Islam, has an abiding commitment to relieve the poor, orphans, the friendless, and the homeless. Sympathy for the unfortunate and admonitions to love one's neighbors and coreligionists extend the meaning of charity to kindness to and consideration for others regardless of their need or faith. It is characteristic of charity to give others the benefit of the doubt. Someone who does not suffer fools gladly may be charitable in deed but probably not in thought.

Philanthropy, secular in origin and emphasizing love of man rather than God, has not been as closely involved with the poor as charity. In the seventeenth century *philanthropy* meant a benevolent disposition and humanistic turn of mind. In the eighteenth and nineteenth centuries it became associated with active participation in humanitarian reforms to improve the treatment of prisoners and the insane, abolish slavery, and obtain rights for women and workers. Toward the end of the nineteenth century philanthropy came to mean contributions of money to a variety of causes intended to benefit all classes of society. In recent years philanthropy has allowed government to assume most of the burden and cost of caring for people below the poverty line. Yet even those who believe this to be a necessary and proper state of affairs recognize that philanthropy can help the poor in a number of ways: by innovating and testing new services directed to those most in need, monitoring government programs for fairness and adequacy, acting as advocate for the neglected, and working for the empowerment of the disadvantaged.

Charity and philanthropy have never lacked critics. Charity has been attacked for spawning the poverty it relieves; both charity and philanthropy have been accused of serving the interests of donors rather than those of recipients. Philanthropy's mild method of reform is scorned by stern advocates of fundamental social change; on the other hand, philanthropic reformers' devotion to particular causes makes less dedicated people question their sanity. Bad motives are attributed to good deeds, and hypocrisy is allegedly as rife among practitioners of charity and philanthropy as among clergy and politicians. All of these charges are voiced, and some of them answered, by the authors whose works are discussed in the book. They are as quick to point out self-interest in the guise of altruism as stinginess hiding behind high principles.

Despite the abundance of footnotes, this is not an aggressively scholarly work. It is mainly a book of stories about giving, asking, and, occasionally, getting. Footnotes are used to give the source of material discussed in the text and, from time to time, to supply the reader with further information. The year in which a book was first published and the birth and death dates of authors are included in the text or notes in order to save readers the trouble of looking them up. In the case of classics that have been published in many editions with different pagination, the notes supply the book and chapter number of the passages quoted or discussed. The bibliography contains major works cited in the notes and consulted in preparing the text.

PART ONE

The Ancient World

Prologue: The First Philanthropist

According to Greek mythology mankind's first benefactor was the Titan, Prometheus, who gave fire, previously the exclusive possession of the gods, to mortal man. For this act Zeus condemned Prometheus to be bound to a mountain peak, forever exposed to burning sun and bitter cold. In *Prometheus Bound* by Aeschylus (525–456 B.C.) Prometheus's captors tell him his punishment is the reward of his *philanthropos*. Scholars have offered various translations for the word: philanthropy, man-loving disposition, loving kindness, love of mankind, human charity, fostering mortal man, championing mankind, and helping men.

1

Classical Attitudes toward
Giving and Begging

In *The Odyssey*, which, with *The Iliad*, is the oldest surviving work
of Greek literature, Homer offers glimpses of attitudes toward begging
and giving in the ninth century B.C. These attitudes, like ours today,
were ambivalent. Both Homer and his characters express contempt for
common vagabonds who lie and cheat, and advocate harsh punishment "to teach beggars not to cheat." On the other hand there is
always the possibility that a beggar might be a god or goddess in
disguise, and so it behooves one to show consideration for him or her.

Toward the end of *The Odyssey* the hero, after years of wandering,
returns to his kingdom of Ithaca to find his estate overrun with suitors
seeking his wife's consent to marriage. Odysseus's guardian goddess,
Athena, disguises him as an old tramp to protect him from the suitors
until he can devise a plan to get rid of them. In shabby clothes and
unrecognizably altered in appearance, Odysseus enters the hall where
the suitors are dining. Only his son Telemachus is aware of his identity. At Telemachus's invitation and Athena's command Odysseus begs
food from each of the suitors. All give him something except Antinous,
who berates the swineherd who has sheltered Odysseus for bringing
an unwanted beggar to the city, and throws a stool at the old tramp.
Neither Antinous nor the other suitors know they are being tested;
Athena has had Odysseus beg from the suitors in order to distinguish
the good from the bad by their response to his appeal. Homer informs
us, however, that even as Athena orders the test she has resolved that
all the suitors, good and bad, are to be destroyed.[1]

Response to beggars may reveal character, but there is no agree-

5

ment on what the response should be. Both Antinous and Odysseus (in
different circumstances) resort to violence against a beggar; Antinous
is criticized, Odysseus congratulated by the suitors for having beaten
one in a fight. Antinous chides the other suitors for taking the easy
way by being generous with other people's property. Homer leaves it
unclear whether Antinous's refusal was based on principled opposition to begging or on personal stinginess.[2]

Some people maintain that it takes more character and is better for
all concerned to say no to beggars than to give to them. Hesiod, a
Greek poet who wrote around 700 B.C., was of that opinion. In *Works
and Days* he tells his brother he has given him enough and will give
no more. "Work foolish Perses," he advises, "for this is what the gods
have decreed for men." Don't pester your neighbors or waste time in
envy and idle dreaming. "Work prospers with care: he who postpones
wrestles with ruin."[3] In similar spirit, Plutarch quoted a Spartan who
rebuffed a beggar by saying, "If I should give, you will be the more a
beggar; and for this unseemly conduct of yours he who first gave to
you is responsible, for he thus made you lazy."[4] Andrew Carnegie,
quoting the Spartan in an essay expanding on his Gospel of Wealth,
added, "There are few millionaires, very few indeed, who are clear of
the sin of having made beggars."[5]

On giving in general, as opposed to giving to beggars or the poor,
Hesiod's advice—this time to the "princes" or large landowners of
Boetia, the district of Greece where he lived—was succinct.

> Love those who love you and help those who help you. Give to those who
> give to you, never to those who do not.

As Hesiod saw it, self-interest should be the guiding principle in
both giving and withholding. On self-indulgence he counseled:

> Drink all you want when your jar is full or almost empty. Sparing is good
> at midpoint and useless when the bottom shows.[6]

In these lines, and in the ones quoted earlier, Hesiod voices what
Thorstein Veblen (1859–1929) called "pragmatic knowledge," which
he defined as "didactic exhortations to thrift, prudence, equanimity,
and shrewd management—a body of maxims of expedient conduct."
Veblen believed that in this field of knowledge there had been "scarcely

a degree of advance from Confucius to Samuel Smiles."[7] Hesiod ante-
dated Confucius by several centuries.

Ennius (239–169 B.C.) was the first major epic poet in Latin. Only
fragments of his work survive in quotations by later writers. Cicero
used the following in his *On Moral Obligations*:

> The man who kindly guides a stranger on his way, Lights as it were
> another's lantern from his own nor is his light the less for kindling the
> other.

The moral Cicero drew from the lines was "whatever kindness can be
done without personal loss should be done, even for a stranger."[8]

Cicero (106–43 B.C.), a statesman, orator, and philosopher, wrote
On Moral Obligations in 44 B.C., ostensibly for the instruction of his
son. In discussing generosity he cited three caveats on giving: first, the
gift should not be prejudicial to the recipient or others; second, the gift
should not exceed the donor's means or impoverish his family; and
third, it should be in keeping with the merits of the recipient, taking
into consideration character, relationship, and attitude to and services
to the donor. Of the three caveats the most important was the first; in
discussing it Cicero emphasized the "others" affected by the gift in
addition to the recipient. Among those he had in mind were the rightful owners of estates seized by Sulla and Caesar and transferred to
favorites or political allies. "No action," he declared, "can be at the
same time generous and unjust."[9]

Because helping others by one's own effort and influence involved
work and courage, Cicero deemed it morally superior to gifts of money.
Kindness dependent on the size of one's purse limits the number of
people who can be helped and may dry up the source of generosity.
Conversely, those who help others in nonmonetary ways gain a double
advantage. "The more they help the more allies they will have in their
good works," and the better prepared and fit they will become for
broader service.[10]

Cicero divided money givers into "the prodigal" and "the generous." He deplored the former's lavish expenditures to flaunt their wealth
and win popularity by sponsoring feasts, distribution of food, gladiato-
rial contests, and fights with animals. These attempts to curry favor
with the public had no lasting results and were soon forgotten. "The
generous" gave money to ransom captives or those held by kidnap-

pers, to provide dowries, or to pay off a friend's debts. Generosity for these purposes was appropriate, providing the beneficiaries were deserving and the gifts were made with care and moderation, avoiding "indiscriminate benevolence" and observing "a happy mean, which means taking our circumstances into account."[11] Nothing struck him as more foolish "than being so generous that further generosity becomes impossible."[12]

Cicero was a contemporary of Julius Caesar (100–44 B.C.) and wrote *On Moral Obligation* in the year of Caesar's death. While Cicero was concerned about giving to individuals, Caesar (who Cicero would have counted among "the prodigals") left large legacies for public purposes.[13] According to Plutarch's account of the assassination of Caesar and the events following the reading of his will — written about a century and a half after the events took place — the announcement of Caesar's "liberal legacie of money, bequeathed unto every citizen of ROME" together with the display of his mangled body inflamed the previously indifferent populace against Brutus and his confederates.[14] Shakespeare, who based *The Tragedy of Julius Caesar* on Sir Thomas North's translation of *Plutarch's Lives* (1579), improved on Caesar's generosity. In the funeral oration, Marc Antony tells the crowd that in addition to money

> he hath left you all his walks, his private arbors and new-planted orchards on this side Tiber; he hath left them to you and to your heirs for ever; common pleasure, to walk abroad in and recreate yourselves.[15]

In this instance a prodigal gift had important consequences and, thanks to literature, has not been forgotten.

On Benefits by Seneca the Younger (4 B.C.–A.D. 65), like Cicero's *On Moral Obligations*, was written late in the author's life, probably in the years A.D. 62–64. Born in Spain and educated in Rome, Seneca was a philosopher and dramatist as well as tutor to and minister to Nero in the early years of the latter's reign (A.D. 54–67). He was out of favor with the emperor when he wrote *On Benefits* and, accused of complicity in a plot against Nero, committed suicide shortly after completing the work. Seneca was about one hundred years younger than Cicero; his views on giving were similar to Cicero's but were expressed in a more urbane and worldly way and with less moral earnestness. He stressed the appropriateness of the gift to the giver as well as the receiver — we should not give a larger or a smaller amount than is proper for someone in our station: "Some gifts are too small to come fitingly from the hands of a great man, and some are too large for the other to take." As an example of an inappropriate and inconsiderate gift he cited the proffer by Alexander — "madman that he was and incapable of conceiving any plan that was not grandiose" — of an entire city to a friend unprepared and unwilling to assume the burden that accepting the gift would entail. Seneca scoffed at Alexander's response: "I am concerned, not in what is becoming for you to receive, but in what is becoming for me to give." There is no such thing as a becoming gift in itself; "it all depends upon who gives it and who receives it — the when, wherefore, and where of the gift."[16]

To a friend who complained of having met with ingratitude Seneca replied that the experience was not uncommon and should not make the donor ungenerous or unduly cautious. "In order to discover one grateful person, it is worthwhile to make trial of many ungrateful ones." The very uncertainty of gratitude, Seneca wrote, "may prompt you to become more charitable. For when the outcome of any undertaking is unsure, you must try again and again in order to succeed ultimately."[17]

In "How To Tell A Flatterer from a Friend" Plutarch tells the story of a man who learns that a friend who has fallen ill has also fallen on hard times. Pretending to rearrange his friend's pillow, he slips money under it. In the morning, when a servant finds the money and expresses surprise, the sick man realizes what has happened and chuckles at his friend's cunning. "So, too, I imagine" Plutarch remarks "the gods confer their benefits, for the most part, without our knowledge, since it is their nature to take pleasure in the mere act of being gracious and doing good." While a flatterer acts as if his efforts on your behalf are onerous, gracious and considerate givers try to convey the impression that what they do is no trouble and hardly worth mentioning. When the Spartans were thanked for having sent corn to Smyrna in a time of famine, they said, "It was nothing of any importance; we merely voted that we and our cattle would go without dinner for one day, and collected the amount."[18]

Notes

1. Homer, *The Odyssey*, translated by E.V. Rieu (Baltimore: Penguin Books, 1962), 268 (Book XVII).

2. Ibid., 276–79 (Book XVIII). Odysseus is provoked into a fight with Irun, a beggar notorious for his appetite for food and wine, and nearly kills him.

3. Hesiod, *Works and Days*, translated by Apostolotos Athanassakis (Baltimore: Johns Hopkins University Press, 1983), 77. Irving Babbitt, an early twentieth century literary critic, quotes Hesiod approvingly in *Democracy and Leadership* (Boston and New York: Houghton Mifflin Company, 1924), 205.

4. Plutarch, "Sayings of Spartans," in *Plutarch's Moralia* with an English translation by Frank Cole Babbitt (Cambridge: Harvard University Press, 1969), 3:415. Plutarch (c. A.D. 50–c. A.D. 125) was a Greek essayist and biographer who lived and taught in Rome.

5. Andrew Carnegie, "The Best Fields for Philanthropy," *North American Review* 148 (1889): 686. Carnegie's "Gospel of Wealth" is discussed in Part Five.

6. Hesiod, *Works and Days*, 76.

7. Thorstein Veblen, "The Place of Science in Modern Civilization" (1906) in Perry Miller, ed., *American Thought, Civil War to World War I* (New York: Holt, Rinehart and Winston, 1963), 312. Samuel Smiles (1812–1904) is best remembered as the author of *Self-Help* (1859).

8. Ennius, "Fragment 140," in *Cicero On Moral Obligations [De Officiis]*, translated by John Higginbotham (Berkeley and Los Angeles: University of California Press, 1967), 57 (bk. 1, ch. 16).

9. Ibid., 54–55 (bk. 1, ch. 14).

10. Ibid., 115–19 (bk. 2, ch. 15).

11. Ibid., 120 (bk. 2, ch. 16).

12. Ibid., 119 (bk. 2, ch. 15).

13. These gifts to the public, although generous, did not exhaust Caesar's estate; he left the bulk of his vast fortune to Octavius (later Augustus Caesar) and the rest to two other great-nephews.

14. Plutarch, "The Life of Julius Caesar," in *Plutarch's Lives of the Noble Grecians and Romans Translated by Sir Thomas North* (Boston and New York: Houghton Mifflin Company, 1928), 5:346–47.

15. William Shakespeare, *The Tragedy of Julius Caesar*, act 3, sc. 2. The play was probably produced in 1599 and printed in 1623. For the funeral oration Shakespeare drew on Plutarch's "The Life of Marcus Brutus" in *Plutarch's Lives* 7:127.

16. Seneca the Younger, *De Beneficiis (On Benefits)* bk. 2, par. 15–16, in *Seneca: Moral Essays*, translated by John W. Basore (Cambridge: Harvard University Press, 1935), 1:77–80.

17. Seneca the Younger, Letter LXXXI, "*On Benefits*" in *Seneca: Epistulae Morales*, translated by Richard M. Gummere (Cambridge: Harvard University Press, 1962), 2:219–21.

18. Plutarch, "How to Tell a Flatterer from a Friend," in *Plutarch's Moralia* 1:337–41.

2

Jewish, Christian, and Islamic Texts
on Giving and Charity

What do you give to an all-powerful God? Cain, one of the sons of Adam, was a farmer and made an offering of "the fruits of the soil"; his brother Abel, a shepherd, brought "the firstlings of his flock and of their fat portions." The Lord scorned Cain's gift but was pleased with Abel's.[1] That God preferred meat to vegetables has never seemed an adequate explanation of why Abel's gift was accepted and Cain's rejected. Recent scholars have pointed out that compilers of the Bible idealized the pastoral, as opposed to the agricultural, stage of Israelite life and deemed the nomadic practice of animal sacrifice more honorable than the peasant custom of offering vegetables or fruit.[2] Other interpreters, past and present, shift the emphasis from the nature of the sacrifice to the character of the donors and the spirit in which they made their offerings. Genesis tells us little about Abel but New Testament writers laud him as "righteous" (Matt. 28:35) and declare that his gift was acceptable to God because it was made "in faith" (Heb. 11:4).

The Jewish Bible (Old Testament) abounds with injunctions to give to the poor and to show kindness to all. The passage in Deuteronomy containing the statement "the poor shall never cease out of the land" commands the faithful to open their hands ungrudgingly to the poor, giving or lending them whatever they need, and promises that the Lord will prosper those who do so.[3] One of the Psalms offers assurance that God himself is "gracious, slow to anger, and plentious in mercy"; another declares that the righteousness of one who has given to the poor will endure forever. The prophet Micah states that God does not demand material sacrifices but requires men to do justice,

11

love kindness, and walk humbly with God.[5] The sayings and writings
of Simeon the Just (fourth century B.C.), one of the fathers of the
Jewish church, emphasize kindness, veneration of the Torah, and faith-
fulness in worship as the three bases of the world.[6]

In the first book of the Christian Bible (New Testament) Jesus (c. 7
B.C.–A.D. 30) tells his disciples, "Give to him who asks you" and "do
not turn away" from him who wants to borrow from you. "When you
do a charitable deed do not sound a trumpet before you."[7] Jesus adhered to the Jewish belief in the duty and rewards of charity, but He
taught that it should be practiced quietly, without ostentatious display
of wealth or piety. It was not the method but the extent of giving Jesus
demanded of his followers that was radical. Instead of "Give what you
can spare" Jesus said "Give all you have." When a rich and pious
young man who had observed all the commandments asked what more
he must do to win salvation, Jesus told him to sell all his possessions
and give the proceeds to the poor. The young man, presumably thinking of his own and his family's security and well-being, went away
"sorrowful, for he had great possessions."[8]

Because of the young man's wealth the poor would have been well
served if Jesus had asked him only to give generously. Instead, Jesus
tested the young man's commitment to the way of life he and his
disciples espoused. Both goal and norm of that way of life were to
share the hardships of, sympathize with, and actively assist the most
miserable and neglected of the needy. Identifying oneself with "the
least of these" (Matt. 25:40) was an inescapable part of the abnegation
of personal interest and selfless love of God, mankind, neighbor, and
even enemy, that Christ's life exemplified. The young man's unreadi-
ness to embrace such a demanding course caused Jesus to wonder
whether the rich, saddled with mundane cares, could ever enter the
Kingdom of Heaven.[9]

Jesus related the parable of the Good Samaritan to answer the question "Who is my neighbor?" The story, often retold in fiction and
depicted in paintings, contrasts the mercy of the Samaritan who puts
himself to trouble and expense to help a wounded stranger with the
indifference of a priest and a Levite who "passed by on the other
side."[10] Another parable, Dives and Lazarus, contrasts the fortunes in
life and death of "a certain rich man," Dives, and the beggar, Lazarus,
yearning for crumbs from his table.[11] Writers like Henry George, who
share Jesus' animus toward wealth and regard for the poor, have cited

the parable to draw attention to the juxtaposition of luxury and want in modern society. On the other hand, the nineteenth century British traveler, Richard Burton, thought it unfair to send Dives to hell merely because he had enjoyed a very modified version of heaven in this life. "If a rich man can hardly enter the kingdom," Burton objected, "What must it be with a poor man whose conditions are far more unfavorable." Instead of preaching and praising "Holy Poverty" we should recognize that "poverty is the root of all evils and the more so as it curtails man's powers of benefitting others."[12]

Jesus measured generosity not by the size of the gift but by the sacrifice it caused the donor. Two coppers put in the treasury by a poor widow were of more significance in His eyes than the magnificent contributions of the rich because they gave out of their abundance, she out of her very subsistence.[13]

It sometimes happens that a person impoverishes himself (more often his estate) by lavish gifts to the poor or the public for spite, whim, self-interest or other reasons having nothing to do with love of God or neighbors. St. Paul, the first great missionary of the Christian faith, may have foreseen such philanthropy when he warned the Christians of Corinth, "Though I bestow all my good to feed the poor . . . and have not love it profiteth me nothing."[14] Of course the gift may benefit the poor or whoever else receives it. As a result of the linkage of charity and love in Christian thought, the motivation of the donor is subject to such intense scrutiny that the equally important and no less debatable issue of the effect of the gift on the recipient is overlooked.

After Jesus' death two of his disciples, Peter and John, entered the temple in Jerusalem just as a man, lame from birth, was being laid at the gate to beg of those who entered. When he asked the disciples for alms, Peter, instead of giving him a coin, miraculously healed his limbs. "And he, leaping up, stood, and walked, and entered with them into the temple, walking and leaping, and praising God."[15] We do not know the sequel. His joy may have been short-lived if he found "honest work" hard to get or less rewarding than begging. In literature, as in popular stereotypes, there are beggars who dread being healed because their infirmities are the source of their livelihood.[16]

In the fourth century a young Roman soldier, receiving instruction in Christianity but not yet baptized, gave half of his cloak to a shivering beggar. The following night Jesus, wearing the half of the cloak given the beggar, appeared to the soldier in a dream, saying, "Martin, yet a catuchmen, has clothed me with this cloak."[17] As soon as possible, Martin (c. 316–397) left the army and joined the church. In 372 he became Bishop of Tours, France. St. Martin is reputed to have worked many miracles and was one of the first persons not a martyr to be venerated as a saint. His youthful act of charity in sharing what little he had with someone less fortunate has been a favorite subject of artists.[18] In some countries the sunny days that sometimes occur in the middle of November are celebrated as St. Martin's summer.

St. Basil the Great (329–79), a younger contemporary of St. Martin, distinguished between charity to the needy poor and casual giving to beggars. Basil, bishop of Caesarea in present-day Turkey and one of the fathers of the Greek Church, founded a hospice in Caesarea for the shelter of travelers and the care of children, the sick, and the aged. He chided the rich for neglect of the poor but also advocated systematic administration and investigation in distribution of relief. In a letter cited approvingly by charity reformers in the nineteenth century he wrote that those who give to the afflicted and people "truly in need" give to the Lord and will be rewarded, whereas one who gives to every wanderer "casts it to a dog, that is troublesome on account of his shamelessness, but not pitiable because of his need."[19]

St. Augustine (354–430), like St. Basil, was a rich and worldly young man who renounced earthly pleasures and possessions for the Christian ascetic ideal. In addition to being a great theologian whose writings profoundly influenced Church doctrines, he was a conscientious parish priest and bishop of Hippo in what is now Algeria. F. Van Der Meer, writing of Augustine's priestly career, notes that "he always has a good word for tramps." One day Augustine closed his sermon — and drew applause from the congregation — by saying that he was asking for alms because on the way to church he met some poor people who urged him to speak on their behalf. We clergy do what we can for them, he told the worshippers, but our means are limited. You must make us your emissaries.[20]

Augustine asserted that "it is only charity that distinguishes the children of God from those of the devil."[21] Yet even in Augustine's day it was impossible for the best intentioned person to do good to all those in need. In *On Christian Doctrine*, written in 397, Augustine proposed a solution: suppose you have an object to give away that can only be given to one person; if two or more people present themselves, none of whom has a greater need than the others and none a greater claim on you, the fairest way to make a choice between them would be by lot. "Just so among men," he concluded, "since you cannot consult for the good of them all you must take the matter as decided for you by a sort of lot according to each man happens to be more closely connected with you."[22]

Among those "more closely connected with you," St. Augustine would probably counsel the giver to choose the neediest. That is the way of charity. Modern philanthropy tends to favor the most promising.

Islam, like Judaism and Christianity, has as its center an all-powerful, inscrutable God (Allah) who exacts submission, love, praise, and faith from his followers. Islam is based on the Koran, which records the tenets revealed by Allah to the Prophet Mohammad (570–632). The canonical text of the Koran was established in 651–52 from a collection of the Prophet's sayings made by his secretary. Generous giving, along with prayer, fasting, pilgrimage, and abstention from certain foods (for example, wine and pork) and practices (including usury) are among the basic tenets of Islam.

In contrast to Christianity, in which the relative merit of faith and works (including almsgiving) has been the subject of recurring debate, Islam sees no conflict between the two; both are essential to piety. The following are among numerous passages in the Koran dealing with faith, charity, kindness, and forgiveness:[23]

> Piety does not lie in turning your face to East or West:
> Piety lies in believing in God,
> the Last Day and the angels
> the Scriptures and the prophets,
> and disbursing your wealth out of love for God
> among your kin and the orphans,
> the wayfarers and mendicants,
> freeing the slaves, observing your devotional obligations,
> and in paying the *zakat* and fulfilling a pledge you have given,
> and being patient in hardship, adversity, and times of peril.
> These are the men who affirm the truth,
> and they are those who follow the straight path.
>
> (2:177)

> Surely the men and women who spend in charity
> and give a goodly loan to God,

will have it doubled for them
and will receive a generous reward.

(57: 18)

O believers, some of your wives and children
are your enemies, so beware of them!
Yet if you forbear, overlook, and forgive,
God is indeed forgiving and kind.
Your wealth and children are surely meant as trial for you:
But with God is the great reward.
So fear God as much as you can,
and listen and obey, and spend in charity
for your own good.
He who is saved from his own avarice
will be successful.
If you lend a goodly loan to God,
He will double it for you, and forgive you.
God knows the worth of good deeds and is clement,
The knower of the unknown and the known,
all-mighty and all-wise.

(64: 14–18)

As the passages indicate, the Koran enjoins two kinds of almsgiving: voluntary charity and payment of *zakat*, a tax on the wealthy. Proceeds of the latter went to the relief of the poor, pay for those who collected and administered the tax, aid to defenders of the faith and recent converts to Islam, help to captives and slaves seeking to buy their freedom, and assistance to debtors and stranded travelers. Voluntary charity helped the donor build treasure in heaven: the compulsory *zakat* led the payer to be less concerned with amassing personal possessions and more sympathetic to the unfortunate.[24] *Zakat*, by rewarding defenders of the faith, promoting conversion, and channeling energy into paths other than personal enrichment, may have been a factor in the rapid spread of Islam. Within little more than a century after the Prophet's death Islam was the dominant religion of the Middle East, North Africa, and southern Spain.

Maimonides, or Moses ben Maimon (1135–1204), born in Cordova, Spain, was a Hebrew scholar, rabbi, philosopher, and physician. At the time of his birth Cordova had been under Moorish rule for almost four centuries, long enough for Moslems and Jews to learn to get along with each other and allow the city to become a center of learning for followers of both faiths. In 1148 a militant Islamic sect captured Cordova, forcing Jews to flee to escape persecution. Maimonides and his family moved from place to place until, after years of wandering, he settled in Cairo. There he became a physician at the court of Sultan Saladin, and leader of the Jewish community. He was fluent in Hebrew and Arabic, writing *Mishneh Torah* in Hebrew and *A Guide to the Perplexed* in Arabic.

Maimonides' most important work, *Mishneh Torah*, completed around 1178, was a systematic guide to the laws and teachings of Judaism from the time of Moses to the author's own day. Book VII of the work codifies the laws and traditions relating to charity developed by the Jewish people over thousands of years. Chapter one deals with "the portion of the poor," the part of a field or orchard to be left unharvested by the owner so that the poor can help themselves. Other chapters treat the collection and distribution of the charity fund and food pantry each Jewish community was expected to maintain. "Charity food is collected daily, and the community fund each Friday. Charity food is for the poor that come from anywhere, while the community fund is intended for the local poor only." The code emphasizes that charity should be given in as kindly and considerate a manner as possible. Chapter seven (on obligations and priorities) states that if a poor man refuses to take charity "he should be given it subtly in the form of a gift or a loan." The same consideration is extended to donors: "It is forbidden to solicit or collect charitable contributions from an over-generous person who donates more than he can afford, or deprives himself and gives to the charity collectors in order not to be embarrassed. Any collector who embarrasses and solicits such a person will eventually be punished, as it is written: 'I will punish those who oppress him' (Jer. 30:20)."[25]

The most frequently quoted part of *Mishneh Torah* is chapter ten in Book VII, in which Maimonides lists 'the "eight degrees of charity." Ranked in order, from the least to the most meritorious, the degrees are:

8. Giving grudgingly
7. Giving cheerfully, but less than you should
6. Giving after being solicited
5. Giving without being solicited
4. Giving to a recipient unknown to you who knows you ("The great sages used to tie money in sheets which they threw behind their

backs, and the poor would come and get it without being embarrassed.")

3. Giving to a recipient you know who does not know you ("The great
   sages used to go secretly and cast the money into the doorway of the
   poor.")

2. Giving to an unknown recipient who does not know your identity (An
   example would be giving to a charity fund or organization. Maimonides
   states, "One should not contribute to a charity fund unless he knows
   that the man in charge of the collection is trust-worthy and intelligent
   and knows how to manage properly.")

1. Helping a needy person become self-supporting by a gift, loan, or entering into partnership with or providing work for him or her[26]

It is not hard to find contemporary examples of each of the eight
degrees of charity. The highest and the four lowest need no comment.
Establishing a philanthropic foundation, fund, or scholarship bearing
the donor's name qualifies for the fourth degree; and an anonymous
gift for purposes designated by the donor represents the third. When
we contribute to a charitable organization we approve of and trust to
use the gift as it sees fit, we attain (although it doesn't seem we have
really done very much) the level just below the highest.

In the paragraph immediately preceding those characterizing the
eight degrees of charity, Maimonides states:

> He who urges and activates others to give *Tsedakah* [aid to the poor] re-
> ceives a greater reward than the donor himself. With regard to the collec-
> tors of charity and the like, Scripture says: "Those who turn many to
> righteousness shall be like the stars" (Dan. 12:3).[27]

In modern times both professional fund raisers and individual volunteers assume the responsibilities and perform the onerous tasks once
performed by the charity fund collectors Maimonides had in mind.

Maimonides' *Guide For the Perplexed*, completed around 1190, is
a philosophical work directed to religious intellectuals familiar with
both Jewish law and classical philosophy, devoted to each, and troubled
by seeming contradictions between them. Maimonides' *Guide* was
translated into Hebrew shortly before his death. It has received study
from Jewish and Christian thinkers including Thomas Aquinas. One
paragraph of the work discusses the use of the term *hesed* (charity) in the
scriptures. In "inspired writings," Maimonides notes, *hesed* is used
mainly to denote loving kindness extended to those who have no claim
to it by relationship or affinity. In this respect charity is like the loving

kindness bestowed on man by God, especially in "the very act of creation."[28]

Notes

1. Gen. 4:2–3.
2. Northrup Frye, *The Great Code, The Bible as Literature* (New York and London: Harcourt, Brace Jovanovich, 1982), 142–43. Cuthbert A. Simpson, "Exegesis," in *The Interpreter's Bible* (New York: Abingdon Press, 1951–57), 1:518.
3. Deuto. 15:7–8, 10–11.
4. Pss. 103:8; 112:9.
5. Mic. 6:8 (Revised Standard Version). The King James version uses "mercy" instead of "kindness".
6. R. Travers Herford, ed., *Pirke Aboth, Commonly called "Sayings of the Fathers"* (New York: Jewish Institute of Religion Press, 1925), 22.
7. Matt. 5:41–42, 6:1–6.
8. Matt. 19:16–22; Mark 10: 23–25.
9. Matt. 19:23–24; Mark 10:23–25.
10. Luke 10:25–37.
11. Luke 16:19–31.
12. Henry George refers to Dives and Lazarus in *Social Problems* (1883) in Perry Miller, ed., *American Thought, Civil War to World War I* (New York: Holt, Rinehart and Winston, 1954), 57. Burton's observations about Dives and Holy Poverty are in *The Book of a Thousand and One Nights* (Benares, India: The Burton Club, 1885), 5:268 nt. 2.
13. Luke 21:1–4; Mark 12: 41–44.
14. I Cor. 13:3 (R.S.V.). In this and other passages in chapter 13 the King James version translates *agape* as "charity" rather than "love."
15. Acts 3:1–8.
16. See Part Two, chapter 3, p. 32 for an instance of beggars' fear of being healed.
17. Mary Caroline Watt, *St. Martin of Tours, The Chronicles of Sulpicius Severus* (London: Sands and Company, 1928), 98–99. The *Chronicles* by Severus (c. 365–425) did much to establish St. Martin's reputation.
18. The representations vary from the simple but moving stick figures in medieval manuscripts to the lofty austerity of El Greco.
19. St. Basil the Great, "Letter CL," in Roy J. Defferari, *St. Basil, the Letters* (Cambridge: Harvard University Press, 1962), 2:369. In E.F. Morison, *St. Basil and His Rule* (Oxford: Oxford University Press, 1912), 126, the concluding part of the last sentence is translated as follows:
    "but he who gives to every vagabond casts to a dog, a nuisance indeed from his importunity, but deserving no pity for plea of poverty."
    W.J. Ashley in *An Introduction to English Economic History and Theory* (New

York: Putnam, 1898, first published in 1888), 2:315, provides another translation of the passage:

> "he who without distinction gives to every beggar that runs up to him, is not really bestowing alms from compassion for need, but is tossing as it were a crust to a troublesome dog."

20. F. Van Der Meer, *Augustine the Bishop, The Life and Work of a Father of the Church*, translated by Brian Battershaw and G.R. Lamb (New York and London: Sheed and Ward, 1961), 138.

21. Ibid., 437–38.

22. St. Augustine, *On Christian Doctrine*, translated by J.F. Shaw in Robert M. Hutchins, editor in chief, *Great Books of the Western World* (Chicago: Encyclopedia Brittanica, 1952), 18: 631–32.

23. *Al Qur'an*. A Contemporary Translation by Ahmed Ali (Princeton: Princeton University Press, 1984), 32, 471, 489.

24. Charles J. White, "Almsgiving," in Mircea Eliade, *The Encyclopedia of Religion* (New York: The MacMillan Publishing Company, 1987), 1:215; Muzzamil H. Siddioi, "Zakat," ibid., 15:550–51.

25. *Mishneh Torah: Maimonides' Code of Law and Ethics*, abridged and translated from the Hebrew by Philip Birnbaum (New York: Hebrew Publishing Company, 1974), 153–59. The quoted passages are from Book VII, chapter 7, paragraphs 9 and 11.

26. Ibid., ch. 10, paragraphs 7–14.

27. Ibid., paragraph 6. Philip Birnbaum in his comments on Book VII observes that the term *tsedakah* is applied, in postbiblical Hebrew, specifically to the relief of poverty as an act of justice and moral behavior. The poor man's right to food, clothing, and shelter is considered by Judaism as a legal claim that must be honored. "*Tsedekah* is not a matter of philanthropic sentiment but an act of justice," (pp. 156–57).

28. Moses Maimonides, *The Guide for the Perplexed*, translated by M. Friedlander, 2nd ed. (London: George Routledge and Sons Limited, 1947), 392–93 (Pt. 3, ch. 53). Isadore Twersky discusses *The Guide for the Perplexed* in his article on Maimonides in Eliade, ed., *Encyclopedia of Religion* 9: 134–35.

PART TWO

Middle Ages and
Early Modern Times

Prologue: A Hospital and Its Patients

The oldest hospital in London is St. Bartholomew's (Barts), founded in 1123 on its present site in Smithfield. The founder was Rahere (d. 1144), a man of "lowly race" whose witty and flattering talk gained him entry to the homes of nobles and the court of King William Rufus, son of William the Conqueror. A follower of Richard de Belmeis, Bishop of London, Rahere gave up minstrelsy for a career in the church. Around 1120 he went on a pilgrimage to Rome — a difficult undertaking at the time — and while in Rome fell ill. Despairing of his life he vowed, if he recovered, to make a hospital for "Ye Recreacion of poure men." Subsequently St. Bartholomew, one of the apostles, appeared to him and asked him to erect a church in Smithfield, a suburb of London where condemned criminals were executed. Rahere's patron, Bishop Richard, helped him obtain a grant of land in Smithfield from Henry I. In 1123 Rahere began to build the hospital and, shortly afterward, a priory, part of which survives as the church of St. Bartholomew's the Great.

Rahere and the eight Augustinian monks and four nuns who tended the patients solicited gifts and begged for food and alms for both the sick poor and the laborers building the church. Heaven smiled on their efforts, for on one occasion

> Edena, wife of Edred, in the parish of St. Giles, was brewing, and had only seven loads of malt, and feared that less would prevent her beer coming off. However, she gave one to the men of St. Bartholomew's, and then found she yet had seven; so counted them again, and there were eight; and again, and there were nine; and a fourth time, and there were ten. She sent off the superabundance to the church.[1]

Rahere remained master of the hospital until 1137, when he retired to the priory. Four centuries after his death, Henry VIII dissolved the religious orders, including the Augustinian canons, but endowed the hospital so that its work could be continued. Subsequent gifts and bequests enabled the hospital to expand its services. In 1918, as St. Bartholomew's approached its eight hundredth birthday, Dr. Norman Moore saluted the benefits received and bestowed by the hospital's patients:

> Children have been restored to their parents, husbands to their wives, wives to their husbands, people of every art to their work, brave defenders of their country to their homes. The pains of incurable illness and of mortal injury have been relieved. Here fruitful observations have been constantly pursued, valuable discoveries often made. The happiness of a full mind, the honour of adding to knowledge, the opportunity of using it for the benefit of mankind, these we owe to the patients. Rahere opened the gates of St. Bartholomew's to the patients for whom the old brethren and sisters worked and prayed. The desire to do all that can be done for the patients in the hospital and for others in like case outside it has continued and enlarged the work he began. The determination to relieve misery and to add to knowledge made Mirfeld look into old treatises and write new ones after the manner of his time. The same motives made Harvey, after reading what was worth study in former writers, observe the human body in health and in sickness and look to such observation as the means of advancing medicine. These motives roused the eloquence of Abernathy to make clear the truths of nature, to stimulate students to apply them, and to love the place where so much knowledge was to be required and so much good to be done. The patient has been the cause of the constant improvement of the physician and of the surgeon, and of the development of the observing student and the well-trained nurse.[2]

Barts survived the Great Depression and suffered only minor damage in the Second World War. At the start of 1993 it continued to operate as a National Health Service teaching hospital for doctors and nurses. Policy decisions made by the Convervative government in 1993 make it likely that the hospital will go out of existence after 870 years of service.

Notes

1. Norman Moore, M.D. *The History of St. Bartholomew's Hospital* (London: C. Arthur Pearson Limited, 1918), 1:21.
2. Ibid., 2:885–86. Moore (1847–1922) was consulting physician to St. Bartholomew's Hospital. Mirfeld (fl. 1373), author of *Breviarium Bartholomae*; William Harvey (1578–1657), discoverer of the circulation of the blood; and John Abernethy (1764–1831), distinguished surgeon and teacher, were all associated with St. Bartholomew's.

3

Begging, Fund Raising, and Charity

Shortly after the year 1200 Giovanni Francisco Berdone, later called Frances of Assisi (1182–1226), began to devote himself to repair of old churches, prayer, charity, and meditation on the tenth chapter of Matthew. His attempt to put into practice in his own life Christ's instructions to the apostles to preach, tend the sick, care for lepers, give freely, and disregard money and personal belongings led to a break with his wealthy family but attracted followers impressed by his sincerity and dedication. The latter became the corps of the Franciscan order of monks recognized by Pope Innocent III in 1210. Francis required the monks, called friars, to accept poverty and to rejoice in the company of "mean and despised persons . . . the poor and weak and infirm and the lepers and those that beg in the street."[1] The friars, having no property of their own, were expected to support themselves by menial labor and by begging from door to door. The order grew so rapidly that Francis was unable to enforce the rule on poverty he had laid down. By 1220, when he resigned leadership of the order, there were 5000 Franciscan monks, but by no means all of them shared the founders' devotion to poverty.

Most of the stories recounted in *The Little Flowers of St. Francis* were written about a century after the Saint's death by Brother Ugolino de Monte Santa Maria. The widely popular collection attests to the affection common people felt for St. Francis and reveals an indulgent attitude toward begging. One of the stories tells of the experience of Francis and one of his companions, Brother Masseo, in a small town where Francis begged on one street, Masseo on another. "Saint Francis because, as a small-built man, and therefore, after human fashion universally despised among strangers, received a few pieces of old bread and small crusts; but more and better bread was given to Brother Masseo because he was a fine looking man and tall in stature." When the two sat down to share their bits of bread Francis was overjoyed at "such treasure" obtained, not by human labor, but provided by God's providence. In another story a young friar belonging to a noble family refused to beg until Francis sternly commanded him to do so. Putting aside his pride or shyness, the young nobleman found his first expedition so rewarding, not so much in goods received as in the joy and grace he experienced as a result of God's bounty, that from then on "he never wanted to do anything but go begging."[2]

Brother Juniper presented a different problem. He was so generous that he would give his tunic or the hood of his cloak to the first poor person he met. Ordered not to give away any part of his habit, Brother Juniper allowed a beggar to strip his tunic from him, subsequently explaining to his superiors: "A good man took it off my back and went away with it." Not content with giving freely of his own possessions, Brother Juniper gave the poor other monks' books, cloaks, and anything he could lay his hands on. "For this reason the brethren took care to leave nothing in the common rooms of the convent, because Brother Juniper gave away everything for the love of God and to the glory of his name."[3]

After the death of Francis, as Brother Juniper's story suggests, the friars, although still bound by vows of personal poverty, were permitted to hold property in common. Franciscans and members of the other mendicant orders founded in the thirteenth century (Dominicans, Carmelites, and Augustinians) continued to seek alms but not so much by begging from door to door as by preaching and hearing confessions, taking special collections in churches, and receiving gifts and bequests. The funds they received built and maintained monasteries and abbeys and supported the schools, colleges, hospitals, and charities conducted by their houses or orders.

One of these mendicants, "the finest beggar of his house," was Hubert, the worldly friar who rode with the Canterbury pilgrims. As a "limiter" Hubert had the exclusive right to beg within a certain district, and as a licentiate of his order he was authorized to hear confessions. Hubert put the latter privilege to good use by granting easy penance to anyone willing to pay money as a sign of repentance. In his love of good living, affinity for the well-to-do, and indifference to the sick and poor, Hubert was the antithesis of St. Francis. He consorted with the rich and "big victuallers," was on good terms with farmers and housewives, knew all the tavern keepers and barmaids, and could coax a penny out of a poor widow, but had no time or pity to waste on lepers and other "poverty-stricken curs."[4]

Hubert's creator, Geoffrey Chaucer (c. 1343–1400), was a younger contemporary of Petrarch (1304–74), Boccaccio (1313–1375), and William Langland (c. 1332–c. 1400). Like them he lived in an era of war, political strife, social unrest, and religious dissension. The Hundred Years' War between England and France began shortly after Chaucer's birth. During his boyhood the Black Death ravaged Europe, in a single year (1349) killing one third of the population of England.

In the Parson Chaucer presents a cleric who has little in common with Hubert. The Parson is poor in earthly goods but "rich in holy thought and work." Learned, patient, and diligent, a shepherd, not a mercenary, he did not gouge his parishioners for tithes, but gave part of his income and possessions to those in need. He went about his widespread parish on foot, in all weather, teaching mainly by his own example but not hesitating to reprove sinners, no matter how high their station.[5]

Possibly because the Parson's views corresponded with his own, Chaucer gave his long discourse on penitence and the seven deadly sins the place of honor at the end of *The Canterbury Tales*. As an adherent of the doctrine of good works, the Parson emphasized general almsgiving as a necessary part of penitence. Unlike Hubert, who as confessor exacted payment in lieu of punishment, the Parson demanded three kinds of almsgiving: sacrificial giving as a sign of contrition, compassionate giving out of sympathy for one's distressed neighbor, and prudential giving in the form of good counsel, on matters material as well as spiritual, to those who needed it. "If you cannot visit the needy" in person, he advised, "visit him by your message and by your gifts."[6] As remedies for the sin of avarice he recommended "mercy and pity in large doses" and "reasonable largess." At the time of death, he reminded the pilgrims, each "must forgo all that he has, save only that which he has invested in good works."[7]

The Summoner and the Pardoner, who rode together, are the last of the pilgrims described in Chaucer's prologue to the tales. The former, an officer of the ecclesiastical courts, viewed the Friar as a rival for gifts of the devout. Angered by the Friar's story of a corrupt summoner, he makes a hypocritical friar the butt of his tale. The Pardoner sells indulgences granted by the Pope that relieve purchasers of the temporal or purgatorial punishment for sins. Chaucer says that as a salesman the Pardoner had no peer; and in the prologue to his story the Pardoner boasts of the use he makes of spurious relics — a pillowcase said to be Our Lady's veil, a piece of the sail of St. Peter's fishing boat, and a miraculous bone capable of healing distemper in animals and jealousy in husbands — to induce giving by the credulous. It is their pence, he says, not their penitence, that counts with him; when they die, for all he cares, their souls can go black-berrying. *Cupiditas* is the theme of all his sermons and of his story as well; firsthand knowledge and practice of avarice makes his preaching against it doubly effective.[8]

Despite Chaucer's and other writers' ridicule of the sale of indulgences, the Papacy continued the practice as a fund-raising device until 1562. In 1517 a campaign by a Dominican monk, Johann Tetzel, to sell indulgences to raise money for the rebuilding of St. Peter's Church in Rome precipitated Martin Luther's break with the Roman Catholic Church. Among Luther's reasons for condemning indulgences was their adverse effect on charity. "He who gives to the poor or lends to the needy does a better deed than he who buys indulgences . . . he who sees a needy man and passes him by, yet gives his money for indulgences, does not buy papal indulgences but God's wrath."[9]

Convinced that faith in Christ was alone sufficient for salvation without necessity for recourse to good works such as almsgiving and pilgrimage, Luther (1483–1546) asked the German nobility to curtail the mendicant orders, including the Augustinians of which he was a member, and to suppress begging. The latter prohibition would extend not only to common beggars but to religious ones such as stationers and palmers. "There is no other business in which so much knavery and deceit are practiced as in beggary," he declared. "Every city should provide for its own poor, and admit no foreign beggars by whatever name they might be called, whether pilgrims or mendicant monks."[10]

About five years after Luther's call for the abolition of begging, at the request of the magistracy of Bruges, Juan Luis Vives (1492–1540), a Spanish humanist, prepared a plan for the registration and management of the poor and the suppression of begging in that city. As the cornerstone of the program, Vives proposed a systematic administration of charity and poor relief with provision and enforcement of labor for all those able to work. Particular objects of his concern were the numerous endowed hospitals and almshouses of the city; in some cases, he suspected, the founders' intention of sheltering the poor and infirm was no longer being carried out because the institutions had come under the control of privileged occupants who lived in idleness and luxury. His model was "a well-ordered home" where everyone, including children, old people, and the handicapped, was assigned appropriate tasks. The blind, for example, were not to be allowed to sit idly or roam aimlessly; there were occupations like teaching, box or basket making, or performing music at which they could be set to work. For those who had fallen into poverty as a result of dissolute living there were to be more irksome tasks and smaller allotments of food. "They must not die of hunger," he said, but they must feel its pangs.[11]

Vives was living in England when he wrote *On Assistance to the Poor*, and his work may have had some influence on English poor law reform. In Bruges the city's economic decline, already under way when Vives wrote, left no work to assign to the poor. A century later Bruges was the locale of "The Beggar's Bush," a play by John Fletcher and Philip Massinger, which depicted life in a camp of beggars, outlaws, and petty thieves on the outskirts of the city.[12]

Between 1535 and 1540 Henry VIII and his minister Thomas Cromwell brought about the dissolution, not just of the mendicant orders as Luther had advocated, but of all the monasteries and nunneries in England. As the religious orders went out of existence their members dispersed and the buildings and lands passed by purchase or royal grant to private landowners. Monks who did not choose to enter the secular clergy received pensions that soon proved inadequate; nuns, except for abbesses, received no pensions and were expected to rejoin their families. For better or worse, the charity dispersed at abbey gates and courtyards came to an end; municipal authorities assumed responsibility for the hospitals and schools thought to be performing useful functions.[13]

Robert Crowley (1518?–88), a religious and social reformer, regretted that the wealth of the monasteries had gone into private pockets rather than to endow religion and education. In his poem "Of Abbeys," written a few years after the dissolution, he commented:

As I walked alone, and mused on things
That have in my time been done by great kings,
I bethought me of Abbeys, that sometime I saw,
Which are suppressed, all by a law.
Oh Lord (thought I then) what occasion was here
To provide for learning and make poverty cheer?
The lands and the jewels that hereby were had,
Would have found godly preachers, which might have led
The people aright that now go astray,
And have fed the poor that famish every day.[14]

In "Of Almshouses" Crowley wrote of one of the corrupted charities that bothered Vives and later reformers. A merchant, returning
from many years overseas, passes a site formerly occupied, as he
recalls, by a "spittelhouse"; now a lordly mansion stands where the
hospital should be.

Good Lord! (said this merchant),
Is my country so wealthy
That the very beggars' houses
Be built so gorgeously?
Then, by the wayside,
He chanced to see
A poor man that craved
Of him for charity.
Why (quoth this merchant)
What meaneth this thing?
Do you beg by the way
And have a house fit for a king?
Alas! sir (quoth the poor man)
We are all turned out,
And lie and die in corners
Here and there about.
Men of great riches
Have bought our dwelling place,
And when we crave of them,
They turn away their face.[15]

Like Crowley, Thomas Fuller (1608–61), whose *Church History of
England* appeared in 1655, deplored the privatization of the resources
the religious orders had possessed for doing good. As a historian,

Fuller was distressed by the breakup and destruction of monastic libraries. Sensitive to the human costs and hardships of the dissolution, Fuller wrote:

> Ten thousand persons were by this Dissolution sent to seek their fortunes in the wide world. Some, indeed, had fathers or friends to receive them, others none at all. Some had twenty shillings given them at their ejection, and a new gown, which needed to be of strong cloth to last so long till they got another. Most were exposed to want . . . and many a young nun proved an old beggar. I pity not those who had hands and health to work; but, surely, the gray hairs of some impotent persons deserved compassion.[16]

Fuller acknowledged that the charitable activities of the monasteries were more effective in producing pauperism than in relieving poverty. "Yea, these abbeys did but maintain the poor which they made," he wrote, but felt compelled to add:

> All this is confessed; yet, by their hospitality, many an honest and hungry soul had his bowels refreshed, which otherwise would have been starved; and better it is, two drones should be fed, than one bee famished. We see the heavens themselves, in dispensing their rain, often water many stinking bogs and noisome lakes, which moisture is not needed by them, (yea, they the worse for it,) only because much good ground lies inseparably intermingled with them; so that, either the bad with the good must be watered, or the good with the bad must be parched away.[17]

Sixteenth-century governments attempted to curb mendicity by sporadic enforcement of harsh laws, particularly against "sturdy"—that is able-bodied—vagabonds, and by efforts to license and regulate begging by people unable to work or suffering from loss of property as a result of war, fire, shipwreck, or natural disaster. In an age rife with poverty and social disorder, when public provision for the poor was still minimal, begging was a way of life for some people, whether in Catholic Spain or Protestant England. In *Lazarillo de Tormes*, an anonymous novel published in Spain in 1564, a young boy, Lazarillo, recounts his adventures and misadventures with various masters. One was a blind beggar "who had endless ways of getting money out of people," often by reciting prayers in their behalf and offering advice on the cure of toothache, fainting spells, and morning sickness. Despite his success, he was stingy and didn't give Lazarillo enough to eat. The boy paid him back by getting into the beggar's provision bag and helping himself to its contents. Another master, a gentleman, was too proud to work but not above eating the bread Lazarillo begged to support them. His best master was a wily pardoner who could have taught Chaucer's pardoner fund-raising tricks.[18]

In England, at about the same time, Robert Crowley reported the conversation of two beggars who sat under a hedge discussing their situation:

> They had both sore legs, most loathsome to see;
> All raw from the foot, well most to the knee.
> "My leg," quoth one, "I thank God is fair."
> "So is mine" (quoth the other) in a cold air;
> For it then looketh raw, and as red as any blood,
> I would not have it healed, for any world's good;
> For were it once whole, my living were gone,
> And for a sturdy beggar I should be taken anon.
> No man would pity me, but for my sore leg;
> Wherefore if it were whole I might in vain beg.
> I should be constrained to labor and sweat.
> And perhaps sometime with scourges be beat."
> "Well" (said the other) "let us take heed therefore
> That we let them not heal, but keep them still sore."

Another beggar, toting up his accounts for the day, finds that he has earned sixteen pence but spent eighteen. Nevertheless, he orders his pot to be filled to the brim:

> The tongue must have boasting, it will the better wag
> To pull a God's penny out of a churl's bag.

In the last two lines Crowley advises his readers:

> Yet cease not to give to all, without any regard;
> Though the beggars be wicked, thou shall have thy reward.[19]

An English nursery rhyme has often been quoted to show the ill feeling that bands of wandering beggars aroused in the respectable classes during the sixteenth century:

Hark! Hark! the dogs do bark,
The beggars are coming to town,
Some in rags and some in tags,
And some in silken gowns.
Some gave them white bread,
Some gave them brown,
And some gave them a good horse-whip,
And sent them out of town.[20]

Some authorities assert, however, that the beggars referred to in the rhyme were soldiers in Prince Rupert's royalist army in the English Civil War (1642–48) or Dutchmen who came to England with William III in 1688.[21] The reference to "a good horse-whip" supports the original interpretation, although the verse may also have been used in connection with later marauders.

Notes

1. Quoted from the Rule of 1221 in M.D. Lambert, *Franciscan Poverty* (London: Society for Promoting Christian Knowledge, 1961), 31.
2. *The Little Flowers of Saint Francis, The Acts of Saint Francis and His Companions*, translated by E.M. Blaiklock and A.C. Keys (Ann Arbor, Mich.: Servant Books, 1985), 35, 151.
3. "The Life of Brother Juniper," in *The Little Flowers of Saint Francis of Assisi*, in the first English translation revised and amended by Dom Roger Huddleston (New York: Heritage Press, The George Macy Companies, Inc., 1965), 191.
4. Geoffrey Chaucer, *The Canterbury Tales*, rendered into modern English by J.U. Nicolson (Garden City, N.Y.: Garden City Publishing Company, 1934), 7–9 ("Prologue," lines 206–57). *The Canterbury Tales*, designed about 1378, was unfinished at Chaucer's death.
5. The Parson is introduced in lines 477–528 of the "Prologue," ibid., 15–17. He rides with his brother, the Ploughman, "a good toiler" who pays his taxes and looks out for his neighbors.
6. "The Parson's Tale," ibid., 621.
7. Ibid., 601. Compare the Parson's belief in the lasting power of "investments in good works" with the sentence quoted by Bernard Shaw: "What I saved I lost: What I spent I had; What I gave I have" ("Socialism for Millionaires," *The Contemporary Review*, 69 (1896):208.
8. Chaucer, "Prologue" and "Prologue to The Pardoner's Tale," ibid., 21–22, 293–96.
9. Martin Luther, "The Ninety-Five Theses" (1517), in Kurt Aland, ed., *Martin*

Luther's 95 Theses (St. Louis: Concordia Publishing House, 1967), 54.

10. Martin Luther, "An Open Letter to the Christian Nobility of the German Nation Concerning the Reform of the Christian Estate," in *Three Treatises by Martin Luther* (Philadelphia: Muhlenberg Press, 1943), 61, 81–82. The "Open Letter" was written in 1520. "Stationers" were beggars who asked donors for alms in the name of a patron saint as insurance against disease or accident; "palmers" were professional pilgrims who supported themselves by begging as they traveled from one place of pilgrimage to another.

11. Juan Luis Vives, "On Assistance to the Poor," translated by Sister Alice Tobriner in Tobriner, *A Sixteenth Century Urban Report* (Chicago: School of Social Service Administration, University of Chicago, 1971), 37–42. Vives defined a hospital as "any place where the sick are fed and nursed, where a given number of indigent persons are supported, boys and girls educated, abandoned infants nourished, the insane confined, and the blind allowed to spend their days" (pp. 37–38).

12. Vives's influence is discussed in the famous chapter "The Relief of the Poor," in W.J. Ashley, *An Introduction to English Economic History and Theory* (New York: Putnam, 1898), 2:343–46. "The Beggar's Bush" was produced in 1622 and printed in 1647. According to Clarence L. Barnhart, ed., *The New Century Handbook of English Literature* (New York: Appleton, Century, Croft, 1956), 111, the play was a favorite of Samuel Taylor Coleridge, who said he could read it every night.

12. G.M. Trevelyan, *English Social History* (London: Longmans, Green and Company, 1942), 105–13, discusses the causes and consequences of dissolution; Joyce Youings, *Sixteenth Century England* (London: Allen Lane, 1984), 202, tells of the dispersal of monks and nuns; on the hospitals see Ashley, *Introduction to English Economic History and Theory*, 2:323.

14. "Of Abbayes," in *The Selected Works of Robert Crowley*, edited by J.M. Cowper (London: Published for the Early English Text Society by N. Trubner and Co., 1872), 7.

15. Ibid., 11–12.

16. Thomas Fuller, *Church History of England* (Oxford: Oxford University Press, 1845) 3:374. First published in 1655.

17. Ibid., 339.

18. Michael Alpert, ed. and trans., *Two Spanish Picaresque Novels Lazarillo de Tormes* (anon.); *The Swindler* (*Francisco de Quevado*) (Harmandsworth, England: Penguin Books, 1969), 28–29, 49–68, 73–75.

19. "Of Beggars," in *The Selected Works of Robert Crowley*, 14–16.

20. The rhyme is quoted in Tobriner, *A Sixteenth Century Urban Report*, 62 n. 8. Ashley, *An Introduction to English Economic History and Theory* 2:352, and Trevelyan, *English Social History*, use it as evidence of hostile attitudes toward beggars.

21. Katherine Elwes Thomas, *The Real Personages of Mother Goose* (Boston: Lothrop, Lee and Shepard Co., 1930); Iona and Peter Opie, eds., *The Oxford Dictionary of Nursery Rhymes* (Oxford: Oxford University Press, 1952), 152–53.

4

Donors and Attributes of Charity

Richard Whittington (d. 1423) and William Sevenoaks (1378?–1433?) were poor boys — the latter a foundling — who achieved wealth and honor as London merchants. Each served as Lord Mayor of London and made substantial and lasting contributions to philanthropy. Whittington endowed a drinking fountain, a public lavatory, a shelter for unmarried mothers, and an almshouse. His will, instead of entrusting the almshouse to a church or religious order, provided for its administration by the Mercers' Company of London.[1] Sevenoaks, having won success as a member of the Grocers' Company in London, and in gratitude for the kindness bestowed on him as an infant, founded a free grammar school and a hospital in Sevenoaks, Kent, where, according to local tradition, he had been found in a hollow tree. In his will dated 4 July 1432, Sevenoaks left property for the support of the two institutions with instructions that the school was to be taught by a "master, an honest man, sufficiently advanced and expert in the science of grammar and a Bachelor of Arts, but by no means in holy orders."[2] The Sevenoaks Grammar School, the first of many schools to be founded by London merchants in succeeding years, is still in existence.

The poet Richard Johnson (1573?–1659) included an account of Sevenoaks' career in his *Nine Worthies of London* (1592) and in 1612 published "A Story of Sir Richard Whittington." The latter was probably based on a popular ballad of an earlier date. Johnson took full advantage of poetic license in romanticizing and perhaps fabricating events in Sevenoaks' life, but he concluded on a sober note:

By testament in Kent I built a town,
   And briefly called it Sevenoak, from my name;
A free school to sweet learning, to renown,
   I placed for those that played at honor's game;
Both land and living to that town I gave,
Before I took possession of my grave.[3]

According to Johnson, "Whittington's Nimble Cat," sold for "heaps of gold" to a king whose lands were overrun by rats and mice, made possible his rise from scullion to merchant prince.

God did thus make him great,
So would he daily see
Poor people fed with meat,
To show his charity.
Prisoners poore cherish'd were,
Widdowes sweet comfort found;
Good deeds, both far and neere,
Of him do still resound.
Whittington Colledge is
One of his charities,
Records reporteth this
To lasting memories.
Newgate he builded faire,
For prisoners to live in;
Christ's Church he did repaire,
Christian love for to win.
Many more such like deedes
Were done by Whittington;
Which joy and comfort breedes,
To such as looke thereon.[4]

In a much later retelling of the story by Osbert Sitwell, the cat survives repeated efforts by Whittington's wife to get rid of her, and the philanthropist leaves his entire fortune for establishment of the "Whittington's Central Cat's Aid Society and Sanitarium."[5]

Izaak Walton (1593–1683), author of *The Compleat Angler* (1653), wrote biographies of his friends, the poets John Donne and George Herbert. Each of the *Lives* is marked by a generous and appreciative attitude toward the subject. The books are models of charity in thought and they throw light on the spirit and methods of religious benevolence in England in the first half of the seventeenth century.

After an adventuresome and promising youth, Donne (1572–1631) fell out of favor with officials of court and church, and for many years he and his wife and children lived on the charity of friends and patrons. The mother of George Herbert was among those who befriended them. In 1621 Donne became Dean of St. Paul's Cathedral and thereafter his income permitted him to give liberally, especially to persons imprisoned for debt and to poor scholars. Walton tells us that at the start of every year after he became Dean Donne drew up a budget showing his anticipated revenues, the portion of it he intended to give to the poor and pious causes, and the amount to be used for himself and family. After discussing Donne's generous bequests Walton states:

> Nor was this blessed sacrifice of charity expressed only at his death, but in his life also, by a cheerful and frequent visitation of any friend whose mind was dejected, or his fortune necessitous; he was inquisitive after the wants of prisoners, and redeemed many from prison that lay for their fees or small debts: he was a continual giver to poor scholars, both of this and foreign nations. Besides that he gave with his own hand, he usually sent a servant, or a discreet and trusty friend, to distribute his charity to all the prisons in London, at all the festival times of the year, especially at the birth and resurrection of our Saviour. He gave an hundred pounds at one time to an old friend, whom he had known live plentifully, and by a too liberal heart and carelessness became decayed in his estate; and when the receiving of it was denied, by the gentleman's saying, "He wanted not;" – for the reader may note, that as there be some spirits so generous as to labour to conceal and endure a sad poverty, rather than expose themselves to those blushes that attend the confession of it; so there be others, to whom nature and grace have afforded such sweet and compassionate souls, as to pity and prevent the distresses of mankind; –which I have mentioned because of Dr. Donne's reply, whose answer was: "I know you want not what will sustain nature; for a little will do that; but my desire is, that you who in the days of your plenty have cheered and raised the hearts of so many of your dejected friends, would now receive this from me, and use it as a cordial for the cheering of your own:" and upon these terms it was received.[6]

George Herbert (1593–1633), a friend of Donne and, like him, a clergyman, made his wife his almoner. He gave her a tenth of the money and grain he received in tithes to distribute to the poor of the parish in the form of blankets and shoes. She "would often offer him an account of her stewardship, and would as often beg an enlargement of his bounty; for she rejoiced in the employment." Herbert repaired the parsonage and church of which he was rector at his own expense and raised money for restoring a dilapidated church in a nearby town. To a friend who cautioned that his generosity might impoverish his family, Herbert replied that his wife was adequately provided for and that all his tithes and church dues were "deodates" from God which, through charity, he was returning to their rightful owner.[7]

Thomas Fuller, whose *Church History of England* has been cited in an earlier chapter, is best known as the author of the encyclopedic and entertaining *The Worthies of England* (1662) which, county by county, reviews the accomplishments of notable men and women in medieval and early modern England. Fuller's book reflects a judicious but magnanimous disposition and reveals a keen interest in works of charity. In outlining the design of the book, Fuller lists the charitable concern of the "worthies" whose activities he sketches: building and repair of churches, support of free schools and colleges, founding of almhouses, and building of bridges and other public improvements. Of the latter he observed:

> Builders of bridges, which are high-ways over water, and makers of caused-ways or causeways, which are bridges over dirt, though last in order, are not least in benefit to the commonwealth. Such conveniences save the lives of many, ease the labour of more painful travellers, and may be said in some sort to lengthen the day, and shorten the way to men in their journeys.

Would that more people would follow the example of Queen Maud, daughter of Henry I, who, after nearly drowning in attempting to ford the river Leo near Stratford, had a beautiful bridge built there! "Far be it from me," Fuller continued:

> to wish the least ill to any, who willingly would not have their fingers to ache, or an hair of their heads lessened. Yet this I could desire, that some covetous churls, who otherwise will not be melted into works of charity, may, in their passing over waters, be put into peril without peril — understand me, might be endangered to fright, but not hurt — that others might fare the better for their fears; such misers being minded thereby to make or repair bridges for public safety and convenience.[8]

Because Fuller believed "we live in an age wherein men begin to be out of charity with charity itself" and the fingers of covetous people "itch to be *nimming* the patrimony of the poor," he began his discussion of almshouses with arguments against and for their establishment or retention. Almshouses may now be a subject of mainly antiquarian interest, but the objections to and defense of them Fuller cites apply equally to many other charitable enterprises. Among the "cavils" is that their founders, "having lived like wolves, turn lambs on their death beds, and part with their fleece to people in want." What they give in charity is insignificant in comparison to the misery they have caused. Fuller replied that not all almshouse builders were guilty of grinding the faces of the poor; as for those who had been unjust and miserly, "Let not envious men repine at that whereat the blessed angels rejoice, the conversion of sinners, and their testifying thereof by such public expressions."

In response to another cavil, "hospitals generally have the rickets, whose heads, their masters, grow over great and over rich, whilst their poor bodies pine away," Fuller answered, "surely there is some other cure for a ricketish body than to kill it; viz. by opening obstructions, and deriving the nutriment to all parts of the same." He acknowledged that there were many faults in almshouses that needed correction yet said that even with their abuses the almshouses should be retained. If those who saw Christ naked would not clothe him, Fuller said, "how much heavier a doom would fall on such who found Christ clothed and stripped him in his poor members of endowments given to their maintenance!"[9]

Mary Dale (d. 1596) and Thomas Sutton (1532–1611) are but two of the many donors to schools and colleges Fuller memorializes. Dale, daughter of a merchant in Bristol, married Sir Thomas Ramsey, a grocer and lord mayor of London, and on his death came into a large fortune. After founding two fellowships at Peterhouse College, Cambridge, she offered the college a large sum of money if it would change its name to Peter and Mary. The master refused the gift, saying, "Peter, who so long lived single, was now too old to have a feminine partner." Unlike "those who in matters of this nature will do nothing, when they cannot do what they would do," Mary Dale continued her charities, directing them in other channels.[10] Sutton, starting life as a soldier, became an army paymaster where "much money therefore passing through, some did lawfully stick on his fingers, which became the bottom of his future estate." The latter, based on income from coal lands in Durham, made him the richest commoner in England. In the last year of his life he endowed a hospital in London on the site of a monastery, Charterhouse, which had been dissolved in 1535. Sutton left funds for a chapel, an almshouse for eighty men, and a school for forty boys. Joseph Addison, Richard Steele, John Wesley, and William Makepeace Thackeray are among the many students at Charterhouse who subsequently became famous.[11]

Of conspicuous givers Fuller wrote:

> I have observed some at the church door cast in sixpence with such ostentation, that it rebounded from the bottom, and rung against both sides of the bason, so that the same piece of silver was the alms and the giver's trumpet; whilst others have dropped down silent five shillings without any noise.[12]

He believed the charitably-minded should be left free "to do what, when, where, how, to whom, and how much" they chose. He recommended for their consideration, however, (1) ransoming of English mariners and other Englishmen held captive in foreign countries; (2) assistance to aged and indigent clergymen deprived of their livings by Cromwell's Protectorate; and (3) aid to servants at the end of their indenture. He also recommended giving in one's lifetime rather than by will. For, as he said, "it is not so kindly charity, for men to give what they can keep no longer; besides, such donations are most subject to abuse."[13]

The case of Sir William Petty (1623–87) illustrates the danger of postponing intended gifts until making a will. Petty was a physician, inventor, cartographer, statistician, and, in the words of J. M. Keynes, "the father of modern economics"; John Aubrey called him "that ingeniose great virtuoso."[14] Once wealthy, he had planned to leave his property to the town of Romsey "for pious uses" and to provide for awards to discoverers of useful knowledge and inventions. By 1685 when he drew up his will, "altered circumstances and the stress of the times" caused him to abandon these plans. His will contained no significant bequests, but it remains an entertaining and edifying document, especially in its stand on gifts to the poor:

> as for beggars by trade and election I give them nothing; as for impotents by the hand of God, the publick ought to maintain them; as for those who have been bred to no calling nor estate they should be put upon their

kindred; as for those who can get no work, the magistrate should cause them to be employed, which may be well done in Ireland, where is fifteen acres of improveable land for every head.

Let compassionate people relieve themselves by relieving such sufferers as seem worthy, he continued, "and for God's sake relieve these several species above mentioned, where the above-mentioned obligees fail in their duties." Satisfied that by previously helping poor relations, by engaging in public works, and by useful inventions he had done his duty to society, Petty warned his heirs that use of his estate for works of charity would be done at their peril. "Nevertheless," he concluded, "to answer custom, and to take the surer side, I give 20 L to the most wanting of the parish wherein I die."[15]

Mercy, forbearance and kindness, and humility are among the qualities seventeenth-century writers associated with charity.[16] Cervantes (1547–1616), speaking through his hero Don Quixote, makes virtue and charity the marks of gentility. In a chapter headed "one of the most important chapters in the whole history," Don Quixote tells his niece and housekeeper the pleasure of wealth comes not from its possession, but from spending it, and spending it well:

> The poor gentleman has no way of showing that he is a gentleman but by virtue, by being affable, well-bred, courteous, gentle-mannered and kindly, not haughty, arrogant or censorious; for by two maravedis given with a cheerful heart to the poor, he will show himself as generous as he who distributes alms with bell-ringing, and no one that perceives him to be endowed with the virtues I have named, even though he knows him not, will fail to recognize and set him down as one of good blood.[17]

Francis Bacon (1561–1626), who, until his fall from power in 1621, held high office under James I, wrote learnedly on both the philanthropic and misanthropic dispositions. The "inclination to goodness" was so deeply implanted in human nature, he asserted, that if not directed to other people it would be bestowed on animals. Thus the Turks, whom Bacon called "a cruel people," gave alms to dogs and cats and, according to a traveler's report, stoned a Christian boy who mischievously bound the bill of a fowl. Bacon had warm regard for charity "directed by right reason" but warned that indiscriminate indulgence was "but facility or softness." Like Cicero, he cautioned against excessive generosity lest "in feeding the streams thou driest the fountain."[18] Just as there is a natural tendency toward goodness in most people, in others there is a "natural malignity," expressed by crossness, "aptness to oppose," envy, and mischief. Misanthropes, haters of men, always enjoy and are ready to take advantage of others' misfortunes. "Such dispositions," said Bacon, "are the very errors of human nature; and yet they are the finest timber to make great politics of; like the knee timber that is good for ships, that are ordained to be tossed; but not for building houses, that shall stand firm."[19]

In the latter years of Bacon's life, the philosopher Thomas Hobbes (1588–1679) occasionally assisted him by taking dictation and translating some of his essays into Latin. In contrast to Bacon, who believed the philanthropic disposition was the norm among human beings, Hobbes maintained that selfishness and self-protection were the dominant motives in human conduct. Hobbes' *The Leviathan* (1651), which prescribed an all-powerful state to establish and preserve peace and order, included philanthropy among the "appetites" that move men. Hobbes defined philanthropy as " 'Desire' of good to another, 'benevolence,' 'good will,' 'charity' if to men generally, 'good-nature.' "[20] In spite of the generous definition, Hobbes could not conceive of anyone practicing philanthropy except to enhance the esteem or "honor" in which he was held in the community or to promote his own security and power.

Anthologists attribute "Charity begins at home" to *Religio Medici* (1642) by Sir Thomas Browne (1605–1662), a physician in Norwich, England. Browne used the phrase as though it were already a common expression, and in an altruistic rather than self-serving sense. He deemed it an "offense unto charity" to defame entire nations or professions with epithets like lying, cheating, or cowardice, because we happen to come across some individuals with those traits. Similarly, he wrote, we should refrain from censuring or condemning other people because their interests, aptitudes, and beliefs differ from our own. "'Tis the general complaint of these times, and perhaps those of the past, that charity grows cold; what I perceive most verified in those which most do manifest the fires and flames of zeal." Charity, in Browne's opinion, required both coolheadedness and humility. Browne had the temerity to include one's self in a plea for good will and tolerance for all:

But how shall we expect charity towards others, when we are uncharitable to ourselves? *Charity begins at home,* is the voice of the World; yet is every man his greatest enemy, and, as it were, his own executioner.

To Browne, uncharitableness meant disregard of and indifference to well-being that, in one's own case, led to self-destruction.[21]

Notes

1. For a history of the trust see Jean Imray, *The Charity of Richard Whittington: A History of the Trust Administered by the Mercers' Company, 1424–1966* (London: Athlone Press, 1968).
2. A.F. Leach, *The Schools of Medieval England* (New York: Benjamin Blom, 1968; first published in 1912), 244; W.K. Jordan, *Social Institutions in Kent, 1480–1660, A Study in Changing Patterns of Social Aspirations,* volume 75 of *Archaeological Cantiana* (1961): 68–69.
3. Richard Johnson, "Sir William Seauenoake," in *The Nine Worthies of London* (1592) in *The Harleian Miscellany* (London, 1811), 12:176–78.
4. Richard Johnson, "A Song of Sir Richard Whittington," in Henry B. Wheatley, ed., *The History of Sir Richard Whittington* by T.H. (London: Villon Society, 1885), ix-xiii.
5. Osbert Sitwell, *The True Story of Dick Whittington, A Christmas Story for Cat Lovers* (London: Home and Van Thal, Ltd., 1945).
6. Izaak Walton, "The Life of Dr. John Donne" (1640), in *Izaak Walton's Lives* (London: Thomas Nelson and Sons Ltd., n.d. [1927], 58–62. Donne's charity did not extend to his son-in-law, Edward Alleyn (1566–1626), actor and founder of Dulwich College, who quarreled with Donne when the latter refused him a loan.
7. Walton, "The Life of Mr. George Herbert" (1670), ibid., 273–74. Herbert and his wife, Jane Danvers, had no children; after his death she remarried and lived until 1656.
8. Thomas Fuller, *The Worthies of England* (London: Thomas Tegg, 1840) 1:45–46. The English statute of Charitable Uses of 1601 (43 Eliz. 4) defined charitable objects to include "the repair of bridges, ports, havens, causeways, churches, sea-banks and highways" as well as "the relief of aged, impotent and poor people," education, and aid to orphans and sick and maimed soldiers and sailors.
9. Ibid., 1:46–48. Anthony Trollope's novel *The Warden* (1855), dealing with Hiram's Hospital and alleged abuse in its administration, is discussed below in Part Four, chapter 9.
10. Thomas Fuller, *The Worthies of England*, edited by John Freeman (London: George Allen Unwin Limited, 1952), 508–9.
11. Ibid., 338–39.
12. Ibid., 508.

13. Fuller, *Worthies of England*, 1:48; Augustus Jessopp, D.D., comp., *Wise Words and Quaint Sayings of Thomas Fuller* (Oxford, 1895), 84–85.
14. Geoffrey Keynes, *A Bibliography of Sir William Petty, F.R.S.* (Oxford: Clarendon Press, 1971), vii; *Aubrey's Brief Lives* edited by Oliver Lawson Dick (London: Clarendon Press, 1950), 115. Samuel Pepys's diary for March 22, 1664/65, records a conversation with Petty about his will. Henry B. Wheatley, ed., *The Diary of Samuel Pepys* (New York: Random House, n.d.), 1, 1063.
15. Petty's will is included in Edmond Fitzmaurice, *The Life of Sir William Petty* (London: J. Murray, 1895), 314.
16. William Shakespeare, *The Merchant of Venice* (1600) act 4, sc. 1 (mercy); Johann Arnett in William Neil, ed., *Concise Dictionary of Religious Quotations* (Grand Rapids, Mich.: Eerdmans, 1974), 14 (forbearance and kindness); Henry Moore, "Hymn to Charity and Humility" in Lord David Cecil, ed., *The Oxford Book of Christian Verse* (Oxford: Oxford University Press, 1965), 215–16 (humility).
17. Miguel de Cervantes, *The History of Don Quixote de la Mancha*, translated by John Ormsby, Pt. 2 (1615), ch. 6 in Hutchins, editor in chief, *Great Books of the Western World*, 29:222.
18. Francis Bacon, "Of Goodness and Goodness of Nature," in *Essays or Counsels Civil and Moral* (1625), in *The Harvard Classics* (New York: F.P. Collier and Son, 1909–10), 3:32–34.
19. Ibid.
20. Thomas Hobbes, *The Leviathan* pt. 1, ch. 6, ibid., 34:354.
21. Sir Thomas Browne, *Religio Medici*, sect. 4, ibid., 3:315–17.

5

God and Neighbor

In the seventeenth century, possibly in reaction to the "fires and flames of zeal" aroused by the Reformation and Counter-Reformation, both Catholics and Protestants reinvoked the doctrine of worshiping God by serving man. In France the work of Saint Vincent de Paul (1581–1660) in forming and organizing charities revived Catholicism. In 1623 he founded the Congregation of the Missions, an order of secular priests (Lazarites), to evangelize the poor in the countryside. Through establishment of Confraternities of Charities in rural and city churches, he gave church members, especially women, opportunities to contribute to and participate in efforts to aid the poor. In 1633, with Saint Louise de Marillac (1591–1660), he founded the Daughters of Charity, an order of uncloistered nuns who visited, fed, and nursed the poor in their own homes, hospitals, orphanages, and institutions for foundlings. Voltaire, who called Saint Vincent de Paul "my saint," said of him that he had left more useful monuments than his sovereign.[1]

St. Vincent, himself of humble birth, achieved his charitable ends by enlisting the support of members of the French aristocracy and the court of Louis XIII. He did not attack wealth, condemn the rich, or call for a more just social order. "On the one hand," observes a student of his charities, "he beheld the need and suffering of the people; on the other hand, he enjoyed the favor of many who were able to furnish means toward the relief of this misery. These . . . he approached with the appeals which under the circumstances, were likely to be the most efficacious."[2] Although his appeals were made to the rich, he did not believe they were under any heavier obligation than the poor to show their love of God through love of neighbor.

45

Literature provides occasional glimpses of the miseries seventeenth-century humanitarians sought to relieve. In *Paradise Lost* (1667), for example, John Milton (1608–74) has the angel Michael reveal to Adam the horrors of a hospital for the poor:

> Immediately a place before his eyes appeared, sad, noisome, dark; A Lazar-house it seemed, wherein were laid numbers of all diseased—all maladies of ghastly spasm, of racking torture, qualms of heart-sick agony, all feverous kinds, convulsions, epilepsies, fierce catarrhs, intestine stone and ulcer, colic pangs, daemoniac phrenzy, moping melancholy,

> And moon-struck madness, pining atrophy, Marasmus, and wide-wasting pestilence, dropsies and asthmas, and joint-racking rheums. Dire was the tossing, deep the groans; Despair tended the sick, busiest from couch to couch; and over them triumphant Death his dart shook, but delayed to strike, though oft invoked With vows, as their chief good and final hope. Sight so deform what heart of rock could long dry-eyed behold? Adam could not, but wept.[3]

In a famous "spital sermon" delivered in London in 1671, Isaac Barrow declared charity "the main point of religion" and mercy and bounty "the chief parts of charity."[4] Barrow (1630–77) was the first professor of mathematics at Cambridge University—a position he relinquished to his student, Isaac Newton; as Master of Trinity College, Cambridge, he commenced the building of the College library, designed by his friend Sir Christopher Wren. Barrow was once chaplain to King Charles II, who admired his scholarship but said he was "an unfair preacher because he exhausted every topic, and left no room for anything new to be said by anyone who came after him." His spital sermon "The Duty and Reward of Bounty to the Poor," which took as its text Psalm 112 ("He hath dispersed, he hath given to the poor"), "required three hours and a half to deliver although it was not preached in full." If long-winded, the sermon was also long-lived, being frequently cited and quoted by latitudinarians in the eighteenth and nineteenth centuries.[5]

Among those who might have attended Barrow's sermon was Thomas Firmin (1632–97), a wealthy London textile manufacturer who, after about 1670, made philanthropy his main concern. According to a biographer, Firmin "was a kind of almoner-general to the metropolis, keeping a register of the poor he visited, recommending their cases, and apprenticing their children."[6] By enlisting the support of others he collected large sums for relief of victims of religious persecution in Poland, assistance to Huguenot refugees from France, and aid to Protestants who fled Ireland in 1688–89. On his own he visited prisons, helped debtors, and prosecuted jailers who abused their authority. Instead of giving alms he attempted to provide work and wages for as many of the poor as he could at a workhouse he established near St. Bartholomew's Hospital. There he employed as many as 1700 spinners and unskilled workers in making linen, which he sold at cost, paying the hands the going (very low) rate. The workhouse was not a paying proposition; Firmin, sometimes with the help of friends, made up the deficit from his own pocket and supplemented the wages of some employees with gifts of coal. He described the undertaking, and overstated its success, in a pamphlet printed in 1681, in which he pointed with particular pride to the benefits resulting from the employment of children in the workhouse:

> I my self have at this time many poor Children, not above five or six years old, that can earn two pence a day, others but a little older, three pence or four pence, by spinning Flax which will go very far towards the maintenance of any poor Child. Not that I would have these Schools confined only to Spinning, but left at liberty to take in any other work that the Children shall be capable of, as knitting of Stockings, winding of Silk, making of Lace or plain Work, or the like: For it matters not so much what you employ these poor Children in, as that you do employ them in some thing, to prevent an idle, lazy kind of Life, which if once they get the habit of, they will hardly leave; but on the contrary, if you train up a Child in the way that he should go, when he is old, he will not depart from it.[7]

Firmin took a benovolent interest in the scholars at Christ's Hospital (a school on the site of a former foundling hospital), of which he was a governor, attending Sunday services there and satisfying himself that the pudding pies the boys received for supper were of adequate size. He was a founding member of the Society for the Reformation of Manners (1691), an organization much admired by the American Puritan, Cotton Mather.

John Bunyan (1628–88), a Baptist imprisoned for nonconformity from 1660 to 1672 and again in 1676–77, was at the other end of the religious spectrum from Barrow, and as far removed from Firmin on the social scale. For most of his life poverty, persecution, and imprisonment made him and his family objects rather than donors of charity. After publication of *Pilgrim's Progress* in 1678 Bunyan became a popular preacher, hailed by Baptists as "Bishop Bunyan"; on his travels through the countryside he collected and distributed alms and mediated quarrels among his followers.

Monica Furlong, discussing the ninety characters Christian meets or hears of in *Pilgrim's Progress*, observes that only seventeen are good; "the rest, and by far the more interesting and more colorful characters are all bad."[8] One of the good, and not very interesting, ones is Charity, who with the three other women, Discretion, Piety, and Prudence, live in the House Beautiful. They extend hospitality to Christian and give him bread, wine, and raisins as he approaches the Valley of Humiliation. The qualities of discretion and prudence were seldom manifested in Bunyan's life, and his piety was not that of the orthodox. The rough and ready charity bestowed on him and his family were best represented in the book by the characters Help, who reaches out a hand to pull Christian from the Slough of Despair, Goodwill, who points out the straight and narrow path to the Celestial City; and Faithful, Christian's cheerful companion who is burnt at the stake in Vanity Fair.

After the Revolution of 1688 William Penn (1644–1718) temporarily lost control of the colony of Pennsylvania because of his continued friendship with the deposed King James II. His *Fruits of Solitude*, written while he was under suspicion of treason, was an attack on censoriousness, an attitude of mind inimical to charity and tolerance whether in public or private matters. Even members of a persecuted sect may be sanctimonious and fault-finding in dealing with one another, to say nothing of outsiders. There is no reason to believe Penn was thinking more of Quakers than anybody else when he condemned censoriousness; his use of "we" makes his comments universal in application.

41. We are apt to be very pert at censuring others, where we will not endure advice our selves. And nothing shews our Weakness more than to be so sharp-sighted at spying other Men's Faults; and so purblind about our own.

. . . .

43. Much of this comes from Ill Nature, as well as from an inordinate Value of our selves: For we love Rambling better than home, and blaming the unhappy, rather than covering and relieving them.

44. In such Occasions some shew their Malice, and are witty upon Misfortunes; others their Justice, they can reflect a pace: But few or none their Charity; especially if it be about Money Matters.

45. You shall see an old Miser come forth with a set Gravity, and so much Severity against the distressed, to excuse his Purse, that he will, e'er he has done, put it out of all Question, That Riches is Righteousness with him. This, says he, is the Fruit of your Prodigality (as if, poor Man, Covetousness were no Fault) Or, of your Projects, or grasping after a great Trade: While he himself would have done the same thing, but that he had not the Courage to venture so much ready Money out of his own trusty Hands, though it had been to have brought him back the Indies in return. But the Proverb is just, Vice should not correct Sin.

46. They have a Right to censure, that have a Heart to help: The rest is Cruelty, not Justice.[9]

On the topic of Frugality or Bounty Penn wrote:

50. Frugality is good if Liberality be join'd with it. The first is leaving off superfluous Expences; the last bestowing them to the Benefit of others that need. The first without the last begins Covetiousness; the last without the first begins Prodigality: Both together make an excellent Temper. Happy the Place where ever that is found.

51. Were it universal, we should be Cur'd of two Extreams, Want and Excess: and the one would supply the other, and so bring both nearer to a Mean; the just Degree of earthly Happiness.

52. It is a Reproach to Religion and Government to suffer so much Poverty and Excess.

53. Were the Superfluities of a Nation valued, and made a perpetual Tax or Benevolence, there would be more Almshouses than Poor; School than Scholars; and enough to spare for Government besides.

54. Hospitality is good, if the poorer sort are the subjects of our Bounty; else too near a Superfluity.[10]

To Penn, charity in its lowest or most basic meaning signified "Commiseration of the Poor, and unhappy of Mankind" and extending them a "Helping-Hand to mend their Condition." In giving to the poor, however, we only return a portion of the bounty with which God has entrusted us. On another level, "Charity makes the best construction of Things and Persons . . . excuses Weaknesses, extenuates Miscarriages, makes the best of every thing; forgives every Body, serves All, and hopes to the End." In "her other and higher senses" (as in 1 Cor. 13:3) charity is "the One Thing Needful, the divine Virtue" which if practiced by "Pretenders to Christianity" would substitute "Love and Compassion" for censuring and persecuting one another in any manner whatsoever.[11]

It remained for an American, Cotton Mather (1663–1728), to enunciate detailed and specific suggestions for serving God by minding one's neighbors' material and spiritual welfare. A righteous person was no better than his neighbor, Mather declared, unless he strove to be more excellent as a neighbor. "Let that man be better than his neighbor who labors to be a better neighbor, to do most good unto his neighbor."[12]

Mather, scion of two eminent Puritan families, was a Boston clergyman of great learning and wide interests. He was aware of and impressed by the work of the German Pietist August Hermann Francke in establishing educational and charitable institutions in Halle. Among Mather's immense output of books and pamphlets on theology, history, biography, philosophy, science, and medicine, *Bonafacius* or *Essays to Do Good* (1710) is probably the most readable and accessible. Benjamin Franklin, a critic of the Mather family's role in Boston affairs in his youth, later acknowledged his indebtedness to the practical piety expounded in the work.

Mather asked the good neighbor not only to think about and pity the widows and orphans of his or her neighborhood, those in "pinching poverty" or heartbroken with bereavements and those under seige by "the wicked one," but to do something to help them. Visit and comfort them with some good word, relieve their necessities, and "lovingly and faithfully" admonish any who seem to be going astray. "If there be any idle persons," he advised, "cure them of their idleness. Don't nourish 'em and harden 'em in that, but find employment for them. Find 'em work, set 'em to work, keep 'em to work. Then as much of your other bounty to them as you please."[13]

Notes

1. Voltaire to Charles Michel, 4 January 1766, in Theodore Besterman, ed., *The Complete Works of Voltaire* 114:16 (Toronto: University of Toronto Press, 1973). For an illustrated biography published on the three hundredth anniversary of Vincent's death see Leonard von Matt and Louis Cognet, *St. Vincent de Paul*, (Chicago: Henry Regnery Company, 1960). His papers have been edited by Pierre Coste and published under the title *Saint Vincent de Paul Correspondences, Entretiens, Documents* (Paris: J. Gabalda, 1920–25).

2. Cyprian William Emanuel, *The Charities of St. Vincent de Paul* (Washington, D.C.: Catholic University of America, 1923), 85–86.

3. John Milton, *Paradise Lost*, Book 11.

4. Isaac Barrow, "Sermon XXXI: The Duty and Reward of Bounty to the Poor," in *The Works of Dr. Isaac Barrow* (London: A.J. Valpy, 1830–31), 2:329–30. "Spital Sermons" were preached on Easter Monday and Tuesday at St. Mary Spital, London, before the Lord Mayor and Corporation of the city.

5. The quotations are from the biographical sketch of Barrow by Robert Edward Anderson in *Dictionary of National Biography*, 1:1221.

6. Biographical sketch of Firmin by Alexander Gordon in *Dictionary of National Biography*, 7:46–49.

7. Thomas Firmin, "Some Proposals for the Employment of the Poor, and for the Prevention of Idleness, Etc." (London, 1681), 2–3.

8. Monica Furlong, *Puritan's Progress* (New York: Coward, McCann and Geoghegan, 1975), 106–7.

9. William Penn, *Some Fruits of Solitude* (1693) in *The Harvard Classics* (New York: F.P. Collier and Son, 1909–10), 1:326–27.

10. Ibid., 1:328.

11. *More Fruits of Solitude* (pt. 2 of *Some Fruits of Solitude*), in *The Harvard Classics*, 1: 396–97 (paragraphs 282–99).

12. Cotton Mather, "Bonafacius" (1710), in Perry Miller, ed., *The American Puritans, Their Prose and Poetry* (Garden City, N.Y.: Doubleday, 1950), 216–17.

13. Ibid., 218.

PART THREE

The Eighteenth Century

Prologue: "The World Is All Alike"

John Gay (1685–1732) wrote his own epitaph twelve years before his death:

> Life is a jest and all things show it;
> I thought so once, but now I know it.

The jest in Gay's "Beggar's Opera" is the "similitude of manners" among denizens of high and low life. The beggar Gay uses as his spokesman in the play says that "it is difficult to determine whether (in the fashionable Vices) the fine Gentlemen imitate the Gentlemen of the Road, or the Gentlemen of the Road the fine Gentlemen." Macheath, a highwayman, is a more honorable character than his adversaries Peachum, a police informer, and Lockit, the prison warden. "The World is all alike," Macheath laments when he learns that he has been betrayed by one of his own men, "and even our gang can no more trust one another than other people." At the end of the play the beggar-author explains that he had intended to have Macheath executed to show that "the lower sort of people have their vices in a degree as well as The Rich, and that they are punish'd for them. Bowing to the "Taste of the Town," he arranges for Macheath's reprieve, and a happy ending.[1]

Note

1. John Gay, "My Own Epitaph" (1720), in Roger Lonsdale, comp, *The New Oxford Book of Eighteenth Century Verse* (Oxford: Oxford University Press, 1984) 129. "The Beggar's Opera" (1728), in John Gay, *Dramatic Works*, edited by John Fuller (Oxford: Clarendon Press, 1983) 2:3, 62–65 (Introduction, act 2, Sc. 14, 15, 16). William Hogarth's painting, *The Beggar's Opera* (1729), emphasizes the similarity between high and low life by depicting both audience and actors in the play.

6

The Age of Benevolence

"We are the most *Lazy Diligent* Nation in the World," wrote Daniel Defoe in 1704. Defoe (1660–1731) acknowledged that England's trade and manufactures had earned her people a deserved reputation for industriousness. "But," he complained, "there is a general Taint of Slothfulness upon our Poor,

> there's nothing more frequent, than for an Englishman to Work till he has got his Pocket full of Money, and then go and be idle, or perhaps Drunk, till 'tis all gone, and perhaps himself in Debt; and ask him in his Cups what he intends, he'll tell you honestly, he'll drink as long as it lasts, and then go to work for more.

Defoe's pamphlet, "Giving Alms No Charity," was an attack not on almsgiving in the ordinary sense but on proposals for establishment of public workhouses for the unemployed. In it he maintained that existing parish relief was adequate to deal with poverty caused by "casualty" (for example, illness, handicap, or inability to work) and argued against public measures to relieve poverty caused by the crimes of "luxury, sloath, and pride."[1]

Shortly after completing *Robinson Crusoe* (1719) and *Moll Flanders* (1722), Defoe traveled through England paying attention both to the state of the economy and to charitable institutions and activities in the places he visited. At Winchester he went to see the Hospital of St. Cross, founded in 1136, the oldest almshouse in England, where every traveler who asked for it received a cup of beer and piece of white bread. It was a wealthy institution but sheltered less than half as many poor brothers as it might have, while the master lived in luxury.[2] At

Saltash, in Cornwall, Defoe heard of a charitable dog that carried the bones or scraps given to him or her to an old blind mastiff that lived in a thicket at the edge of town. On Sundays and holidays the dog brought the mastiff to the city for handouts and then led him back to his nest. In Oxford and Cambridge Defoe, a Dissenter, took pride in the thought that more scholars had been produced, more libraries stocked, and more fine buildings erected in the 200 years since the Reformation than in the 800 years of papacy. In contrast to gifts of Catholics, he said, those of Protestant donors were "acts of charity to the world, and acts of bounty, in reverence to learning and learned men, without the grand excitement of the health of their souls, and of the souls of their fathers, to be pray'd out of purgatory and get a ready admission into heaven."[3]

One act of charity whose magnificence impressed Defoe and his contemporaries was the gift of Thomas Guy (1644–1724) for establishment of a hospital for incurables in London. Defoe ranked it with the founding of Charterhouse as "the greatest of its kind . . . that ever was founded in this nation by one person, whether private or public, not excepting the kings themselves." How the donor, a printer and seller of Bibles who had never held a public office of trust or profit, became so immensely rich that in addition to great public benefactions he was able to leave his heirs generously provided for was a matter of keen interest to Defoe. Noting that Guy never married, that he lived to be more than eighty years of age, and that interest on his money added to its accumulation, Defoe concluded, "'Tis enough to say, he was a thriving, frugal man, who God was pleased exceedingly to bless, in whatever he set his hand to, knowing to what good purpose he laid up his gains."[4]

Bernard de Mandeville (1670–1733), a Dutch physician who settled in London in the 1690s, defined charity so strictly as to exclude any action bearing the faintest whiff of self-regard. This rigorous definition, combined with a pessimistic view of human nature, allowed Mandeville to discount the role of altruism and benevolence in human affairs. At about the same time Defoe was exclaiming over the generosity of Thomas Guy, Mandeville declared, "Pride and vanity have built more hospitals than all the virtues together."[5]

Mandeville's pronouncement was consistent with his argument in *The Fable of the Bees* (1714) that private vices such as greed, ostentation, and even intemperance conferred public benefits by increasing demand for labor and commodities; virtues such as thrift, sobriety, and consideration for others, on the contrary, produced no tangible benefits for society. Mandeville's unorthodox views found favor with distillers who rewarded him for his writings endorsing the social benefits of drunkenness.[6]

Mandeville's readers included the young Samuel Johnson (1709–84). In 1778 he told James Boswell and other friends that he had read Mandeville forty or fifty years earlier and that the reading "opened my views into real life very much." The fallacy of the book, as Johnson saw it, was Mandeville's failure to define vices and benefits; the benefits tavern keepers, brewers, and farmers derived from the vice of drunkenness was outweighed by the harm it did to the drunkard and his family. On one point, however, Johnson continued to agree with Mandeville. "You cannot spend money in luxury without doing good to the poor," Johnson said in 1778. "Nay, you do more good to them by spending it in luxury than by giving it; for by spending it in luxury you make them exert industry, whereas by giving it, you keep them idle." Johnson conceded that there might be more virtue in giving for charity than in spending for luxury, "though" he added, echoing Mandeville "there may be pride in that too."[7]

In 1712 Richard Steele (1672–1729), co-founder of *The Spectator*, hailed charity schools as "the greatest instance of public spirit the age has produced." The movement for their establishment had been launched in 1698 by the Society for the Promotion of Christian Knowledge (SPCK), which urged parish churches to organize schools where poor children could be taught to read the Bible and catechism and could receive instruction in religion and morality. The schools were an example of application of joint stock enterprise to philanthropy, seeking support from shopkeepers, artisans, and other small donors as well as the wealthy. By 1715, 25,000 boys and girls in London and other parts of England were enrolled in charity schools. While attending the schools, the children wore uniforms; as soon as feasible they were apprenticed to learn a trade. Advocates of the schools, including Steele, pointed out their usefulness to donors in producing "a race of good and useful servants."[8] Bernard de Mandeville called the movement "this present folly"; he opposed the schools partly because he distrusted the motives of the sponsors but mainly because he thought education of poor children was inimical to the public interest; in order to keep the poor "laborious," it was essential to keep them ignorant.[9]

Henry Fielding (1707–54) also distrusted the motives of some seemingly respectable people, but there was a world of difference between his view of life and that of Mandeville. Like Charles Dickens, who named a son after Fielding, he revered charity, goodness, and kindness and kept his faith in them throughout a career that brought him into frequent contact with the seamy side of "real life." A member of a distinguished but not wealthy family, educated at Eton and the University of Leiden, Fielding was by turn dramatist, journalist, novelist, and justice of the peace in two sections of London. In politics he opposed the government of Robert Walpole; as justice of the peace he fought corruption and crime; in religion he supported the latitudinarianism of Isaak Barrow and John Tillotson. The latter doctrine, often introduced into Fielding's novels, emphasized the religious value of morality and good works, notably charity, as opposed to the rival doctrine of justification by faith alone, taught both in the Church of England and by the evangelist George Whitefield. Charity helped Fielding over some hard spots in his own life: when he was in financial straits his friends Lord George Littelton, a whig politician, and the philanthropist Ralph Allen (1694–1764) came to his assistance. Allen provided for the support and education of Fielding's children after his death.

Because of Fielding's sincere regard for charity, he poked fun at hypocrisies practiced in its name. The hero's father in *Joseph Andrews* (1742) was unable to get Joseph admitted to a charity school because, as Fielding explained, "a cousin of his father's landlord did not vote on the right side for a churchwarden in a borough-town."[10] The book contains repeated examples of people finding excuses for not giving to or helping the needy. Early in the story Joseph, a handsome and virtuous youth of about 18, loses his job as footman for spurning the advances of his mistress. While he is trying to make his way to the country, thieves beat him, rob him of his money and clothes, and leave him for dead along the highway. The driver and passengers in a coach who hear his moans and discover his body, like the priest and Levite in the Parable of the Good Samaritan, are inclined to "pass by on the other side." Only fear that if Joseph dies they may be accused of complicity in his murder makes them grudgingly come to his aid. The driver does not want to let him into the coach unless someone agrees to pay his fare; a lady passenger objects to having a naked man in the coach; neither driver nor passengers are willing to give Joseph a coat for fear of getting blood on it. Only the postilion, a young man soon afterward transported for robbing a henhouse, takes pity on Joseph and gives him his coat.[11]

After Joseph recovers and resumes his travels, he makes a speech on charity, intended for the ears of his curate and companion, Parson Adams. More or less in the spirit of Hobbes and Mandeville, Joseph asserts that "an ambition to be respected more than other people" is what makes a man build a fine house, and buy fine pictures, furniture, and clothes. But when we admire his house, pictures, furniture, and clothes it is the architect and builder, the painter, the craftsman, and the tailor who made them that we honor, not the man who bought them. Would not some noble act of charity such as relieving a poor family of the miseries of poverty or helping a debtor or tradesman to become independent create more honor for a man than the accumulation of possessions? Not only the object of his charity but all who heard of it would "reverence him infinitely more than the possessor of all those other things."[12]

Parson Adams does not hear the speech because he falls asleep just as Joseph begins speaking. Adams, a kindly, unworldly figure who shares and expounds Fielding's religious views, plays an increasingly important role in the story. His request for assistance made to another clergyman, an expert in finding high-minded reasons for not giving, leads to a spirited debate on the subject of faith versus works. Adams concludes his side of it by declaring that in the Scriptures "there is no Command more express, no Duty more frequently enjoined than Charity. Whoever therefore is void of charity, I make no scruple of pronouncing that he is no Christian."[13] On another occasion, denouncing the Calvinistic views of George Whitefield, Adams states his own belief that "a virtuous and good Turk, or heathen, are more acceptable in the sight of their creator than a vicious and wicked Christian, though his faith was as perfectly orthodox as St. Paul's himself."[14]

In *Tom Jones* (1749) the author's spokesman on religious matters is Squire Allworthy, a character modeled after Fielding's benefactor Ralph Allen. Allworthy and Captain Blifil, who believes in salvation by faith and grace rather than by works, argue about the meaning of charity. Blifil proves, at least to his own satisfaction, that nowhere in the Scriptures is the word charity used to denote benevolence or generosity. Distribution of alms, even if it exhausts one's fortune, can never help more than a handful of people; but charity in its true sense — "that sublime Christian-like Disposition, that vast Elevation of Thought, in Purity approaching to Angelic Perfection, to be attained, expressed, and felt only by Grace — can be extended to all Mankind."[15]

Allworthy responds that in his opinion charity involves action, such as almsgiving; in its most meritorious form charity means bestowing what we really want or need for ourselves to lessen the distress of another. As if in response to Joseph Andrews's speech on charity that Parson Adams did not hear, Allworthy calls expending our surplus on works of charity rather than on fine pictures or other luxuries an instance of our being "humane creatures." Replying to Blifil's warning that one must be on guard against imposition by the undeserving, Allworthy says, "I do not think a few or many examples of ingratitude can justify a man's hardening his heart against the distress of his fellow-creatures; nor do I believe it can ever have such effect on a truly benevolent mind."[16]

Fielding's working title for *Tom Jones* was *The Foundling*. His inclusion of the word in the book's title, *The History of Tom Jones, a Foundling*, struck some critics, including Samuel Richardson, author of *Pamela* (1740), as "coarse."[17] Tom's history would probably have been much shorter had he been found anywhere but in the bed of the kindly Mr. Allworthy. Even so, if Allworthy had permitted, the servant summoned to the care of the baby would have put it in a basket and left it at the churchwarden's door, where it might or might not have survived the night.[18]

One of Fielding's contemporaries, Thomas Coram (1668–1751), distressed by the sight of abandoned babies left alive, dying, or dead on the streets of London's East End, undertook a campaign to establish a hospital to receive and care for foundlings. In seeking support for the project Coram, a retired sea captain, had to overcome prejudice against bastardy and belief that the hospital would encourage promiscuity. After seventeen years of struggle, to which Coram devoted his fortune as well as his powers of persuasion, he received a royal charter for the Foundling Hospital, and the institution opened in 1745. Coram attributed the success of the project to support received from "the ladies."[19]

As Justice of the Peace, Fielding engaged in a daily battle with crime and poverty, problems he believed to be interrelated. Fielding blamed the sorry state of the times (1750s) to the "Torrent of Luxury" that had engulfed the nation, corrupting all classes, high and low. The moral results on the rich were deplorable; the social, economic, and moral consequences for the poor were disastrous. Unable to achieve the standard of living they saw others enjoying on the wages offered them, many gave up the struggle to make ends meet. "The more simple and poor spirited," Fielding reported, "betake themselves to a state of starving and beggary, while those of more art and courage become thieves, sharpers and robbers."[20]

In the introduction to a pamphlet entitled "A Proposal for Making Effectual Provision for the Poor, For Amending their Morals, and for Rendering them Useful Members of the Society" (1753), Fielding expressed sympathy for the suffering of the poor. If we were to walk through the outskirts of London, Fielding declared:

> and look into the Habitations of the Poor, we should there behold such Pictures of human misery as must move the Compassion of every Heart that deserves the Name of human. What indeed must be his Composition who could see whole Families in Want of every Necessary of Life, oppressed with Hunger, Cold, Nakedness, and Filth, and with Diseases, the certain Consequence of all these; what, I say, must be his Composition, who could look into such a Scene as this, and be affected only in his Nostrils?

Unfortunately, society was better acquainted with the misdeeds of the poor than their suffering. "They starve, and freeze, and rot among themselves; but they beg, and steal, and rob among their betters." Fielding asserted:

> There is not a Parish in the Liberty of Westminster which doth not raise Thousands annually for the Poor, and there is not a Street in that Liberty which doth not swarm all Day with Beggars, and all Night with Thieves. Stop your Coach at what Shop you will, however expeditious the Tradesman is to attend you, a Beggar is commonly beforehand with him; and if you should not directly face his Door, the Tradesman must often turn his Head while you are talking to him, or the same Beggar, or some other Thief at hand, will pay a Visit to his Shop![21]

Fielding's attitude toward the poor was sympathetic but not indulgent. A mercantilist in economics, he believed (in this respect like Mandeville) that the only thing of value the working class had to contribute to the nation was labor. With the exception of the "impotent and infirm"—the proper objects of charity—poor people had an obligation to work. Conversely, society had the double duty of providing them with the means of labor and compelling them to undertake it.[22]

Fielding cited neglect, abuse, and defects in England's poor laws (in modern terms, "welfare") for the nation's failure to discharge its duty to the poor. In contrast to Defoe, he advocated transferring responsibility for their care from parishes, many of which were too small and poverty-stricken to make "effectual provision," to larger administrative units such as counties. For Middlesex County, where he was Justice of the Peace, and where the problems of poverty and crime were particularly acute, he urged establishment of a huge county workhouse, capable of providing segregated lodgings and work space for 3,000 men and 2,000 women, with an adjoining county house of correction for 600 prisoners. Contractors would train and employ the inmates in manufacturing different products, improving their skills and preparing them for independence. Since the objective was not only to put the inmates to work but to reform their morals, the plan (which, as Fielding foresaw, was never carried out) called for prayers every morning and regular hours for religious worship. On this point Fielding quoted his favorite theologian, John Tillotson, archbishop of Canterbury toward the end of the seventeenth century: "Religion hath a good influence on the people, to make them obedient to government, and peaceable towards one another" not only out of fear, "but out of Conscience which is a firm, and constant, and lasting Principle, and will hold a man fast when all other Obligations will break."[23]

In considering the options available to the desperately poor—begging or crime—Fielding failed to take note of a self-help movement already stirring among them. This was Methodism, inspired by the preaching of John Wesley (1703–1791), and put into practice by his leadership and organizational ability. Wesley's self-imposed mission was to "preach the gospel to the poor." The gospel was that salvation was open to all, no matter how wretched and sinful, who unreservedly accepted Jesus as their Savior, sincerely repented of their sins, and conscientiously mended their ways. Wesley was not interested in "persons of quality," that is, members of his own social class. All his concern and love went to the poor, disreputable as well as reputable; the former were special favorites since their redemption was particularly challenging and rewarding. The people he sought out and attracted to meetings held outdoors or in makeshift chapels were those on whom the established church had given up hope and those who, because of poverty or indifference, had ceased attending or had never gone to church.[24]

Wesley organized his converts into "classes" of from five to twelve members with a leader chosen by him or an associate. The leader was responsible for seeing that the members held to Methodist doctrine and led upright, temperate, and charitable lives. The "classes" merged into "bands" and "meetings", an extended but intimate family, with the leaders acting as father and members regarding and calling each other "sisters" and "brothers".[25]

In contrast to the latitudinarianism taught by Tillotson and favored by Fielding and his characters, Wesley made justification (salvation) by faith alone, without regard to works, the doctrine of Methodism. Nevertheless, he placed heavy emphasis on charity. His personal creed, which he urged his followers to adopt, was to gain all he could without harm to others — in his case by writing; to save all he could by living modestly and frugally; and to give all he could — which to Wesley meant all he had other than his books.[26]

Wesley's attitude toward charity reflected his fear of wealth and hostility to self-indulgence. Giving generously to the needy and to good causes — for example, building of chapels, orphan homes, and hospitals — was a preventive of and remedy for the accumulation of riches and worldly temptations. Throughout his career Wesley recognized that wealth was inimical to Methodism, "the religion of the heart." He foresaw, and lived long enough to see, that frugality and industry would make some Methodists rich. Only by giving virtually to the extent Jesus recommended to the rich young man could such Methodists remain true to their faith.[27]

Wesley urged his followers to assume that same responsibility for guarding their physical as their spiritual health. Although opposed to finery in dress, he believed "cleanliness is next to godliness." He was the author of *Primitive Physic* (1747), cited by historians of medicine as "the century's most popular medical self-help text."[28] In *Adam Bede* (1859), George Eliot's novel of "old-fashioned Methodist" life in the 1790s, a woman takes raw bacon from her scant larder to a neighbor's child "to stop the fits." Wesley, whatever he thought of the remedy, would have approved the manifestation of neighborly concern and kindness.[29]

The first Methodist given a prominent and sympathetic role in fiction was Humphrey Clinker in Tobias Smollett's novel of that name

(1771). Smollett (1721–71), a physician as well as author, had been critical of Methodism in his *History of England* (1764); he treats Clinker as a somewhat comic figure but always as a person of honesty, sincerity, and upright character. Humphrey is about the same age as Joseph Andrews and, in his initial appearance in the book, is nearly as naked as Joseph was when left for dead by the robbers and discovered by people in a passing coach. Humphrey has lost his job as stableman, been evicted, and has had to pawn his clothes because of six months' illness. He has no shirt and his breeches are so thin that they split when he is pressed into service as postilion for Squire Matthew Bramble's carriage. The squire's sister is affronted by the exposure of his back, but her maid observes that his skin is "as fair as alabaster." When Squire Bramble hears Humphrey's story he tells him, "Clinker, you are a most notorious offender — you stand convicted of sickness, hunger, wretchedness, and want."[30]

Humphrey, having been given money to redeem his clothes, is hired by Squire Bramble as footman and joins Bramble's party on its travels through England and Scotland. From time to time, much to the Squire's annoyance, Humphrey gives vent to his religious fervor and reforming zeal. When wrongfully thrown into prison, he applies himself to the reform of the prisoners, a task Methodists of the time often attempted. In London he preaches at a Methodist meeting attended, the furious Squire Bramble discovers, by the Squire's sister, her maid, and his niece. When the Squire discovers Humphrey exhorting a group of footmen and porters, he accuses him of selling medicine and drugs. Humphrey replies that he is selling nothing but is freely offering advice to his listeners on giving up profane swearing. The Squire objects that if Clinker gets the vulgar to give up their vile language there will be "nothing left to distinguish their conversation from that of their betters." As always in these exchanges, Smollett allows Humphrey Clinker the last word: "But then your honour knows, their conversations will be void of offense; and, at the day of judgment, there will be no distinction of persons."[31]

Hannah More, in an essay on "Religions of the Fashionable World" published in 1791, bestowed the appellation *"the age of benevolence"* on the eighteenth century. More (1745–1833) was a member of the "Blue Stocking Circle," a group of women of wit and learning in London who held receptions attended by an equal number of women and men (including Johnson and Boswell) at which current topics were discussed. Politics and scandal were excluded from the conversations, but arguments for and against charity probably received attention. "Liberality flows with a full tide through a thousand channels," declared More. Scarcely a day passes that "men of fortune" do not meet "for the most salutary purposes." Subscriptions for hospitals and other eleemosynary institutions are quickly obtained. "The noble and numberless structures for the relief of distress, which are the ornament and glory of our metropolis, proclaim a species of munificence unknown to other ages." And yet, More continued, "it is scarcely a paradox to say that there was probably less misery when there was less munificence."[32]

The reason More gives for the multiplication of bounty and distress is that the age of benevolence was simultaneously an age of licentiousness and corruption. Munificence in charitable giving went hand in hand with habits of luxury and dissipation: the good the former did was overcome by the evils loosed by the latter.[33]

By the 1790s, judging by More's essays and other writings that will be discussed in chapter 7, benevolence was losing favor in England. With the coming of the French Revolution, censoriousness replaced benevolence in the thought of the upper classes and their literary allies. "What is *benevolence*?" asks a speaker in More's pamphlet "Village Politics" (1793). His companion replies, "Why in the new-fangled language, it means contempt of religion, aversion to justice, overturning of law, doting on all mankind in general, and, hating everybody in particular."[34]

Notes

1. Daniel Defoe, "Giving Alms No Charity" (1704), in *Defoe's Writings* (Boston and New York: Houghton Mifflin Company, 1927), 13:186.
2. Daniel Defoe, *A Tour Through England and Wales* (London: J.M. Dent and Son, 1948), 1:187–88 (first published 1724–26). Allegations of mismanagement of the affairs of St. Cross Hospital in the 1850s form part of the background of Anthony Trollope's novel *The Warden* (see Part Four, chapter 9).
3. Ibid., 1:231–32 (Saltash) and 2:27 (Oxford and Cambridge).
4. Ibid., 2:370–71.
5. Mandeville's definition of charity is in "An Essay on Charity and Charity Schools" (1723), in Bernard de Mandeville, *The Fable of the Bees, or Private Vices, Public Benefits* (Oxford: Oxford University Press, 1924), 1:253–54; his statement on

hospitals is ibid., 264. The "Essay" was bound with the second edition of *The Fable of the Bees* (1714).

6. John Malcolm Mitchell, "Bernard de Mandeville," in *The Encyclopedia Brittanica*, 11th ed., (London, 1911), 17:559–60.

7. All quotations are from James Boswell, *Life of Samuel Johnson* (1791) edited by R.W. Chapman, revised by J.D. Fleeman (Oxford: Oxford University Press, 1980), 947–48 (April 15, 1778). For a similar observation by Johnson about the superiority of wages to charity see pp. 775–76 (May 1776).

8. Richard Steele, *The Spectator* 4:294 (February 6, 1712). M.G. Jones, *The Charity School Movement* (Cambridge: Cambridge University Press, 1938), is an excellent account of the origin, development, and significance of the movement.

9. Bernard de Mandeville, "An Essay on Charity and Charity Schools," in *The Fable of the Bees*, 277–80, 286–88.

10. Henry Fielding, *Joseph Andrews and Shamela*, edited with an introduction and notes by Martin C. Battestin (Boston: Houghton Mifflin Company, 1961), 18 (bk. 1, ch. 3).

11. Ibid., 42–44 (bk. 1, ch. 12).

12. Ibid., 197–99 (bk. 3, ch. 6).

13. Ibid., 139–42 (bk. 2, ch. 14).

14. Ibid., 68 (bk. 1, ch. 17).

15. Henry Fielding, *Tom Jones, An Authoritative Text* edited by Sheridan Baker (New York: W.W. Norton, 1973), 71 (bk 2, ch. 5).

16. Ibid., 72.

17. Ibid., 775. Fielding had parodied *Pamela* in *Joseph Andrews*.

18. Ibid., 31 (bk. 1, ch. 3).

19. John Brocklesby, "Memoir" of Coram in John Brownlow, *History and Objects of the Foundling Hospital* (London: The Foundling Hospital, 1865), 114–17, 120–21; R.H. Nichols and F.A. Wray, *History of the Foundling Hospital* (London: Oxford University Press, 1935).

20. Henry Fielding, *An Enquiry into the Causes of the Late Increase of Robbers and Related Writings*, edited by Malvin R. Zirker (Middletown, Conn.: Wesleyan University Press, 1988), 77.

21. Ibid., 230–31.

22. Ibid., 228.

23. Tillotson is quoted, ibid., 269; Fielding's "Proposal" is discussed in Martin C. Battestin with Ruthe R. Battestin, *Henry Fielding, A Life* (London and New York: Routledge, 1989), 565–70.

24. Robert Southey, *The Life of Wesley and the Rise and Progress of Methodism*, edited by M.H. Fitzgerald (London: Oxford University Press, 1925), 1:349–50; Gertrude Himmelfarb, *The Idea of Poverty* (New York: Alfred A. Knopf, 1984), 33. Southey's biography of Wesley was first published in 1820.

25. Himmelfarb, *The Idea of Poverty*, 34.

26. "Sermon XLIV, The Use of Money," in *John Wesley's Fifty-three Sermons*, edited by Edward H. Sugden (Nashville, Tenn.: Abingdon Press, 1983), 633. Wesley's Rule states:

> Do all the good you can,
> By all the means you can;
> In all the ways you can,
> In all the places you can,
> At all the times you can,
> To all the people you can,
> As long as ever you can.

Justin Kaplan, General Editor, *Bartlett's Familiar Quotations*, 16th Edition (Boston: Little, Brown and Company, 1992), 309:2.

27. Southey, *Life of Wesley*, 2:305–6. For Jesus' advice to the Young Man, see chapter 2, p. 12. Wesley's attitude toward wealth recalls Francis Bacon's maxims: "Riches is a good handmaid but the worst mistress" and "Money is like muck, not good except to spread around." Kaplan, ed., *Bartlett's Familiar Quotations*, 158:19 and 159:17.

28. Roy and Dorothy Porter, *In Sickness and Health, The British Experience, 1650–1850* (London: Fourth Estate Limited, 1988), 26, 36.

29. George Eliot, *Adam Bede*, edited by Stephen Gill (New York: Viking Penguin, 1980), 82 (ch. 3). Eliot [Mary Ann/Marian Evans] (1819–80) contrasts the "old-fashioned Methodists" of the eighteenth century with the more worldly Methodists of her own day.

30. Tobias Smollett, *The Expedition of Humphrey Clinker* (Athens: University of Georgia Press, 1990), 1:78–80 (Letter of Jeffrey Melford to Sir Watkins Phillips, May 24, 17—).

31. Ibid., 1:97–98 (Letter of Melford to Phillips, June 2, 17—).

32. Hannah More, "Estimate of the Religion of the Fashionable World," in *Works of Hannah More* (London: Henry G. Bohn, 1853), 2:302–3.

33. Ibid., 303. More's attitude toward the social consequences of luxury was like Fielding's and unlike Samuel Johnson's.

34. Hannah More, "Village Politics" (1793), in *Works of More*, 2:233–34. This unlikely dialogue between two workmen, a mason and a blacksmith, sounds like a conversation between members of the Blue Stocking Circle.

7

Poets and Philanthropists

To Alexander Pope (1688–1744) charity was the embodiment of "social love" or concern for others, which, in the divine scheme of things, balanced "self-love" or concern for one's own well-being. Epistle III of "An Essay on Man" (1733) states Pope's view of charity's central place in human affairs:

> For forms of government let fools contest;
> whater'er is best administer'd is best:
> For modes of faith, let graceless zealots fight;
> His can't be wrong whose life is in the right:
> In faith and hope the world will disagree,
> But all mankind's concern is charity:
> All must be false that thwart this one great end;
> And all of God, that bless mankind, or mend.
> Man, like the gen'rous vine, supported lives;
> The strength he gains is from th' embrace he gives.
> On their own axis as the planets run,
> Yet make at once their circle round the sun;
> So two consistent motions act the soul;
> And one regards itself, and one the whole.
> Thus God and nature link'd the gen'ral frame,
> And bade self-love and social be the same.[1]

Pope addressed Epistle III of his "Moral Essays" to his long-time and long-lived friend Allen Apsley, Lord Bathurst, who, although several years older than Pope, outlived him by thirty years, mingling "freely in society till past ninety, [and] living to walk in the shade of lofty trees he and Pope had planted."[2] The title of the Epistle was "On the Use of Riches." Pope, after speaking of

> The sense to value Riches, with the art
> T'enjoy them and the virtue to impart

asks Bathurst to draw the line between "mad Good-nature" and "mean Self-love." Bathurst replies (of course in words supplied by Pope):

> To Worth or Want well-weigh'd, be Bounty giv'n,
> And ease, or emulate, the care of Heav'n;
> (Whose measure full o'erflows on human race)
> Mend Fortune's fault, and justify her grace.
> Wealth in the gross is death, but life diffus'd;
> As Poison heals, in just proportion us'd:
> In heaps, like Ambergrise, a stink it lies,
> But well-dispers'd, is Incense to the Skies.[3]

Pope cited Bathurst and Edward Harley, second earl of Oxford (1689–1741), a patron of letters, as examples of benevolent noblemen. He reserved his greatest praise, however, for John Kyrle (1637–1724) a landowner, who lived simply and used his income of no more than 600 pounds a year to improve his community, Ross on Wye. "Rise, honest Muse!" Pope commanded, "and sing the Man of Ross:

> Who hung with woods yon mountain's sultry brow?
> From the dry rock who bade the waters flow?
> Not to the skies in useless columns tost,
> Or in proud falls magnificently lost,
> But clear and artless, pouring thro' the plain
> Health to the sick, and solace to the swain.
> Whose Cause-way parts the vale with shady rows?
> Whose Seats the weary Traveller repose?
> Who taught that heav'n-directed spire to rise?
>
> The Man of Ross, each lisping babe replies.
> Behold the Market-place with poor o'erspread!
> The Man of Ross divides the weekly bread:
> Behold yon Alms-house, neat, but void of state,
> Where Age and Want sit smiling at the gate:
> Him portion'd maids, apprentic'd orphans blest,

The young who labour, and the old who rest.
Is any sick? the Man of Ross relieves,
Prescribes, attends, the med'cine makes, and gives.
Is there a variance? enter but his door,
Balk'd are the Courts, and contest is no more.[4]

Pope may have exaggerated the extent of Kyrle's good deeds since, as Samuel Johnson pointed out, Kyrle could not have accomplished them all on his modest income. William Warburton, Pope's literary executor, said the listing was intended to indicate not only what Kyrle personally donated but what he achieved by enlisting the support of his neighbors. The park on a hill overlooking the river Wye that Kyrle laid out, planted with trees, and dedicated to the town can still be visited. His memory is kept alive not only by Pope's poem but by the Kyrle Society, founded in 1877 by Miranda and Octavia Hill, to beautify waste spaces in cities.[5]

Like Fielding, Pope admired Ralph Allen, a man of humble birth who made a fortune by reforming the rural postal service and quarrying operations in the vicinity of Bath. Allen had a much larger income than Kyrle and tended to give unobtrusively as an individual—"by stealth," as Pope put it—rather than in association with others, as was Kyrle's way. He gave generous support to architecture and literature and churches in Bath and especially to aid to the poor. Kyrle and Allen struck Pope as "noble" because of their sense of responsibility and willingness to respond to need, whether individual or social. Pope wrote of Allen, "God made this man rich, to shame the Great; and wise to humble the learned."[6]

If Kyrle's income was deemed modest, what of that of Oliver Goldsmith's brother, Rev. Henry Goldsmith, to whom the poet (1730?–74) dedicated "The Traveller"? Goldsmith's dedication tells us the brother was "a man who despising fame and fortune . . . retired early to happiness and obscurity, with an income of forty pounds a year." Yet even that meager sum was sufficient to enable a happy and hospitable family to experience "the luxury of doing good":

Bless'd that abode, where want and pain repair
And every stranger finds a ready chair.
Bless'd be those feasts with simple plenty crown'd,
Where all the ruddy family around
Laugh at jests or pranks that never fail,

Or sigh with pity at some mournful tale,
Or press the bashful stranger to his food,
And learn the luxury of doing good.[7]

In two elegies, one on the death of a pawnbroker, the other on that of a mad dog, Goldsmith satirized the then fashionable verse form in which poets lavished insincere praise on someone and glossed over his or her faults. In the late 1750s when Goldsmith was trying to eke out a living as a physician and hack writer in London he may have dealt with pawnbrokers like "That Glory of Her Sex, Mrs. Mary Blaize" (1759).

The needy seldom pass'd her door,
And always found her kind;
She freely lent to all the poor, —
Who left a pledge behind.
She strove the neighbourhood to please,
With manners wond'rous winning,
And never follow'd wicked ways, —
Unless when she was sinning.
At Church, in silks and satins new,
With hoop of monstrous size,
She never slumber'd in her pew, —
But when she shut her eyes.
Her love was sought, I do aver,
By twenty beaux and more;
The king himself has follow'd her, —
When she has walk'd before.[8]

"The Elegy on The Death of a Mad Dog" (1766) first appeared in Goldsmith's novel, *The Vicar of Wakefield* (1766), where it was sung by the Vicar's youngest son.

In Islington there was a man,
Of whom the world might say,
That still a godly race he ran,
Whene'er he went to pray.
A kind and gentle heart he had,
To comfort friends and foes;
The naked every day he clad,
When he put on his clothes.

When the pious man is bitten by a mad dog the neighbors are sure he will die

> But soon a wonder came to light,
> that showed the rogues they lied:
> The man recovered of the bite,
> The dog it was that died.[9]

Goldsmith's "The Deserted Village" contains the lines (51–52)

> Ill fares the land, to hastening ills a prey
> Where wealth accumulates and men decay.

The village preacher, like Goldsmith's father, uncle, and brother; Parson Adams in *Joseph Andrews*; and Dr. Primrose in *The Vicar of Wakefield*, was an "inferior" — that is, low-ranking — clergyman whose generosity and conscientious performance of duty were not lessened by miserly pay. Goldsmith's preacher bears a strong resemblance to Chaucer's Parson in *The Canterbury Tales*.

> Near yonder copse, where once the garden smiled,
> And still where many a garden flower grows wild;
> There, where a few torn shrubs the place disclose,
> The village preacher's modest mansion rose.
> A man he was to all the country dear,
> And passing rich with forty pounds a year;
> Remote from towns he ran his godly race,
> Nor e'er had changed, nor wished to change, his place;
> Unpractised he to fawn, or seek for power,
> By doctrines fashioned to the varying hour;
> Far other aims his heart had learned to prize,
> More skilled to raise the wretched than to rise.
> His house was known to all the vagrant train,
> He chid their wanderings, but relieved their pain;
> The long-remembered beggar was his guest,
> Whose beard descending swept his aged breast;
> The ruined spendthrift, now no longer proud,
> Claimed kindred there and had his claims allowed;
> The broken soldier, kindly bade to stay,
> Sat by his fire and talked the night away;
> Wept o'er his wounds or tales of sorrow done,

Shouldered his crutch and showed how fields were won.
Pleased with his guests, the good man learned to glow,
And quite forgot their vices in their woe;
Careless their merits or their faults to scan,
His pity gave ere charity began.
Thus to relieve the wretched was his pride,
And even his failings leaned to virtue's side;
But in his duty prompt at every call,
He watched and wept, he prayed and felt for all.[10]

Early in William Cowper's "Charity" (1782) the poet advises students of the subject:

Who seeks to know thee, and make thee known
To other hearts, must have thee in his own.[11]

Cowper (1731–1800), who suffered periods of extreme depression, was a beneficiary of the charity of John Thornton (1720–90), a contributor to evangelical religious causes who printed and distributed at his own expense large numbers of Bibles and other religious books. According to Cowper, Thornton was an example of a man God had made rich for the benefit of humanity.

Some men make gain a fountain, whence proceeds
A stream of liberal and heroic deeds;
The swell of pity, not to be confined
Within the scanty limits of the mind,
Disdains the bank, and throws the golden sands,
A rich deposit, on the bordering lands;
These have an ear for His paternal call,
Who makes some rich for the supply of all,
God's gift with pleasure in his praise employ,
And Thornton is familiar with the joy.[12]

A different kind of giver is the Squire who takes his time and makes sure the congregation sees the gold coin he contributes to a collection for victims of a disaster that has left many homeless. Cowper says that in disaster relief

Extravagance and avarice shall subscribe
While fame and self-commplacence are the bribe

As for the Squire's contribution

> From motives such as his, though not the best,
> Springs in due time supply for the distressed,
> Not less effectual than what love bestows,
> Except — that office clips it as it goes.[13]

Although Cowper believed "all zeal for reform that gives offense/to peace and charity is mere pretense" (lines 533–34), his poem paid generous tribute to a philanthropic reformer. John Howard (1726–90) began his career as a prison reformer in 1773 when, as sheriff of the county of Bedford, England, he took action to have jailers paid out of county funds. Previously jailers had supported themselves by levying fees on prisoners and refusing to release anyone — even those not prosecuted or found innocent — until payment of "jail delivery" fees. After 1774, acting as a private citizen, Howard investigated prisons in Great Britain and on the continent, publishing his findings in *The State of Prisons in England and Wales* (1777). In the 1780s Howard visited and collected information on conditions in plague and quarantine hospitals, voluntarily submitting to incarceration in the lazaretto at Venice to obtain firsthand knowledge of the situation. He died in Russia of a fever contracted while on a tour of military hospitals. In the following lines Cowper addresses Howard, who at the time was still alive.

> Patron of else the most despised of men,
> Accept the tribute of a stranger's pen;
> Verse, like the laurel, its immortal meed,
> Should be the guerdon of a noble deed;
> I may alarm thee, but I fear the shame
> (Charity chosen as my theme and aim)
> I must incur, forgetting HOWARD's name.
> Blest with all wealth can give thee, to resign
> Joys doubly sweet to feelings quick as thine,
> To quit the bliss thy rural scenes bestow,
> To seek a nobler amidst scenes of woe,
> To traverse seas, range kingdoms, and bring home,
> Not the proud monuments of Greece or Rome,
> But knowledge such as only dungeons teach,
> And only sympathy like thine could reach,
> That grief, sequester'd from the public stage,
> Might smooth her feathers, and enjoy her cage,

Speaks a divine ambition, and a zeal
The boldest patriot might be proud to feel.
Oh, that the voice of clamour and debate,
That pleads for peace till it disturbs the state,
Were hush'd in favour of thy gen'rous plea,
The poor thy clients, and Heaven's smile thy fee.[14]

Edmund Burke, speaking about ten years before Howard's death, called his investigations of prisons and lazarettos "a circumnavigation of charity" undertaken "to take the gauge and dimensions of misery, depression, and contempt; to remember the forgotten, to attend to the neglected, to visit the forsaken, and to compare and collate the distresses of all men in all countries."[15]

The admiration Howard won in his own day for exchanging a life of comparative comfort and ease for arduous and dangerous service as an advocate for prisoners and victims of dreaded diseases survived his death and extended across the Atlantic. In the United States, where numerous relief societies took his name, he was known as "Howard the Philanthropist." Almost a century after he began his work the Reverend Henry W. Bellows, president of The United States Sanitary Commission, declared, "the name of Howard has become the synonym for philanthropy. It stands for universal mercy, worldwide sympathy, and absolute consecration to human service."[16]

Beginning in 1704 charity-school children, wearing their uniforms, attended special church services celebrating the anniversary of the founding of the schools. The sight and sound of the children marching, singing, and praying provided those who had donated to the schools an opportunity for pride and satisfaction in their gifts and encouraged further contributions to the work. In London after 1782, the observance, involving hundreds of children, took place in St. Paul's Cathedral. William Blake (1757–1827) wrote two poems entitled "Holy Thursday" dealing with the ceremonies. The first, published in 1789 in *Songs of Innocence*, strikes a happy note:

Twas on a Holy Thursday, their innocent faces clean,
The children walking two and two in red and blue and green;
Grey-headed beadles walked before with wands as white as snow,
Till into the high dome of Paul's they like Thames' waters flow.

Oh, what a multitude they seemed, these flowers of London Town!
Seated in companies they sit, with radiance all their own.
The hum of multitudes was there, but multitudes of lambs,
Thousands of little boys and girls raising their innocent hands.

Now like a mighty wind they raise to heaven the voice of song,
Or like harmonious thunderings the seats of heaven among
Beneath them sit the aged men, wise guardians of the poor:
Then cherish pity, lest you drive an angel from your door.[17]

The second, in *Songs of Experience* (1794), reflects a very different reaction:

> Is this a holy thing to see
> In a rich and fruitful land,
> Babes reduced to misery,
> Fed with cold and usurous hand?
>
> Is that trembling cry a song?
> Can it be a song of joy?
> And so many children poor?
> It is a land of poverty!
>
> And their sun does never shine,
> And their fields are bleak and bare,
> And their ways are filled with thorns:
> It is eternal winter there.
>
> For where'er the sun does shine,
> And where'er the rain does fall,
> Babe can never hunger there,
> Nor poverty the mind appal.[18]

Like many people, Blake felt differently at different times and in
different moods about human nature and the rival pull of kindness and
altruism agains't cruelty and selfishness. "The Divine Image" (1789)
evokes the hopeful view:

> To mercy, pity, peace and love
> All pray in their distress;
> And to these virtues of delight
> Return their thankfulness.

For mercy, pity, peace and love
Is God our father dear;
And mercy, pity, peace and love
Is man, his child and care.

For mercy has a human heart,
Pity, a human face;
And love, the human form divine,
And peace, the human dress.

Then every man of every clime
That prays in his distress,
Prays to the human form divine —
Love, mercy, pity, peace.

And all must love the human form
In heathen, Turk or Jew.
Where mercy, love and pity dwell
There God is dwelling too.[19]

"The Human Abstract" (1794) reveals the other, darker side of the picture:

Pity would be no more,
If we did not make somebody poor;
And mercy no more could be,
If all were as happy as we;

And mutual fear brings peace,
Till the selfish loves increase.
Then Cruelty knits a snare
And spreads his baits with care.

He sits down with holy fears
And waters the ground with tears;
Then humility takes it root
Underneath his foot.

Soon spreads the dismal shade
Of mystery over his head;
And the caterpillar and fly
Feed on the mystery;

And it bears the fruit of deceit,
Ruddy and sweet to eat,
And the raven his nest has made
In its thickest shade.

The gods of the earth and sea
Sought through nature to find this tree.
But their search was all in vain:
There grows one in the human brain.[20]

Poets, no less than pundits and politicians, responded to the French Revolution by embracing exuberant radicalism or pessimistic conservatism and sympathizing with or disdaining common people. Robert Southey's "The Widow" (1797), a dolorous poem about a poor woman whose death from exposure went unheeded by a horseman and the occupants of a coach, prompted a derisive reply by two Tory politicians, George Canning (1770–1827) and John Hookham Frere (1769–1846). Their poem "The Friend of Humanity and the Knife-grinder" (1797) presaged the antiphilanthropic bias of much nineteenth- and twentieth-century literature. The Friend of Humanity, anticipating a pitiable tale of oppression by the rich and powerful, is annoyed when the shabby knife-grinder cheerfully admits that he, by his drinking and brawling, is alone responsible for his miserable appearance. When he asks for money to buy beer the Friend of Humanity kicks him, overturns his grinding wheel, and departs "in a transport of republican enthusiasm and universal philanthropy."[21]

In "New Morality" (1798) Canning and Frere distinguished between British charity, "who dries/The orphan's tears, and wipes the widow's eyes," and "French Philanthropy," whose "baneful sway" subverts patriotism and undermines morality. The authors allege that the teachings of Condorcet and Tom Paine make a man

A steady Patriot of the World alone,
The friend of every country — but his own.

Rousseau's "Sweet Sensibility" induced his followers to weep over a crushed beetle, widowed dove, drooping flower, or dead jackass while leaving them unmoved by the atrocities of the French Revolution — "Foul crimes . . . sicklied o'er with Freedom's name."[22]

Percy Bysshe Shelley (1792–1822), an infant during the French

Revolution, carried the spirit of "republican enthusiasm and universal philanthropy" into the nineteenth century. In the introduction to *Prometheus Unbound* (1820) he acknowledged that he had a passion to reform the world. Like Aeschylus, he saw Prometheus as the champion of mankind, Zeus (and God) as the tyrannical oppressor. "Prometheus," he wrote, "is the type of the highest perfection of moral and intellectual nature impelled by the purest and truest motives to the best and noblest ends." A radical, Prometheus is ready

> To suffer woes which Hope thinks infinite;
> To forgive wrongs darker than death or night;
> To defy Power, which seems omnipotent;
> To love, and bear; to hope till Hope creates
> From its own wreck the thing it contemplates;
> Neither to change, nor falter, nor repent;
> This, like thy glory, Titan, is to be
> Good, great and joyous, beautiful and free;
> This is alone Life, Joy, Empire, and Victory![23]

Both Shelley's ardor for philanthropy and Canning's and his friend's suspicion of it would find expression in nineteenth century literature. Some of the writers most critical of particular philanthropists, however, were themselves staunch friends of humanity.

Notes

1. *The Complete Poetical Works of Alexander Pope*, edited by Henry W. Boynton (Boston: Houghton Mifflin Company, 1903), 150, lines 303–18.
2. *The Poetical Works of Alexander Pope*, edited by Adolphus William Ward (New York: St. Martin's Press, 1964), 244 nt. 2.
3. *The Complete Poetical Works of Alexander Pope*, edited by Henry W. Boynton, 168, lines 218–36. Walter Rauschenbusch (1861–1918), an American leader of the social Gospel movement, used a similar analogy to advocate more equal distribution of wealth: Money, like manure, does more harm than good if heaped in piles; both should be spread evenly over the ground.
4. Ibid., 168, lines 249–72.
5. *The Poetical Works of Alexander Pope*, edited by Adolphus William Ward, 252, nt. 3. On Kyrle see Howard Erskine-Hill, *The Social Milieu of Alexander Pope* (New Haven: Yale University Press, 1975), 8, 15–41.
6. Erskine-Hill, *Social Milieu of Alexander Pope*, 232, quoting letter from Pope to William Fortescue, 23 January 1739/40. Pope's lines on Allen:

Let humble Allen, with an awkward Shame

Do Good by stealth, and blush to find it Fame

are in "Epilogue to the Satires," *The Complete Poetical Works of Alexander Pope*, edited by Henry W. Boynton, 209, lines 135–36.

7. Oliver Goldsmith, "The Traveler" (1764–65), in Austin Dobson, ed., *The Poetical Works of Oliver Goldsmith* (London: Oxford University Press, 1939), 3–6, lines 15–22.

8. "An Elegy on That Glory of Her Sex, Mrs. Mary Blaize," ibid., 47, lines 5–20.

9. "An Elegy on the Death of a Mad Dog," ibid., 65–66, lines 5–12, 29–32.

10. "The Deserted Village," ibid., 27–28, lines 137–66.

11. "Charity," in *The Complete Poetical Works of William Cowper*, edited by H.S. Milford (London: Oxford University Press, 1913), 76, lines 9–10.

12. Ibid., 81, lines 244–53. Thornton was the great-great-grandfather of the novelist E.M. Forster. Forster, *Commonplace Book*, edited by Philip Gardner (Stanford: Stanford University Press, 1985), 115.

13. "Charity," in *Complete Poetical Works of William Cowper*, 86, lines 467–68, 481–84.

14. Ibid., 82–83, lines 290–312.

15. "Speech at Bristol, Previous to the Election, 1780" in *The Works and Correspondence of Edmund Burke* (London: Francis and John Rivington, 1852), 3:422.

16. Henry W. Bellows, "John Howard: His Life, Character and Services," in Edwin Pears, ed., *Prisons and Reformatories at Home and Abroad* (London: International Penal and Prison Conference, 1872), 739. For Thomas Carlyle's less enthusiastic assessment of Howard's work see Part Four, chapter 11.

17. "Holy Thursday" (1789) in Roger Lonsdale, comp., *New Oxford Book of Eighteenth Century Verse* (Oxford: Oxford University Press, 1984), 690.

18. "Holy Thursday" (1794), ibid., 696–97.

19. "The Divine Image" (1789), ibid., 692. Quoted by permission of Oxford University Press.

20. "The Human Abstract" (1794), ibid., 695.

21. "The Friend of Humanity and the Knife-grinder," ibid., 824–25. Canning later became foreign secretary and prime minister of Great Britain.

22. "New Morality," ibid., 827–30 lines 21–27, 45–46, 69, 74–79.

23. Shelley, "Prometheus Unbound" (1820), in Newell B. Ford, ed., *The Poetical Works of Shelley* (Boston: Houghton Mifflin, 1974), 206. (act 4, lines 570–78).

8

Beggars, Importunate and Long
Remember'd

Sir Andrew Freeport, Addison and Steele's exponent of mercantil-
ism in *The Spectator* (1711–12), denounced giving to beggars as bad
for business, especially that of merchants like himself who made their
living by buying and selling. To make a profit they had to have a
supply of labor large enough to keep wages low. Giving money to
beggars was worse than throwing it away; it was like hiring them to do
nothing. "The very Alms they receive from us," he exclaimed, "are the
Wages of Idleness." Sir Andrew departed from his principles, however, when beggars hung on either side of his coach and made it
impossible for him to proceed until he had given them something for
their allegedly sick spouses and starving children.[1]

Bernard de Mandeville denied that giving to beggars was charity.
Pity, not love, inspires our giving, and we give to ease the discomfort
we experience in seeing their afflictions, hearing their tales of woe,
and imagining ourselves in their place. Pride and avarice also figure in
the exchange: the beggar's plea flatters our ego and makes us feel both
obliged to give and expectant of a reward for our generosity. But with
pity, as with fear, the more people are exposed to circumstances and
situations that excite those emotions, the less they are disturbed by
them. Exposure to too much misery makes people indifferent to beggars. In such cases, said Mandeville, the only thing the industrious
beggar can do "is to follow close and with uninterrupted Noise tease
and importune them to try if he can make them buy their peace. Thus
thousands give money to beggars from the same motive as they pay
their corn-cutter, to walk easy."[2]

The subject of begging came up often in Samuel Johnson's conversations with friends. His observation that "one might give away five hundred pounds in a year to those that importune in the streets, and not do any good" is well known. According to James Boswell, however, Johnson's conduct belied his words:

> He frequently gave all the silver in his pocket to the poor, who watched him, between his house and the tavern where he dined. He walked the streets at all hours, and said he was never robbed for the rogues knew he had little money, nor had the appearance of having much.[3]

One reason Johnson gave to beggars, although he doubted it would do any good, was that he recognized there were more people in need than work to support them. He once estimated that in London at least twenty people a week — more than a thousand a year — died of hunger, "not absolutely of immediate hunger; but of the wasting and other diseases which are the consequences of hunger." The notion that some people earned large sums by begging was false: "the trade," he told Boswell, "is overstocked."

> And, you may depend upon, it (he continued) there are many who cannot get work. A particular kind of manufacture fails: those who have been used to work at it, can, for some time, work at nothing else. You meet a man begging; you charge him with idleness: he says, "I am willing to labour. Will you give me work?: — "I cannot." — "Why, then you have no right to charge me with idleness."[4]

According to James Prior, an early biographer of Oliver Goldsmith, in rural Ireland, where there was no public provision for the poor, beggars were a privileged class with "a prescriptive claim, amounting nearly to a right, to the compassion of the poorer and middling classes of people." The "long-remember'd beggar" in Goldsmith's "The Deserted Village" belonged to a class of people who year after year "traversed the same tract of country, stopped at every house not protected by a gate and porter's lodge, asked for and received food from the family, and even [found] an occasional resting place for the night, or from severe weather, in the chimney corner of respectable farmers."[5]

Thomas Leland, writing in 1773, reported that in Ireland hospitality was deemed an obligation as well as a virtue. Wandering beggars entered the house of a gentleman or farmer "with as much ease and freedom as an inmate." Leland attributed the custom to the benevolent spirit of Christianity. " 'The most holy men of heaven,' say the Irish laws, 'were remarkable for hospitality, and the Gospel commands us to receive the sojourner, to entertain him, and to relieve his wants.' "[6] In practice this meant that members of poor families who had only one bed in their houses sometimes shared it with a traveling peddlar, tailor, or beggar.[7]

Some beggars, by virtue of their regular visits, became familiar figures, treated with affection and even respect. William Wordsworth's "The Old Cumberland Beggar," written in 1798, depicted a man the poet had observed in childhood, "with great benefit to my own heart." Late in life Wordsworth said that beggars like the old man were almost extinct. They were poor and "mostly old and infirm persons, who confined themselves to a stated round in their neighborhood, and had certain fixed days, in which at different houses, they regularly received alms, sometimes in money, but mostly in provisions." Wordsworth (1770–1850) remembered him not only for his infirm and solitary condition but also for the kindness and consideration shown him:

> Him from my childhood have I known; and then
> He was so old, he seems not older now;
> He travels on, a solitary Man,
> So helpless in appearance, that for him
> The sauntering Horseman throws not with a slack
> And careless hand his alms upon the ground,
> But stops, — that he may safely lodge the coin
> Within the old Man's hat; nor quits him so,
> But still, when he has given his horse the rein,
> Watches the aged Beggar with a look
> Sidelong, and half-reverted. She who tends
> The toll-gate, when in summer at her door
> She turns her wheel, if on the road she sees
> The aged Beggar coming, quits her work,
> And lifts the latch for him that he may pass.
> The post-boy, when his rattling wheels 'ertake
> The aged Beggar in the woody lane,
> Shouts to him from behind; and, if thus warned
> The old man does not change his course, the boy
> Turns with less noisy wheels to the road-side,

And passes gently by, without a curse
Upon his lips or anger at his heart.[8]

Wordsworth's "The Beggars" (1802) was based not on his own experience but on his sister's encounters with a woman who asked for and received alms, and later with the woman's two little boys; the latter interrupted their play to beg for money, saying their mother was dead. As Wordsworth told the story the beggars were parts of a well-loved landscape, the mother "a weed of glorious feature," the boys "joyous vagrants." In 1817 he wrote a sequel, reliving the day and the scenery, and asking "where are they now, those wanton boys?"[9]

Wordsworth's long autobiographical poem, "The Prelude," written between 1798 and 1805 but not published in his lifetime, contains a passage telling how profoundly he was affected by the sight of a blind beggar bearing a sign to identify himself amid the crowd of a London street:

Amid the moving pageant, I was smitten
Abruptly, with the view (a sight not rare)
Of a blind Beggar, who, with upright face,
Stood, propped against a wall, upon his chest
Wearing a written paper, to explain
His story, whence he came, and who he was.
Caught by the spectacle my mind turned round
As with the might of waters; an apt type
This label seemed of the utmost we can know,
Both of ourselves and of the universe;
And, on the shape of that unmoving man,
His steadfast face and sightless eyes, I gazed,
As if admonished from another world.[10]

Eighteenth-century wars left in their train countless broken soldiers like the one welcomed by the village parson in "The Deserted Village." Institutions such as Les Invalides in Paris (founded in 1670) and the Royal Hospital at Chelsea, England (opened in 1690), provided refuge for a few old soldiers, but most of the survivors had to fend for themselves, even if burdened with physical and psychological wounds. Some found the struggle to make a living by their own labor so difficult or irksome that they resorted to begging.[11]

In 1786, at a Scottish inn patronized by poor travelers and vagrants,

Robert Burns (1759–96) witnessed — and may have joined in — the carousing of a band of jolly beggars. "Nearest the fire in old red rags," Burns reported in "Love and Liberty — a Cantata," was a one-armed, one-legged veteran of the battles of Quebec (1759), Santiago, Cuba (1762), and Gibraltar (1782). He lay with his callet (doxy or beggar's mistress) who "held up her greedy mouth/ just like an alms dish" to receive his kisses and her dram of whiskey. "Staggering and swaggering" the soldier rose and boasted of his military exploits in a ditty that finished on a note of pride and satisfaction in his current life:

> And now though I must beg, with a wooden arm and leg,
>   And many a tattered rag hanging over my bum,
> I'm as happy with my wallet, my bottle and my callet,
>   As when I used in scarlet to follow a drum.
>
> What though, with hoary locks, I must stand the winter shocks,
>   Beneath the woods and rocks oftentimes for a home,
> When the tother bag I sell and tother bottle tell,
>   I could meet a troop of hell at the sound of a drum.[12]

The soldier's mistress, when it was her time to sing, recalled the happy days when she had "the regiment at large for a husband":

> But the peace it reduced me to beg in despair,
> Till I met my old boy in a Cunningham fair:
> His rags regimental they fluttered so gaudy,
> My heart it rejoiced at a sodger laddie.
>
> And now I have lived — I know not how long,
> And still I can join in a cup and a song;
> But whilst with both hands I can hold the glass steady,
> Here's to thee, my hero, my sodger laddie.[13]

Sir Walter Scott (1771–1832), noting Burns's affinity for beggars, said that he "seems to have looked forward with gloomy firmness to the possibility of himself becoming one day or another a member of their iterant society." Burns ended the poem with a rousing chorus in which the beggars rejoiced in the liberty and pleasure of their careless life and declared, "Let them rant about decorum/Who have character to lose."[14]

Decorum and dignity were essential elements in the character of Edie Ochletree, a beggar who plays an important role in Scott's novel set in late-eighteenth-century Scotland, *The Antiquary* (1816). As a King's Bedesman, receiving alms from the King of Scotland in return for prayers for his and the country's welfare, Edie stood at the very top of the begging profession. He wore a blue gown or cloak and a pewter pin authorizing him to beg anyplace in the country, even in places where local ordinances forbade mendicancy. He begged, but he also carried news and gossip from one farmstead to others, helped repair fiddles, mended pots and pans, offered advice on the cure of sick cows and horses, and knew hundreds of songs and tales. "I canna lay down my vocation," he told a young woman; "it would be a public loss."[15]

Edie, of course, was a fictional character; he was modeled after Andrew Gemmells, an old mendicant Scott had known in his youth. As Scott remembered him,

> Andrew Gemmells had little of the cant of his calling; his wants were food and shelter, or a trifle of money, which he always claimed, and seemed to receive, as his due. He sung a good song, told a good story, and could crack a severe jest with all the acumen of Shakespeare's jesters. . . . It was some fear of Andrew's satire, as much as a feeling of kindness or charity, which secured him the general good reception which he enjoyed everywhere. In fact, a jest of Andrew Gemmells, especially at the expense of a person of consequence, flew round the circle which he frequented, as surely as the bon-mot of a man of established character for wit glides through the fashionable world.

On one occasion a country gentleman reported to be close with his money told Andrew he could not offer him the accustomed sixpence because he had no silver in pocket. "'I can give you change for a note, Laird,' Andrew replied."[16]

Late in Andrew's career — probably around 1800 — he complained that begging was not as profitable as formerly; he estimated that he received forty pounds a year less than when he had entered the trade. Scott attributed the decline of mendicancy to the "utterly degraded class of beings" who had invaded the field in recent years.[17] Others — Wordsworth, for one — put the blame not on the character of the beggars but on the harsh doctrines of political economists that disparaged begging and alms-giving.[18]

One of the articles in Charles Lamb's *Essays of Elia* (1823) defended beggars and denounced political economists and charity reformers. Deploring periodic efforts to get beggars off the streets of London, Lamb (1775–1834) hailed beggars for their freedom from the constraints and concerns of polite society. He called attention to the plight of

> those old blind Tobits that used to line the wall of Lincoln's-inn Garden, before modern fastidiousness had expelled them, casting up their ruined orbs to catch a ray of pity, and (if possible) of light, with their faithful Dog Guide at their feet, — whither are they fled? or into what corners, blind as themselves, have they been driven, out of the wholesome air and sun-warmth? immersed between four walls, in what withering poor-house do they endure the penalty of double darkness, where the chink of the dropt halfpenny no more consoles their forlorn bereavement, far from the sound of the cheerful and hope-stirring tread of the passenger? Where hang their useless staves? and who will farm their dogs? — Have the overseers of St. L — caused them to be shot? or were they tied up in sacks and dropt into the Thames, at the suggestion of B- the mild rector of — ?[19]

Lamb also spoke in behalf of a beggar who, having lost the lower part of his body in the Gordon riots of 1780, wheeled himself about the city on a wooden machine propelled by his hands and arms. He had followed his out-of-door trade for forty-two years, his hair turned grey but his good spirits unimpaired when, because of his refusal to enter a poorhouse, he was sent to a house of correction. Lamb maintained that the daily spectacle of him pursuing "his chosen, harmless, nay, edifying way of life" was not a nuisance but "a salutary and a touching object to the passers-by in a great city." This man, "half a Hercules," "the man-part of a centaur," was one of the sights of London; beggars in general were among the shows, museums, and curiosities that made the city interesting. "And what else;" Lamb asked, "but an accumulation of sights — endless sights — *is* a great city; or for what else is it desirable?"[20]

Notes

1. *The Spectator* III, No. 232 (November 26, 1711).
2. Mandeville, "An Essay on Charity and Charity Schools," in *The Fable of the Bees* (Oxford: Oxford University Press, 1924), 257–59. A French visitor to eighteenth-

century Dublin found that the abundance and insolence of beggars in the city hardened his heart and made him feel indisposed to alsmgiving. Chevalier de La Tocnaye, *A Frenchman's Walk Through Ireland, 1796–7*, translated by John Stevenson (Belfast, Ireland: Blackstaff Press, 1984), 17.

3. James Boswell, *Life of Samuel Johnson*, edited by R.W. Chapman, revised by J.D. Fleeman (Oxford: Oxford University Press, 1980), 1067–68 (1780).

4. Ibid., 1031 (October 10, 1779).

5. James Prior, *Life of Oliver Goldsmith* (London: J. Murray, 1837), 2:268–69.

6. Thomas Leland, *The History of Ireland from the Invasion of Henry II* (London: J. Nourse, T. Longman, 1773), xxxiv-xxxv.

7. Edward MacLysaght, *Irish Life in the Seventeenth Century, After Cromwell* (Cork, Ireland: Cork University Press, 1950), 66–67.

8. William Wordsworth, "The Old Cumberland Beggar," in *The Complete Poetical Works of Wordsworth*, edited by A. J. George (Boston: Houghton Mifflin Company, 1904), 93–96 (lines 22–43).

9. Ibid., 275–76, 563–64.

10. Wordsworth, "The Prelude," bk. 7, lines 637–49, ibid., 177. The passage quoted is from the 1850 version of the often-revised poem.

11. The hostility and indifference of public authorities to crippled veterans who had to resort to begging was satirized by John Wolcot (1738–1819) in "George III and the Sailor" (1795), Roger Lonsdale, comp., *New Oxford Book of Eighteenth Century Verse* (Oxford: Oxford University Press, 1984), 745–47.

12. Robert Burns, "Love and Liberty – A Cantata" ["The Jolly Beggars"], ibid., 713 (lines 42–49). The poem, written in 1786, was first published in 1799.

13. Ibid., 714 (lines 71, 75–82).

14. Ibid., 715 (lines 105–106). Scott discusses Burns's affinity for beggars and his recognition of the possibility of becoming one in "Advertisement," in *The Antiquary* (New York: Harper and Brothers, 1901), 1:12–16.

15. Scott, *The Antiquary* 1:196 (ch. 12).

16. Ibid., 1:18–22.

17. Ibid., 1:12.

18. Note to "The Old Cumberland Beggar," in *The Complete Poetical Works of William Wordsworth*, 93.

19. Charles Lamb, "A Complaint of the Decay of Beggars in the Metropolis," in *The Essays of Elia* (London: G. Bell and Sons, 1913), 149–55. First published in 1823.

20. Ibid.

PART FOUR

The Nineteenth Century

Prologue: If All Were as Happy as We

One day in 1776 as Samuel Johnson and James Boswell were leaving church, the sight of beggars in the street made Boswell wonder aloud whether any country in the world protected its lower classes from misery. "I believe, Sir, there is not," Johnson replied, "but it is better than some should be unhappy, than that none should be happy, which would be the case in a general state of equality."[1]

William Blake's poem "The Human Abstract" (1794), quoted in chapter 7, acknowledges, in derision and despair, a perverse streak in human nature:

> Pity would be no more
> If we did not make somebody poor;
> And mercy no more could be,
> If all were as happy as we.[2]

Charles Dickens's *Martin Chuzzlewit* (1843–44) presents two characters with different perceptions of inequality, one from below, one from above. In the eyes of society Chevy Slyme, a distant and disreputable relative of the Chuzzlewits, is an inferior being; in his own estimation, however, he is vastly superior to everyone else. "He hated two sorts of men; all those who did him favors, and all those who were better off than himself; as in either case their position was an insult to a man of his stupendous merits." Slyme was "too insolent to lick the hand that fed him in his need, yet cur enough to bite and tear it in the dark."[3] The architect, Mr. Pecksniff, on the other hand, approves of inequality for its spiritual and material advantages. As Pecksniff and his daughters settle down in a stagecoach, windows closed, feet burrowed in straw, and bodies wrapped in cloaks, they find added comfort in the thought that not everyone is as warm as they are. How beautifully fate arranges things, thinks Mr. Pecksniff, because " 'if everyone were warm and well fed, we should lose the satisfaction of admiring the fortitude with which certain classes of men bear cold and hunger. And if we were no better off than anybody else, what would become of our sense of gratitude; which' he continued, tears welling in his eyes as he shook his fist at a beggar who was trying to get on the back of the coach, 'is one of the holiest feelings of our common nature.' "[4]

Julian West, the narrator of Edward Bellamy's utopian novel, *Looking Backward, 2000–1887* (1888), uses the analogy of a coach to give readers an impression of the way people lived together in 1887 and of the relations between rich and poor at that time. The driver of the coach was hunger and the poor pulled it along a difficult road, sometimes losing their footing and their lives in the struggle to keep the coach moving. Some people, by desperate effort or stroke of fortune, had won places in the coach and, like the Pecksniffs, rode at ease and in comparative comfort. They never got down to help but when the coach came to a particularly difficult place in the road, they would call down encouragement to the straining team and take up collections for liniments and salves.

If it had not been for the possibility and fear that the coach might turn over, the occupants would have given little thought to those who pulled. The former took it for granted that they were somehow different from and better than the latter. Everyone agreed that those who pulled the coach had a hard lot, but that was the way things had to be in order to have the coach proceed and make progress possible. Any interference with the process would lead to a general breakdown, with everybody mired in chaos. Seats in the coach, although comfortable, were precarious, and with every jolt some riders might fall to the ground and be compelled to grasp a rope. A feeling of insecurity, therefore, clouded the happiness of the fortunate occupants of the seats.[5]

Notes

1. James Boswell, *Life of Samuel Johnson* (1791), edited by R.W. Chapman, revised by J.D. Fleeman (Oxford: Oxford University Press, 1980), 736 (April 10, 1776).
2. William Blake, "The Human Abstract," *Songs of Experience* (1794), in Roger Lonsdale, comp., *The New Oxford Book of Eighteenth Century Verse* (Oxford: Oxford University Press, 1984), 695.

3. Charles Dickens, *Martin Chuzzlewit* (New York: Grosset and Dunlap, 1935), 112 (ch. 7).
4. Ibid., 119 (ch. 8).
5. Edward Bellamy, *Looking Backward, 2000–1887* (New York: Random House, 1960), 3–6 (ch. 1).

9

Relief of Need

During the lifetime of Sir Walter Scott (1771–1832) Scotland levied no taxes for the relief of the poor, relying instead on donations collected at church doors. At one point in Scott's novel *The Antiquary*, Jonathan Oldbuck (the antiquary of the title), provoked by the insolence and familiarity of Edie Ochletree, declares, "I have always been against poor's rates and a workhouse—I think I'll vote for them now to have that scoundrel shut up."[1] Scott's preference in relieving the needy was personal charity, which he said "blesses him that gives and him that takes" and awakens kindly feelings in the minds of both donors and recipients. Scott believed, however, that in the existing state of society "a system of compulsory charity by poor's rates" (that is, tax-supported poor relief) was "an absolute necessity." He recognized but rued the need for a compulsory assessment for the poor, foreseeing that the system would cause resentment among those from whom the tax was "extorted" (Scott's word) and those for whose benefit it was levied. The former would wish the "annihilation" rather than the relief of the distressed; the latter, "sensible of ill-will with which the pittance is bestowed," would claim it as a right rather than a favor and find revenge by "becoming impudent and clamorous."[2]

In England parishes had imposed taxes for the relief of the poor since the Tudors, and the money raised had sometimes (as in the late eighteenth and early nineteenth centuries) been used to supplement the low wages of agricultural laborers. A reform of the Poor Laws enacted in 1834 required adoption by all parishes of methods of administering relief that, as Scott foretold, were intentionally calculated to humiliate persons unfortunate enough to need assistance. The reformers pro-

posed to annihilate pauperism by denying relief to able-bodied persons
and their families except in "well-regulated workhouses" where they
could be set to and kept at work and could be housed, fed, clothed, and
otherwise maintained at a bare subsistence level. Under such a system — already in existence in some parishes — the reformers reasoned
that parish (public) relief would become the last rather than the first
resort of the indigent; on the other hand, since relief of a sort was
provided in the workhouse, vagrants and beggars would lose their best
weapon, "the plea of impending starvation."[3]

The emphasis of the *Poor Law Report*, which enunciated the principles incorporated in the law of 1834, was to get and keep the able-
bodied off relief. The impotent poor — those unable to work — remained
a parish charge, but young children of the able-bodied were consigned
to workhouses until released by apprenticeship. Edwin Chadwick
(1800–90) and Nassau W. Senior (1790–1864), the principal authors
of the *Report*, admitted that the workhouse test might cause hardship
for some poor people, but they deemed it "a hardship to which the
good of society requires the applicants to submit." The remedy for
cases of real hardship was the charity of individuals, "a virtue for
which no system of compulsory relief can or ought to be a substitute."[4]

Shortly after passage of the *New Poor Law*, William Wordsworth, an
enemy of the economists and utilitarians who had framed the act,
attacked its provisions intended to deter applications for poor relief by
making assistance available only under harsh and demeaning circumstances. The provisions, in Wordsworth's opinion, violated the proposition, accepted in principal in the *Poor Law Report*, that "all persons
who cannot find employment, or procure wages sufficient to support
the body in health and strength, are entitled to maintenance by law."
Just as the state has the right to compel its subjects to fight and
perhaps die in the common defense, subjects have a right to public
support when, "from any cause," they are unable to support themselves. Acceptance of relief, far from degrading the recipients,
strengthens them by protecting them from misery and death and enables
them to avoid resort to charity, violence, or breach of law.[5]

Even before the *Poor Law Report* one of Sir Walter Scott's coun-
trymen and contemporaries, Thomas Chalmers (1780–1847), had demonstrated that voluntary charity could be as systematic and uncompromising in dealing with the poor as a tax-supported system of relief. In

the 1820s, as minister of the largest and poorest parish in Glasgow, Chalmers obtained authority to manage all funds for relief of the parish poor. He divided the parish into districts and subdistricts, each supervised by "laymen of Christian character" who established Sunday schools, visited and counseled the poor, investigated applications for relief, and made decisions about granting or withholding it. According to Chalmers, their strict investigation of applicants' character and condition exerted "a preventive influence — and they simply cease to apply." Over a period of about four years Chalmers reduced parish expenditures for poor relief by seventy-five percent. He was unable to prevent Scotland from adopting a tax-supported relief system, but his writings stressing the financial, moral, and social (for example, reducing the poor to "a habit of most mild and manageable quiescence") benefits of his experiment were well known and highly regarded in both England and America.[6]

The authors of the *Poor Law Report*, while relying on individual charity to alleviate "cases of real hardship" caused by the new law, looked with disfavor on the charity of earlier centuries that had dotted England with almshouses, hospitals, and foundations regularly or occasionally distributing alms, bread, and beer to the poor. Four commissions established by Parliament in the fifteen years after 1819 to investigate charities in England and Wales reported that most charitable trusts had been conscientiously administered, even though the purposes and methods of many were inconsistent with the stern measure poor-law reformers recommended to "dispauperize" the country. The reports also showed that in a number of instances charity funds had been lost, misappropriated, or applied to uses other than those the donor had intended. Consequently between 1835 and 1853, when Parliament created a permanent charity commission, numerous efforts were made to correct such abuses and obtain closer supervision of endowed charities.[7]

Conservatives resented the reforming spirit of the 1820s and 1830s and questioned the necessity of investigating familiar, long-established institutions and practices. In *Crotchet Castle* (1831) Thomas Love Peacock, essayist, poet, and novelist, included an account of the Commissioners' visit to a village to inquire into the payment of one pound a year for the endowment and repair of an almshouse. The vicar and churchwarden deny knowledge of the almshouse or its support, but the aged parish clerk testifies:

> I do remember, gentlemen, to have been informed, that there did stand at the end of the village a ruined cottage, which had once been an alsmhouse, which was endowed and maintained, by an annual revenue of a mark and a half, or one pound sterling, charged some centuries ago on the farm of Hautbois; but the means, by the progress of time, having become inadequate to the end, the almshouse tumbled to pieces.

The clerk recalls that many years ago, by unanimous vote of the vestry, the pound was given to the minister; Farmer Seedling, present owner of Hautbois, lumps the pound in every year with his tithes. "A flagrant perversion of a charitable donation," exclaims one of the Commissioners. They admonish the parish officers for the improper proceedings and promptly depart, leaving matters as they found them.[8]

Beginning in 1849 *The Times* of London exposed misuse of income from endowments at Rochester Cathedral School and St. Cross Hospital, Winchester, both of which were administered by the Church of England. Anthony Trollope (1815–82) recalled that he had been distressed both by the diversion of funds intended for charitable purposes to incomes for church officials, and by the ferocity with which the newspaper attacked the recipients of the incomes. "When a man is appointed to a place," Trollope wrote in his *Autobiography* (1883), "it is natural that he should accept the income allotted to that place without much inquiry. It is seldom that he will be the first to find out that his services are overpaid."[9]

The main character in Trollope's *The Warden* (1855), the Reverend Septimus Harding, is preceptor (choir director) of Barchester Cathedral; his position as warden of Hiram's Hospital, an almshouse for twelve bedesmen founded in 1434, is a sinecure providing Mr. Harding with a pleasant residence and a good salary with only nominal duties and responsibilities. He is an old friend of the bishop and the father-in-law of the archdeacon. Trollope depicts Harding as an upright and kindly man, more interested in and concerned about the old men in the almshouse than their self-appointed champion, who believes the warden's salary should be divided among the bedesmen. Harding, a mild, unworldly person, finding himself involved in a lawsuit and the target of newspaper abuse, resigns as warden. His adversary drops the lawsuit and, soon after, marries Harding's younger daughter. Harding remains preceptor and the bishop finds another "living" for him in a small church in Barchester.

Contemporary critics objected that Trollope's ending left the rights and wrongs of church reform unresolved.[10] No one is rewarded, and no one punished, although the bedesmen are left worse off (the bishop declines to name a new warden or successor to Harding) and more disgruntled than at the start of the book. In a critical scene early in the novel, Harding tells John Bold, the young surgeon who has instigated the publicity and legal action about the hospital accounts, "I shall never attribute to you base motives because you hold an opinion opposed to my own, and adverse to my interests."[11] Trollope himself, as we shall see in chapter 11, "Philanthropy and Reform," makes a point of the purity of Bold's motives. Trollope does not impose his opinions on readers or ask them to change their convictions, but he encourages them to be less hasty and more charitable in their judgments.

A more splendid almshouse for old *gentlemen* figures in *The Newcomes, Memoirs of a Most Respectable Family* (1853–55) by William Makepeace Thackeray (1811–63). Col. Newcome, a retired army officer reduced to poverty by business losses, is nominated for a place among the eighty poor brothers of Charterhouse Hospital by a friend who is a governor of the institution. Thackeray, an alumnus of Charterhouse School, part of the same foundation, writes lovingly of the chapel with the ornate tomb of Thomas Sutton, the founder; the beautiful Jacobean Hall; and the "old staircases, old passages, old chambers decorated with old portraits, walking in the midst of which we walk as it were in the early seventeenth century." Each year on the anniversary of the founder's death, poor brothers, scholars, governors, and alumni meet for oratory, sermon and prayers, and feasting. Thackeray describes the ceremony in the candlelit chapel, "this scene of age and youth, and early memories, and pompous death."[12]

As American consul in Liverpool (1853–57) Nathaniel Hawthorne (1804–64) was fascinated by charitable foundations established hundreds of years earlier that were still functioning in the middle of the nineteenth century. "There is something altogether strange to an American in these charitable institutions," he wrote after visiting several in Coventry "— in the preservation of antique modes and customs which is effected by them; insomuch that, doubtless without at all intending it, the founders have succeeded in preserving a kind of model of their own long past age, down into the midst of ours, and how much later nobody can tell."[13]

At Ford's Hospital in Coventry, Hawthorne caught glimpses of little rooms, each with a fireplace, bed, and chair or two for one old woman.

They are destitute old widows, who have their lodging and home here — a little room for every one to sleep, cook, and be at home in — and three and sixpence a week to feed and clothe themselves with; a cloak being the only garment bestowed on them. When one of the sisterhood dies, each old woman has to pay two-pence towards the funeral; and so they slowly starve and wither out of life, and claim each their two-penny contribution in turn.[14]

The twelve old soldiers in the Leicester (or Lord Leycester) Hospital, an almshouse founded in the reign of Queen Elizabeth, were more fortunate: each had a parlor and bedroom of his own; if married, their wives lived with them. Hawthorne said the hospital seemed "an abode where a war worn veteran, satiated with adventure, might spend the remnant of his life as happily as anywhere else." He was so intrigued by this "patch of old times surviving sturdily into the new" that he visited it on two occasions.[15] In *Our Old Home* (1863), written after Hawthorne's return to the United States, he said of the Leicester Hospital, "It is such a pleasant kind of dream for an American to find his way thither, and behold a piece of the sixteenth century set into our prosaic times, and then to depart, and think of its arched door-way as a spell-guarded entrance which will never be accessible to him any-more."[16]

Neither Hawthorne nor later visitors could fail to notice the founder's determination to glorify his family and himself by having the Leicester coat of arms prominently displayed wherever it could be carved or painted on the exterior and interior of the building and sewn on the garments of the hospital bretheren. Hawthorne charitably observed that "this may not indicate his individual vanity, but belonged to the manners and feeling of the age." He was reminded of the fuss made over William Brown (1784–1864), a Liverpool banker, in 1857 when he presented a library and museum to Liverpool. Hawthorne was present at the laying of the cornerstone and gave a speech at the ceremony. "In their several ways, and according to the fashion of the times," he concluded, the Earl of Leicester and Mr. Brown wanted recognition. "Both wanted to do a good thing, and were willing to have the credit of it."[17]

Writers — Trollope for one — find it difficult to make conventional charity and morality interesting. Mr. Harding in *The Warden* is interesting because he is not, as people might expect someone in his position would be, selfish and corrupt. Near the end of the novel Trollope admits that he has not done justice to archdeacon Grantly, having emphasized his faults rather than his virtues. It is true that Grantly is domineering, determined to have his own way, bigoted in his religious views, and desirous of power and money. But he is a gentleman, is conscientious and capable in performance of his duties, upholds propriety in conduct by example as well as precept, and is "generous to the poor and hospitable to the rich."[18] Trollope is less scrupulous with Miss Thorne in *Barchester Towers* (1857). After paying a good deal of attention to her eccentricities he notes that she divides her considerable income among younger relatives, her milliner, and the poor, giving much the largest share to the last. "All her follies . . . have been told," Trollope writes. "Her virtues were too numerous to describe, and not sufficiently interesting to deserve description."[19]

One of Hawthorne's early stories touches briefly on the charities of a New England village. It was not a flourishing town, Hawthorne tells us, having neither a jail nor a distillery, but there were cottage industries and reading societies, "and the females actually raised ten dollars and fifty-two cents for the emancipation of the Greeks." The exemplar of benevolence is the clergyman (the village seems to have had only one church) who, in the tradition of Chaucer's and Goldsmith's parsons, squeezes an "overplus" from his modest salary to apply to the need of the poor.[20] In this respect he is like the old minister and unlike the new vicar in Trollope's *Can you Forgive Her?* (1864–65). The old man was known for both his charity and the brevity of his religious services. The newcomer adds an afternoon service. He was "a close-fisted man, with higher ideas of personal comfort, who found it necessary to make every penny go as far as possible, who made up in preaching for what he could not give away in charity."[21]

"The females" in Hawthorne's story may have raised the money for Greek independence by holding a "fancy fair" or charity bazaar. Women on both sides of the Atlantic made and contributed articles to be sold at such occasions to raise money for church and community projects. "Fancy fairs," wrote Frances Trollope (the mother of Anthony) in *The Vicar of Wrexhill* (1837) took advantage of "that great object of all English Christian enthusiasm—the disbursement of money."[22] They were social as well as charitable events, giving participants an opportunity to dress up, be seen, and perhaps be admired. A charity bazaar held in the beautiful hall of a historic building in George Eliot's *The*

Mill on the Floss was the culmination of the ill-fated heroine's brief career as a member of polite society in the town of St. Ogg's. "The perfect fitness of this ancient building for an admirable modern purpose . . . made charity truly elegant, and led through vanity up to the supply of a deficit." Maggie Tulliver's beauty and simplicity contrast with the "artificial airs" of many of the other young women and attract young men — one of whom would be her undoing — to the booth where she is selling dressing gowns.[23]

One way of obtaining money for individuals in need of assistance was by subscription letters circulated by the needy persons themselves or by their friends. At Nicholas Nickleby's first meeting with the Cheeryble brothers, they are adding their names to a subscription list and writing checks for the relief of the family of a workman killed in an accident on the docks — and thanking the collector for calling the matter to their attention.[24] Among the wayfarers in Hawthorne's "The Seven Vagabonds" (1833), one subsists "on the casual charity of the people" and one presents the narrator with a circular "signed by several distinguished gentlemen I have never heard of, stating that the bearer had encountered every variety of misfortune and recommending him to the notice of all charitable people." The narrator offers to make a donation if the man can change a five-dollar bill; like Scott's friend Andrew Gemell, the old man has more than enough coins in his well-filled purse to change the bill.[25] In 1842, while Hawthorne was living at the Old Manse in Concord, Massachusetts, a woman came to his door with a certificate saying she was destitute because of the death of her husband, son, and friends; she had a list of the people who had helped her, with the amounts — seldom more than twenty-five cents — they had donated. Hawthorne's reflection on the import of her visit will be examined in chapter 12. He had a less favorable reaction to the bearers of subscription letters who pestered him while he was American consul in Liverpool, calling them "rats that nibble at the honest bread and cheese of the community, and grow fat by their petty pilferings." Nevertheless, he often gave them what they asked, privately admitting he was a simpleton for doing so.[26]

"A sympathetic person," declared Ralph Waldo Emerson, "is placed in the dilemma of a swimmer among drowning men, who all catch at him, and if he gives so much as a leg or finger, they will drown him." Emerson (1803–82), briefly a clergyman, seldom had anything good to say about charity. "They wish to be saved from the mischief of their vices, but not from their vices." By "they" he seems to have meant the needy in general rather than any particular poor persons. It would be a waste of charity, he said, assuming for the moment that charity might occasionally be justified, to lavish it on the symptoms while ignoring the cause.[27]

Emerson's observations and advice might more often be heeded if the only object of charity were to relieve the needs of others. It is no secret, however, that people give not only to help others but in response to their own need or wish for forgiveness, reward, love, and recognition. Speculation about why they give — the motives for philanthropy — is a favorite pastime of observers, whether scholars or people in the street. Authors have the advantage of being able to assign motives, creditable or discreditable, to their characters. In Victor Hugo's *Les Miserables* (1862), the townspeople speculate about the reasons why M. Madeleine, the manufacturer, is so extremely generous to the poor and has endowed the hospital and built two schools. Is it ambition for office, desire for official recognition, or social acceptance? According to Hugo (1802–85), none of these explanations is correct. M. Madeleine — Jean Valjean in disguise — gives to atone for his abuse of the confidence of a kindly bishop and a mean trick played on a little boy, misdeeds he committed after his release from nineteen years in prison for stealing a loaf of bread.[28]

If remorse is at one end of the spectrum of motivation, pride and display are at the other. The prodigal givers deplored by Cicero, who spent money on public feasts and entertainments, were interested not in the needs of the populace but in showing off their wealth and winning popular favor. For similar reasons Aladdin, after finding the magic lamp, has slaves throw money to the crowds that line the street as he passes on his way to mosque or court. "This generosity gained him the love and blessings of the people."[29]

Mr. Bulstrode, the banker in George Eliot's *Middlemarch* (1871–72), doesn't throw his money around, but he uses his charity, like his loans, to increase his power in the community. He held positions of authority in all the public charities, and his personal giving augmented the influence he exercised: His beneficence was "at once ready and severe — ready to confer obligations, and severe in watching the result." He was an intensely pious man. "It was a principle with Mr. Bulstrode to gain as much power as possible, that he might use it for the glory of

God."[30] For all his good works he was not well liked, and, from time to time, aware of his unpopularity, he reexamined his motives without altering his practice.

Notes

1. Scott, *The Antiquary* (New York: Harper and Brothers, 1901), 1:77 (chapter 14). Edie Ochletree is discussed in Part Three, chapter 8, page 90.
2. Scott, *St. Ronan's Well* (New York: G.D. Sproul, 1901) 2:250–52. First published in 1824.
3. "Report for Inquiring into the Administration and Practical Operation of the Poor Laws," sect. 4, "Remedial Measures," in Roy Lubove, ed., *Social Welfare in Transition Selected English Documents, 1834–1909* (Pittsburgh: University of Pittsburgh Press, 1966), 52–56.
4. Ibid., 57.
5. William Wordsworth, "Postscript," in *Yarrow Revisited and Other Poems* (London: Longman, 1835), 323–26. William Pultney Alison, M.D. (1790–1859), whose reports on the influences of poverty and bad social conditions on the spread of disease were influential in the adoption (1845) of a tax-supported system of poor relief in Scotland, used Wordsworth's argument in *Observations on the Management of the Poor in Scotland and its Effect on the Health of Great Towns* (Edinburgh: William Blackwood and Sons, 1840), 62–64.
6. Quotations are from Thomas Chalmers, D.D., *Statement in Regard to Pauperism in Glasgow* (Glasgow: Chalmers and Collins, 1823), 28–45.
7. Ibid., 112–13. For an informative and entertaining account of the findings of the earlier commissions see C.E.P. Lascelles, "Charity," in G.M Young, ed., *Early Victorian England* (London: Oxford University Press, 1934), 2:340–41. In *English Philanthropy, 1660–1960* (Cambridge: Harvard University Press, 1964), 182–208, David Owen reviews efforts to reform and supervise endowed charities in England between 1812 and 1860.
8. Thomas Love Peacock, *Crotchet Castle* (1831), in *The Pleasures of Peacock*, edited by Ben Ray Redman (New York: Farrar, Straus, 1947), 335–37.
9. Anthony Trollope, *An Autobiography* (London: William and Northgate, Limited, 1946), 96–97. First published in 1883.
10. N. John Hall discusses the background of *The Warden* and contemporary criticism of it in *Trollope, A Biography* (Oxford: Clarendon Press, 1991), 134–35.
11. Anthony Trollope, *The Warden* (London: Oxford University Press, 1952), 33 (chapter 3). First published in 1855.
12. William Makepeace Thackeray, *The Newcomes, Memoirs of a Most Respectable Family* (Cambridge: Cambridge University Press, 1954), 717–20 (chapter 75). First published in 1853–55.

13. Nathaniel Hawthorne, *The English Notebooks*, edited by Randall Stewart (New York: Modern Language Association of America, 1941), 140.
14. Ibid., 579.
15. Ibid., 584–85, 587.
16. Nathaniel Hawthorne, *Our Old Home* (Columbus, Ohio: Ohio State University Press, 1970), 84. First published in 1863. For a recent description of the hospital see Jonathan Keats, *The Companion Guide to the Shakespeare Country* (Englewood Cliffs, N.J.: Prentice Hall, 1983), 53.
17. Hawthorne, *The English Notebooks*, 588–89.
18. Trollope, *The Warden*, 266–67 (chapter 20).
19. Anthony Trollope, *Barchester Towers* (London: The Zodiac Press, 1975), 186 (chapter 22). First published in 1857.
20. "The New England Village" (1831), in *The Complete Short Stories of Nathaniel Hawthorne* (Garden City, N.Y.: Hanover House, 1959), 584.
21. Anthony Trollope, *Can You Forgive Her?* (London: Oxford University Press, 1948), 2:135 (chapter 53).
22. Frances Trollope, *The Vicar of Wrexhill* (London: Richard Bentley, 1837), 3:217.
23. George Eliot, *The Mill on the Floss* (Oxford: Oxford University Press, 1980), 377–78 (chapter 9). First published in 1860. In a sketch written while a student at the University of Edinburgh, Robert Louis Stevenson satirized the uselessness of articles sold at fancy fairs: "The Charity Bazaar" (1868), in The *Works of Robert Louis Stevenson* (New York: Charles Scribner's Sons, 1925), 24:171–74.
24. Charles Dickens, *The Life and Adventures of Nicholas Nickleby* (Oxford: Oxford University Press, 1950), 452 (chapter 35). First published in 1838–39.
25. "The Seven Vagabonds" (1833), in *The Complete Short Stories of Nathaniel Hawthorne*, 176–77.
26. Hawthorne, *Our Old Home*, 293.
27. "Experience," in *Essays: Second Series* (1844), in *The Collected Works of Ralph Waldo Emerson* (Cambridge: Harvard University Press, 1971–83), 3:46–47.
28. Victor Hugo, *Les Miserable*, translated by Norman Denny (Harmandsworth, England: Penguin Books, 1987), 156–59 ("Fantine," book 5, chapter 2). "Fantine" is the first segment of *Les Miserables*. The episode takes place around 1820.
29. On Cicero's condemnation of prodigal givers see Part One, chapter 1. "Aladdin and the Wonderful Lamp," in Rupert S. Holland, *The Arabian Nights* from the translation by William Lane (New York: Grosset & Dunlap, n.d.), 212–13. Lane's "expurgated but scholarly" translation was first published in 1838–41.
30. George Eliot, *Middlemarch, A Study of Provincial Life* (New York: The Modern Library, 1992), 146 (book 2, chapter 16). The novel takes place around 1830.

10

The Good Samaritan: Charles Dickens on Public Relief and Private Charity

Over a span of thirty years, from *Sketches by Boz* (1836–37) to *Our Mutual Friend* (1864–65), Dickens (1812–70) denounced English poor relief policy and practice as a violation of the religious injunction — exemplified in the parable of the Good Samaritan — to deal with the needy in a kind, considerate, and helpful way. His first book begins with a section entitled "Our Parish." The first two sentences are exclamations: "How much is conveyed in those two short words — 'The Parish!' and with how many tales of distress and misery, of broken fortune and ruined hopes, too often of unrelieved wretchedness and successful knavery, are they associated!" A poor man falls behind in his taxes, and then cannot pay them; the parish seizes his possessions; his wife dies and the parish buries her; the parish binds out his children; the man, destroyed by worry and drunkenness, ends his days in the parish asylum.

"The Parish" includes the rector, churchwardens, vestry, and the parish infirmary, surgeon, overseers, and beadle. "Excellent institutions, and gentle kind-hearted men." Dickens has nothing to say about the rector and mentions the churchwardens and overseers only in passing, but he looks closely at the officials directly responsible for the care of the local poor: the beadle, pauper schoolmaster, and workhouse master. The first, the chief administrative officer of the temporal affairs of the parish, is a self-important man whose chief concern is maintaining the dignity of his office. The schoolmaster, once talented and still conscientious, is an old man whose career has been a succession of disappointments and misfortune. The workhouse master is poorly paid, but probably better off than ever before in his life. "He lives free of house-rent, has a limited allowance of coal and candles, and an almost unlimited allowance of authority in his petty kingdom." When you pass his window he looks at you as though he wishes you were a pauper so that he could show you his power. "He is an admirable specimen of a small tyrant: morose, brutish, and ill-tempered; bullying to his inferiors, cringing to his superiors, and jealous of the influence and authority of the beadle." In Dickens's novels we meet men of his stripe again and again.[1]

When first published in 1838, *Oliver Twist* was subtitled *The Parish Boy's Progress*. The boy was born in a workhouse in the late 1820s, his mother dying at his birth. When we meet him he is crying lustily. Dickens tells us, "If he could have known that he was an orphan, left to the tender mercies of churchwardens and overseers, perhaps he would have cried the louder."[2] Dickens gave Oliver his first name; as was customary with foundlings, Mr. Bumble, the beadle and workhouse warden, supplied the surname, Twist. Mr. Bumble named foundlings in alphabetical order: the one before Twist was Swubble, the next was to be Unwin.[3]

On his ninth birthday Oliver, having spent his infancy and early childhood "farmed" to a woman who never gave him a kind word or look, returns to the workhouse where he was born. For six months it has been operating under new rules and regulations. Dickens describes the regimen matter-of-factly and in a tone of sweet reasonableness: a starvation diet, skimping on the other necessities of life, separation of sexes and families, strict discipline, and enforced labor (picking oakum) under the name of "education in a useful trade." Dickens might have said that the board was simply following instructions laid down by the New Poor Law of 1834, but he sharpened his criticism by personalizing the issue, attributing the new policies to the meanness of the local board. "It was rather expensive at first, in consequence of the increase in the undertaker's bill, and the necessity of taking in the clothes of all the paupers, which fluttered loosely on their wasted, shrunken forms, after a week or two's gruel. But the number of workhouse inmates got thin as well as the paupers; and the board were in ecstasies."[4]

The parochial seal shows the Good Samaritan tending the wounded man; Mr. Bumble, the chief instrument in carrying out the policies of the workhouse board, proudly displays a replica of the seal on a lapel pin. He starts Oliver on his post-workhouse adventures by apprenticing him to an undertaker, from whom Oliver runs away. Like the workhouse master in "Our Parish," Mr. Bumble is an example of the arbitrary, incompetent, hypocritical minor public official Dickens detested. Later in the novel he takes revenge on Bumble for his cruelty to Oliver and the other occupants of the workhouse by having him become an inmate of the institution over which he had once presided.[5]

In later works *Our Mutual Friend*, for example Dickens recognized that methods and standards of poor relief were set by national rather than local policy. He deplored the practice of treating all able-bodied paupers, regardless of character or cause of distress, whether vicious and violent or blameless and meek, as if they were alike. The rough, idle, and disorderly poor could survive the workhouse, but respectable and deserving souls like Betty Higden in *Our Mutual Friend* would rather die than go or be sent to one. "The best of the poor," he wrote of Betty, an old woman who tries to make a living by selling trinkets, "detest our mercies, hide their heads from us, and shame us by dying of starvation in the midst of us." Of the New Poor Law of 1834, the pride of tough-minded political economists, he wrote, "This boastful handiwork of ours, which fails in its terrors for the professional pauper, the sturdy breaker of windows and the rampant tearer of clothes, strikes with a cruel and wicked stab at the stricken sufferers, and is a horror to the deserving and unfortunate." After a long passage dealing with Betty Higden's fear of the workhouse and official charity, Dickens comments, "It is a remarkable Christian improvement to have made a pursuing Fury of the Good Samaritan; but it was so in this case, and it is a type of many, many, many."[6]

Dickens recognized and accepted what Scott called the "absolute necessity" of tax-supported poor relief. Like Wordsworth, he condemned the policies that caused suffering within and outside the workhouse. "With an enormous treasure at disposal to relieve the poor" we have devised ways to administer it so that people — Betty Higden is just one example — die of neglect and exposure rather than accept our bounty. Dickens's final words on the Poor Law appear in the "Postscript in Lieu of Preface" in *Our Mutual Friend*:

> I believe there has been in England, since the days of the STUARTS, no law so often infamously administered, no law so often openly violated, no law habitually so ill-supervised. In the majority of the shameful cases of disease and death from destitution that shock the Public and disgrace the

country, the illegality is quite equal to the inhumanity — and known language could say no more of their lawlessness.[7]

Individual benevolence — kindly and generous assistance offered by someone out of the goodness of his or her heart — was Dickens's favorite way of rescuing his characters from want and despair. Good Samaritans like Mr. Brownlow in *Oliver Twist*, the Cheeryble brothers in *Nicholas Nickleby* (1839), Mr. and Mrs. Garland in *The Old Curiosity Shop* (1841), and the Boffins in *Our Mutual Friend* play key roles in many of Dickens's novels. Neither Dickens nor his heroes and heroines question their benefactors' motives; it is enough that they are ready to help and that their aid is appreciated and put to good use. "The key to their character is benevolence," observes a Dickens scholar, Humphrey House. "They are all good natured and seem to act as they do because they cannot act otherwise."[8]

In real life the cherubic Cheeryble brothers who give Nicholas Nickleby a chance to prove his merit might have learned that a reputation for helpfulness and civic spirit, like being known for making a superior product and paying bills on time, is good for business. Dickens modeled them after William and Daniel Grant, textile manufacturers and philanthropists in Manchester. The brothers' achievements are among the success stories recounted by Samuel Smiles in *Self-Help* (1859).

Dickens himself was generous toward people in need, contributed to a variety of charitable organizations, helped them raise funds, and served on the board of many charitable agencies.[9] Among those he served was The Hospital for Sick Children on Great Ormond Street in London. His praise of the hospital in *Our Mutual Friend* is one of the few, possibly the only, instance of a flattering portrait of a charitable institution in his works. In this case he recognized that institutional care was superior to that provided by well-intentioned individuals. Betty Higden first opposes and then consents to the removal of her sick grandchild to the hospital where, Mrs. Boffin assures her, he will receive closer medical attention than would be possible at home.[10]

In 1853 Dickens wrote a long article on the Foundling Hospital, established a century earlier by Thomas Coram. His attitude to it was respectful, but he was put off by its size, impersonality, and bureaucratic administration. In one respect, however, he found it a model for other public charities. "Canvassing and electioneering are the disgrace of many public charities at this time," he declared, referring to the practice of making appointments by favoritism or sale. The Governors of the Foundling Hospital, Dickens reported, held themselves "strictly aloof from any canvassing for an office connected with it, or a benefit derivable from it."[11]

Because Dickens placed such a high value on personal kindness and benevolence, he condemned harshness, hypocrisy, and self-interest in charity as well as in public relief. Instead of heaping praise on charity in the abstract, he called attention to its all too frequent flaws and shortcomings in practice. Similarly, because of his sympathy for the deserving poor, he delighted in exposing fakes, professional beggars, and "charlatan traders on compassion."[12]

One of the last stories in the "Our Parish" section of *Sketches By Boz* deals with the parish ladies' charitable societies. These include separate organizations for the distribution of soup, coal, and blankets; a dispensary and sick-visitation committee; the child's examination society (to drill the charity-school pupils), the Bible and prayer book distribution society (for the poor who sit in the free seats in the church), and, for mothers and newborn babies, the childbed-linen monthly loan society. The two latter, judged by the "greater stir and more bustle" they create, are the most important. The sketch examines the rivalry between the two associations and the challenge posed to each by the bumptious child's examination society. Dickens pokes fun at all three. It is possible that Dickens finds them amusing just because they are *ladies'* societies, which men (and many women) often regard as innately humorous. Dickens's point, however, is that the three societies are self-serving charities. Helping others is only an incidental purpose. Their main function is to advertise the virtue of their members and to promote their self-esteem.[13]

The Charitable Grinders School in *Dombey and Son* (1847–48) is an example of a demeaning charity. Mr. Dombey, to ensure that his infant son's nurse will give undivided attention to the boy, nominates *her* son, Biler, to a place in a school established by the worshipful company of Charitable Grinders. "I am far from being friendly," Dombey explains, "to what is called by persons of levelling sentiments, general education. But it is necessary that the inferior classes should continue to be taught to know their position, and to conduct themselves properly. So far I approve of schools."[14] Boys attending the school, as a sign of their lowly status, have to wear a badge and an absurd uniform. They are taught "as parrots are, by a brute jobbed into his place as schoolmaster with as much fitness for it as a hound." (The schoolmaster's appointment is an instance of the favoritism Dickens saw as the "disgrace" of some public charities.) Outside of school the uniform exposes the students to the contempt of adults and the bullying of other boys. After a day at the school, beaten and jeered at, Biler's "social existence had been more like that of an early Christian, than an innocent child of the nineteenth century."[15]

One of Dickens's best-known creations, Mrs. Jellyby in *Bleak House* (1852–53), practices "telescopic philanthropy." Distressed by the plight of suffering people in remote parts of the world, and devoting all her energies to helping them, she neglects her own family and shows no sympathy for the suffering in her own community. "The African project at present employs my whole time," she explains to visitors. "We hope by this time next year to have from a hundred and fifty to two hundred healthy families cultivating coffee and educating the natives of Borrioboola-Gha, on the leftbank of the Niger."[16]

Esther Summerson, who narrates the part of *Bleak House* in which Mrs. Jellyby appears, uses the expression "rapacious benevolence" to characterize another famous character, Mrs. Pardiggle. Esther describes her as "a formidable style of lady . . . who had the effect of wanting a great deal of room." When she enters a house "she seems to come in like cold weather." Unlikely as it seems, Mrs. Pardiggle is a "friendly visitor" to the poor. Esther and her friend Ada accompany her to the miserable hovel of a brick maker who, in a memorable outburst, makes plain that he wants nothing to do with Mrs. Pardiggle's advice or tracts. In recounting the incident Esther says that she and Ada "both felt painfully sensible that between us and these people there was an iron barrier, which could not be removed by our new friend. By whom or how, it could be removed, we did not know; but we knew that." Taking no notice of the hostile reception, Mrs. Pardiggle tells the family, "I shall come to you again, in your regular order," expresses the hope that the house will be in neater condition then, and proceeds to another cottage.[17]

John Stuart Mill (1806–73), philosopher and economist, did not find Mrs. Jellyby and Mrs. Pardiggle laughable. He resented the implication that woman's sphere was the home rather than philanthropy and critized Dickens's portrayal of the two women as an attack on the rights of women done "in the very vulgarest way."[18]

In considering Mill's objection it is useful to keep in mind that Dickens presented Mrs. Jellyby and Mrs. Pardiggle through the eyes of Esther Summerson, one of the more level-headed of his heroines. She was conventional and goody-goody, but she also possessed the qualities Dickens admired in both women and men: honesty, kindness, generosity, sympathy for and willingness to help others, and modesty about one's own abilities and attainments. She can't help noticing that Mrs. Jellyby is a poor housekeeper and untidy in dress and appearance; what distresses Esther more is Mrs. Jellyby's indifference to her son and exploitation of her daughter. Esther comments on Mrs. Pardiggle's loud voice, formidable appearance, and a hoop skirt that demands too much room; these might be overlooked if it were not for Mrs. Pardiggle's overbearing manner and assumption that she has the right, duty, and ability to tell other people how to manage their affairs. Esther acknowledges that she herself does not possess "that delicate knowledge of the heart which must be essential to such a work. That I had much to learn, myself, before I could teach others, and that I could not confide in my good intentions alone."[19]

Dickens's targets were "telescopic philanthropy" and "rapacious benevolence." These failings can be found in men as well as women. Dickens chose to represent the failings through women rather than men, possibly because he believed that by doing so he could make them seem more ludicrous. He was capable of making up men as all-absorbed in distant projects and as unconcerned about everyday events as Mrs. Jellyby and as aggressive and insensitive as Mrs. Pardiggle. But Mr. Jellyby and Mr. Pardiggle would not have been as effective as Mrs. Jellyby and Mrs. Pardiggle because their faults were, and to a certain extent still are, considered less reprehensible in men than in women.

From time to time even someone as responsive as Dickens became irritated by the demands on his generosity. Esther Summerson echoes Dickens's exasperation in commenting on the charitable appeals received by John Jarndyce. His correspondents

> wanted everything. They wanted wearing apparel, they wanted linen rags, they wanted money, they wanted coals, they wanted soup, they wanted interest, they wanted autographs, they wanted flannel, they wanted whatever Mr. Jarndyce had — or had not. Their objects were as various as their demands. They were going to raise new buildings, they were going to pay off debts on old buildings, they were going to establish in a picturesque

building (engraving of proposed West Elevation attached) the Sisterhood of Mediaeval Marys; they were going to give a testimonial to Mrs. Jellyby; they were going to have their Secretary's portrait painted, and presented to his mother-in-law, whose deep devotion to him was well known; they were going to get up everything, I really believe from five hundred thousand tracts to an annuity, and from a marble monument to a silver teapot.[20]

Mr. Boffin in *Our Mutual Friend* is also the recipient of a multitude of opportunities to give for the erection of churches, parsonages, and orphanages. "And then the charities, my Christian brother! And mostly in difficulties, yet mostly lavish, too, in the expensive articles of print and paper." Then, as now, fund raisers used "names" and appealed to snobbery to induce giving. Plain Mr. Boffin received letters addressed to Nicodemus Boffin, Esquire, signed by the Duke of Linseed, and sealed with the ducal crest; the letter had been lithographed by the hundred and the envelope addressed by a hand other than that of the Duke.[21]

Despite the frenzy of fund raising, charity is neglectful. To succeed, it needs an object in which donors can take an interest. Jo, the boy crossing-sweeper in *Bleak House*, is not such an object. He is just a dirty, vermin-infested boy who is ignored by society, and charitable societies, until he is near death. There is nothing exotic about Jo.

He is not one of Mrs. Pardiggle's Tockahoopo Indians; he is not one of Mrs. Jellyby's lambs; being wholly unconnected with Borrioboola-Gha; he is not softened by distance and unfamiliarity; he is not a genuine foreign-grown savage; he is the ordinary home-made article. Dirty, ugly, disagreeable to all the senses, in body a common creature of the common streets, only in soul a heathen. Homely filth begrimes him, homely parasites devour him, homely sores are in him, homely rags are on him: native ignorance, the growth of English soil and climate, sinks his immortal nature lower than the beasts that perish. Stand forth Jo, in uncompromising colours! From the sole of thy foot to the crown of thy head, there is nothing interesting about thee.[22]

Jo dies while saying "The Lord's Prayer," seemingly for the first time in his life. "Dead, your Majesty," intones Dickens, "Dead, my lords and gentlemen. Dead, Right Reverends and Wrong Reverends, of every order. Dead, men and women, born with Heavenly compassion in your hearts. And dying thus around us every day."[23]

Notes

1. Charles Dickens, *Sketches by Boz Illustrative of Every-day Life and Every-day People* (Oxford: Oxford University Press, 1987), 1–6 (chapter 1).
2. Dickens, *The Adventures of Oliver Twist* (Oxford: Oxford University Press, 1987), 1–3 (chapter 1).
3. Ibid., 4–5 (chapter 2).
4. Ibid., 10–11 (chapter 2).
5. Ibid., 23–24 (chapter 4) and 538–39 (chapter 53). Dickens suggests that Mr. Bumble was grateful for being separated from his wife.
6. Dickens, *Our Mutual Friend* (Oxford: Oxford University Press, 1987), 503–6 (book 3, chapter 8).
7. Ibid., 821–22.
8. Humphrey House, *The Dickens World* (London: Oxford University Press, 1941), 39.
9. Dickens's charitable activities are summarized in Norris Pope, *Dickens and Charity* (New York: Columbia University Press, 1978), 10–11, an excellent guide to Dickens's attitude toward charity and treatment of it in his work.
10. *Our Mutual Friend*, 327–30 (book 2, chapter 9).
11. Dickens's article "Received, A Blank Child" originally appeared in *Household Words*, March 19, 1853. It is reprinted in R.H. Nichols and F. A. Wray, *The History of the Foundling Hospital* (Oxford: Oxford University Press, 1935), 285–91.
12. This phrase is used by Humphrey House in a discussion of Dickens's and his contemporaries' views on the deserving and undeserving poor, *The Dickens World*, 81–82. Norris Pope in *Dickens and Charity*, 246, says that Dickens believed his criticisms of charity were "of more pressing urgency than the sort of praise routinely bestowed on charitable enterprises."
13. Dickens, "The Ladies' Societies," in *Sketches by Boz*, 34–39.
14. Dickens, *Dombey and Son, Wholesale, Retail, and for Exportation* (Oxford: Oxford University Press, 1987), 59 (chapter 4).
15. Ibid., 279 (chapter 20); 67–68 (chapter 6).
16. Dickens, *Bleak House* (Oxford: Oxford University Press, 1987), 34–39 (chapter 4).
17. Ibid., 99–108 (chapter 8).
18. Quoted in Edgar Johnson, *Charles Dickens, His Tragedy and His Triumph* (New York: Simon and Schuster, 1952), 761.
19. Dickens, *Bleak House*, 104 (chapter 8).
20. Ibid., 99–100 (chapter 8).
21. Dickens, *Our Mutual Friend*, 210–11 (book 1, chapter 17).
22. Dickens, *Bleak House*, 640–41 (chapter 47)
23. Ibid., 649 (chapter 47). In 1853 in New York City Charles Loring Brace founded the Children's Aid Society to help homeless children like Jo.

11

Philanthropy and Reform

Throughout most of the nineteenth century, philanthropy meant not financial support for educational, charitable, and cultural institutions but advocacy of humanitarian causes such as improvement in prison conditions; abstinence or temperance in use of alcohol; abolition of slavery, flogging, and capital punishment; and recognition of the rights of labor, women, and nonwhite people. Because these reforms were often unpopular, philanthropists who championed them received as much criticism as praise, if not more.

Evangelical Protestants who supported the abolition of slavery and the slave trade, temperance, and missionary activities to Christianize Africa and Asia and to put the love of Jesus and the fear of God into the hearts of the lower classes at home, were the butt of derision such as Dickens's attack on "telescopic philanthropy and rapacious benevolence." The evangelical missionary and benevolent societies met at Exeter Hall in London where, their detractors alleged, they whipped up enthusiasm for their cause by hearing lurid tales of barbarity and depravity and heaped praise on themselves and vituperation on their godless enemies. "The Philanthropists," an unsigned poem published in *Blackwood's Edinburgh Magazine* in 1841, satirized these assemblies, calling the meeting place "Puffington Hall" and revealing the prejudices of the philanthropists' critics:

> Come all ye philanthropists, tender of souls,
> Who feel for the pangs of the North and South poles,
> Who groan for the perils, by land and by water,
> Of the wearers of black skins beneath the Equator,
> Though the sons of your country may pine at your feet,

Though the daughters may make their last bed in the street;
   But, Humbug for ever! and humbug for all!
   So, come to our field-day in Puffington Hall.

     . . . . .

If you'd furnish your fancies with stories of niggers,
Of floggings and fetters, musquitoes, and jiggers;
Of Mumbo and Jumbo, by preaching struck dumb;
Of the wonders of tracts, and the woes of new rum;
Of Cannibal monarchs with five hundred wives,
Which they bake in hot pies every day of their lives —
   All told in a style that would soften Fox Maule,
   You have only to pop into Puffington Hall.[1]

When Thomas Carlyle (1795–1881) called John Howard, the eighteenth century prison reformer, "a beautiful Philanthropist," he did not mean to praise him. Although professing to have "nothing but respect, comparatively speaking, for the dull solid Howard, and his 'benevolence,'" Carlyle regarded Howard "as the unlucky fountain of that tumultuous frothy ocean-tide of benevolent sentimentality . . . which is threatening to drown human society as in deluges, and leave . . . a continent of fetid ooze inhabitable only by mud-gods and creatures that walk upon their belly."[2] Attempting "to cure a world's woes" by "rosewater and charity" was not Carlyle's way. He belongs in the company of social critics who disparage philanthropic efforts to improve society ("the mild method," in his words) and assert the necessity for "fundamental reforms" of a sterner and more drastic nature. In his opinion the iniquities caused by "the deranged condition of our affairs" required replacement of popular government by a dictatorship of a ruler like Cromwell or Frederick the Great whose ideas of right and wrong coincided with Carlyle's own.

Dickens, very much a believer in "the mild method," disliked extremism in reform and the tendency of some reformers to concentrate on a single solution to all problems. "It has been discovered," he wrote in an article in *Household Words* in 1851, "that mankind at large can only be regenerated by a tee-total society, or by a Peace Society, or by always dining on vegetables." As Dickens saw it, one trouble with the Regenerators was that they would throw overboard every effort for the betterment of man except their own nostrum; another was that they vilified workers for the general good who did not adhere to their particular orthodoxy. He denied that those who declined to join the

Tee-Total, Peace, or Vegetarian societies were drunkards, militarists, or scorners of spinach and carrots. Dickens's observation, "A man, to be truly temperate, must be temperate in many respects — in the rejection of strong words no less than strong drinks," expressed his preference for moderation over radicalism, at least in the issues under discussion. In a subsequent article he dealt unkindly with "Bloomerism" (women's dress reform) and showed coolness to women's involvement in public affairs.[3]

Dickens recorded with equal relish the stand-pat resistance to reform of Mr. Podsnap in *Our Mutual Friend* and the "gunpowderous" philanthropy of Mr. Honeythunder in *The Mystery of Edwin Drood* (1870). "Mr. Podsnap was well to do, and stood very high in Mr. Podsnap's opinion." He had begun with a good inheritance, married a good inheritance, and prospered in the marine insurance business. He was satisfied with himself and with things as they were. When anyone suggested to him that not all was right with the world he would say, "I don't admit it; I don't want to hear about it; I don't choose to discuss it." Pressed further about hunger or homelessness he would deny that it existed but said that if it did, it was the sufferers' fault, it was in accord with the working of providence, and he was opposed to Centralization. With a flourish of his right hand he would sweep the matter behind him, thus "clearing the world of its most difficult problems."[4]

Mr. Honeythunder's philanthropy was of such a militant sort "that the difference between it and animosity was hard to determine:

> You were to abolish military force, but you were first to bring all commanding officers who had done their duty, to trial by court-martial for that offence, and shoot them. You were to abolish war, but were to make converts by making war upon them, and charging them with loving war as the apple of their eye. You were to have no capital punishment, but were first to sweep off the face of the earth all legislators, jurists, and judges, who were of contrary opinion. You were to have universal accord, and were to get it by eliminating all the people who wouldn't, or conscientiously couldn't, be concordant. You were to love your brother as yourself, but after an indefinite interval of maligning him (very much as if you hated him), and calling him all manner of names.

Honeythunder was an officer of a charitable society having some features similar to the London Charity Organization Society founded in 1867. The first rule of his society was that you were to commit no charity "in private or on your own account." You paid your subscription, got your membership card, and left all decisions on giving up to Mr. Honeythunder and his colleagues.

At a dinner party attended by Mr. Honeythunder "nobody could talk to anybody, because he held forth to everybody at once, as if the company had no individual existence, but were a Meeting." His hosts contrive to serve him his coffee early and thrust him into his greatcoat and out into the night "as if he were a fugitive traitor with whom they sympathized, and a troop of horse were at the back door." Escorts took him to the omnibus and, concerned that he might catch cold, "shut him up in it instantly and left him, with still half-an-hour to spare."[5]

John Bold, the idealistic young surgeon whose zeal for justice stirs up all the trouble in Trollope's *The Warden*, is a different breed of reformer from the evangelical philanthropists or Dickens's Regenerators and Mr. Honeythunder—more (according to Trollope) like a French Jacobin. "His passion is the reform of all abuses: state abuses, church abuses, corporation abuses, . . . abuses in medical practice, and general abuses in the world at large." In respect to Hiram's Hospital, Bold believes that the bedesmen are legally entitled to one hundred pounds a year rather than a shilling and sixpence a day and that the warden's salary should be no more than three hundred pounds a year instead of the eight hundred he receives.

On the whole, Trollope treats Bold kindly. He represents him as intelligent, sincere, and energetic in his efforts to correct evil and stop injustice. Trollope's main objection is that Bold's impetuosity and conviction of rectitude lead him to intervene in matters about which he is not fully informed, and without carefully considering the possible consequences of his intervention. "It would be well if one so young had a little more diffidence himself, and more trust in the honest purposes of others—if he could be brought to believe that old customs need not necessarily be evil, and that changes may possibly be dangerous."[6]

For all his good intentions and purity of motive, Bold succeeds only in making matters worse. His moral indignation makes him do rash things and unleash journalistic furies that cause undeserved unhappiness to a good man, Mr. Harding, and result in loss rather than gain for the bedesmen. At least that is the way Trollope tells the story. In the hands of an author more sympathetic to youth and receptive to change it might have a different ending.

In the 1830s and 1840s New England writers had a good deal to say about reform, as well they might, since, as Emerson exclaimed, "What a fertility of projects for the salvation of the world!" the time and place yielded. On October 7, 1835, Hawthorne jotted an idea for a story in his notebook: "a modern reformer, — a type of the extreme doctrines on slaves, cold water, and other such topics." The reformer goes about the streets haranguing eloquently and persuasively and is about to make many converts when he is apprehended by the keeper of a madhouse from which he has escaped. "Much may be made of this idea," Hawthorne told himself.[7]

Emerson, like most people, had mixed feelings about reform. He was impressed by the "great activity of thought and experimenting" that had gone on in New England within his memory, and, in principle, he approved of "this din of opinion and debate," "keener scrutiny of institutions and domestic life," and "sincere protesting against existing evils." He also appreciated "restless, prying, conscientious criticism," as long as it was original with the thinker and not borrowed from someone else.[8] But Emerson's sympathies were limited to the select group of people for whom he felt "spiritual affinity," and he denied any obligation to give as much as a penny to improve the lot of the poor he did not know, or, who, as he put it, "do not belong to me." He told a "foolish philanthropist" that he had no use for "your miscellaneous popular charities; the education at college of fools; the building of meeting-houses to the vain end to which many now stand; alms to sots; and the thousandfold Relief Societies."[9]

Slavery, *the* issue in reform in the mid-nineteenth-century United States, was a subject on which someone like James Russell Lowell, normally conservative in his opinions, could take a radical stance. Possibly under the influence of his wife, Maria White, an abolitionist, Lowell became for a while a champion of William Lloyd Garrison (1805–79), editor of *The Liberator* and leader of the most uncompromising wing of the antislavery movement. In a letter in verse addressed to the editor of the *Pennsylvania Freeman* Lowell reported on the 1846 fund raiser for the Massachusetts Anti-Slavery Society:

> The great attraction now of all
> Is the "Bazaar" at Faneuil Hall
> Where swarm the anti-slavery folks
> As thick, dear Miller, as your jokes.
> There's Garrison, his features very

> Benign for an incendiary,
> Beaming forth sunshine through his glasses
> On the surrounding lads and lasses,
> (No bee could blither be, or brisker), —
> A Pickwick somehow turned John Ziska,*
> His bump of firmness swelling up
> Like a rye cupcake from its cup.

Maria Weston Chapman, treasurer of the Anti-Slavery Society, was the person most responsible for making the fairs successful:

> There was Maria Chapman, too,
> With her swift eyes of clear steel-blue,
> The coiled-up mainspring of the Fair,
> Originating everywhere
> The expansive force without a sound
> That whirls a hundred wheels around,
> Herself meanwhile as calm and still
> As the bare crown of Prospect Hill;
> A noble woman, brave and apt,
> Cumaean sibyl not more rapt,
> Who might, with those fair tresses shorn,
> The Maid of Orleans' casque have worn,
> Herself the Joan of our Ark,
> For every shaft a shining mark.[10]

Lowell's poem "On the Death of Charles Turner Torrey" (1846) saluted an antislavery martyr:

> He strove among God's suffering poor
> One gleam of brotherhood to send;
> The dungeon oped its hungry door
> To give the truth one martyr more,
> Then shut, — and here behold the end![11]

Torrey (1813–46), a native of Massachusetts and a graduate of Yale, was a conservative (that is, anti-Garrisonian) abolitionist. In 1844, while living in Baltimore, he was found guilty of helping slaves es-

---

* John Ziska (d. 1424), who led the Hussite forces in the religious wars of the fifteenth century, lost his only remaining eye in battle. Totally blind for the last four years of his life, he continued to fight the Catholics.

cape from Maryland and Virginia and was sentenced to prison at hard labor for six years. He died after serving a little more than a year of his sentence.

At the head of a tribute "To W.L. Garrison" (1848) Lowell quoted a letter of Harrison Gray Otis, a Federalist-Whig opponent of abolitionism, stating that Garrison's "office was an obscure hole, his only visible auxillary a negro boy, and his supporters a very few insignificant persons of all colors." The poem depicts Garrison in 1831 when he began printing *The Liberator*:

> In a small chamber, friendless and unseen,
> Toiled o'er his types one poor, unlearned young man;
> The place was dark, unfurnitured, and mean;
> Yet there the freedom of a race began.
> Help came but slowly; surely no man yet
> Put level to the heavy world with less:
> What need of help? He knew how types were set,
> He had a dauntless spirit, and a press.
> . . .
> O small beginnings, ye are great and strong,
> Based on a faithful heart and weariless brain!
> Ye build the future fair, ye conquer wrong,
> Ye earn the crown, and wear it not in vain.[12]

In a personal letter Lowell assessed Garrison as he saw him in 1848: "Garrison is so used to standing alone that like Daniel Boone, he moves away as the world creeps up to him, and goes further into the wilderness. He considers every step a step forward, though it be over the edge of a precipice." Garrison's faults were those of his position, and despite them Lowell believed him an extraordinary man who had done a great work. "Garrison was so long in a position where he alone was right and all the world wrong, that such a position has created in him a habit of mind which may remain, though circumstances have wholly changed." That cast of mind, Lowell believed, "is essential to a Reformer. Luther was as infallible as any man that ever had St. Peter's keys."[13]

"I confess I have hitherto indulged very little in philanthropic enterprises," wrote Henry David Thoreau (1817–62) in *Walden* (1854). Doing good to others was one of the pleasures he had sacrificed to the stern duty of minding his own business. On those rare occasions when he had been persuaded to offer help to one or another poor family of the town "they have one and all unhesitatingly preferred to remain poor." Although not much impressed by philanthropy, which he called "the only virtue which is sufficiently appreciated by mankind," Thoreau had a live-and-let-live attitude toward it. "You must have a genius for charity as well as for anything else. As for Doing good, that is one of the professions which are full." Philanthropy was not for him. "But I would not stand between any man and his genius; and to him who does this work, which I decline, I would say Persevere, even if the world call it doing evil, as it is mostly like they will."[14]

The most famous portrait of a philanthropist in the nineteenth-century sense of a lover of mankind, especially its least lovely and most unlikeable representatives, is Hollingsworth in *The Blithedale Romance* (1852). Hawthorne based the novel in part on his reminiscences of Brook Farm, the utopian community he had joined for a few months in 1841. His portrayal of Hollingsworth is believed to incorporate features of many contemporary reformers including Bronson Alcott, Albert Brisbane, Orestes Brownson, Elihu Burritt, Richard Henry Dana, Horace Mann, and Theodore Parker. Nearly a decade before publication of *The Blithedale Romance*, Hawthorne had outlined his objection to reformers in "The Procession of Life" (1843) and sketched a figure very similar to Hollingsworth:

> When a good man has long devoted himself to a particular kind of beneficence — to one species of reform — he is apt to become narrowed into the limits of the path wherein he treads, and to fancy that there is no other good to be done on earth but that self same good to which he has put his hand, and in the very mode that best suits his own conceptions. All else is worthless; his scheme must be wrought out by the united strength of the whole world's stock of love, or the world is no longer worthy of a position in the universe.[15]

Before Hollingsworth makes his appearance in the novel, Zenobia, a spirited and intelligent woman, tells the narrator, Miles Coverdale, that she would like Hollingsworth better if the philanthropic streak had been left out of his character. "To tell you a secret," she says, "I never could tolerate a philanthropist, before. Could you?" Coverdale replies, "By no means, neither can I now."[16] On meeting Hollingsworth, Coverdale is impressed by his gentleness and warmth. As he becomes better acquainted with Hollingsworth he recognizes that the latter's all-consuming desire to achieve his philanthropic goal has debased his benevolence into egotism. What a difference there is, Coverdale reflects, between a philanthropic man, God's truest image, and "that steel engine of the Devil's contrivance, a philanthropist!"[17]

The monster that is consuming Hollingsworth is "a plan for the reformation of criminals, through an appeal to their higher instincts." The reader is spared details of the plan because Coverdale finds Hollingsworth's discussion of them too boring to record. The scheme involves moral, intellectual, and industrial methods; to put it in operation will require a lot of money (Hollingsworth plans to use Zenobia's) and a large tract of land (Hollingsworth intends to use Blithedale Farm as its site).[18]

Not far into the story Coverdale becomes convinced that Hollingsworth is fast growing mad. Hawthorne does not, as in his much earlier journal entry, have the reformer returned to a madhouse, but he makes much of the aberration Hollingsworth suffers as a result of his obsession with his "rigid and unconquerable scheme." People who have Hollingsworth's illness "have no heart, no sympathy, no reason, no conscience. They will keep no friend, unless he make himself the mirror of their purpose; they will smite and slay you, and trample your dead corpse under foot, all the more readily, if you take the first step with them, and cannot take the second, and the third, and every other step of their terribly straight path."[19]

In a crucial passage Coverdale tells Hollingsworth, "The besetting sin of a philanthropist is apt to be moral obliquity. His sense of honor ceases to be the sense of honor of other honorable men. At some point of his course — I know not exactly when nor where — he is tempted to palter with the right, and can scarcely forbear persuading himself that the importance of his public ends renders it allowable to throw aside his private conscience." Hollingsworth, instead of denying the charge that he is willing to sacrifice honor and loyalty to friends in order to foster his grandiose plans for the reformation of criminals, asks Coverdale to join him in the great scheme. If they succeed, as he is confident they will, "we shall have done our best for this miserable world; and happiness (which never comes but incidentally) will come to us unawares!"[20]

Seekers after wealth and power, and even ordinary persons determined to have their own way, may use dubious methods to gain their objective. In Hollingsworth, however, Hawthorne makes the philanthropist peculiarly insensitive to others and indifferent to conventional morality. What may have been brilliant insight into the character of a particular philanthropist becomes, in Emerson's words, "dull and suspicious" when adopted at second- or third-hand to explain the attitude and behavior of other philanthropic reformers. " 'Oh, that's the way with these philanthropists,' " exclaims the heroine of William Dean Howells' *Annie Kilbourne* (1888), "thinking of Hollingsworth in *The Blithedale Romance*, the only philanthropist she had ever really known. 'They are always ready to sacrifice the happiness and comfort of anyone to the general good.' "[21]

If, as Coverdale muses at the end of the novel, Hollingsworth's ruination was an overplus of purpose, Coverdale's problem is want of one, which "has rendered my own life all an emptiness."[22] Hawthorne's Bowdoin classmate, Henry Wadsworth Longfellow (1807–82), jotted down thoughts in his notebooks or on scraps of paper, sometimes incorporating them in his books. In *Driftwood* (1857) he included a comment on criticism of philanthropy: "We often excuse our own want of philanthropy by giving the name of fanaticism to the more ardent zeal of others."[23]

Henry James (1843–1916) used the phrases "barbarian fanatic" and "omnivorous egotism" to describe Hollingsworth. "There is much reality in the conception of the type to which he belongs," James wrote in *Hawthorne* (1879), " — the strong-willed, narrow-hearted apostle of a special form of redemption of society."[24] *The Bostonians* and *Princess Casamassima*, both published in 1886, midway in James's career, deal respectively with reform, notably feminism, and revolutionary terrorism. Miss Birdseye, an old-fashioned New England philanthropist, although not one of the leading characters in *The Bostonian*, was, in James's opinion, the best figure in the book. He takes elaborate pains in describing her appearance: a little old lady with a large head, a wide, protuberant brow, and "weak, kind, and tired-looking eyes." Unlike Hollingsworth, she has devoted her energies and sympathy not to one overriding purpose but to a superabundance of causes. "The long practice of philanthropy had not given accent to her features; it had rubbed out their transitions, their meanings. The waves of sympathy, of enthusiasm, had wrought upon them in the same way in which the waves of time modify the surface of old marble busts, gradually washing away their sharpness, their details." She always wore a black jacket whose pockets were stuffed with letters and papers. In contrast to Mrs. Pardiggle's vast aggressive skirt, Mrs. Birdseye wore a simple, businesslike dress. She belonged to the Short-Skirts League, just as she belonged "to any and every league that had been founded for almost any purpose whatever." In summary, "she was a confused, entangled, inconsequent, discursive old woman, whose charity began at home and ended nowhere, whose credulity kept pace with it, and who knew less about her fellow-creatures, if possible, after fifty years of humanitarian zeal, than on the day she had gone into the field to testify against the iniquity of most arrangements."[25]

Some readers of *The Bostonians* identified Miss Birdseye with Elizabeth Palmer Peabody (1804–94), Hawthorne's sister-in-law, an author, reformer, and educator best remembered today as founder of one of the first kindergartens in the United States. In a letter to his brother William James, Henry denied any intention to caricature Miss Peabody, asserted that Miss Birdseye evolved entirely from his own moral consciousness, and maintained that throughout the book Miss Birdseye was treated with respect and was "represented as the embodiment of pure, the purest philanthropy."[26] James's indulgent attitude toward Miss Birdseye contrasts with his lack of sympathy for Olive Chancellor, one of the major characters of *The Bostonians*. He cannot spare Miss Chancellor the charity of a pleasant smile. Miss Birdseye's dim smile "seemed to say she would smile more if she had more time, but you could see, without this, that she was gentle and easy to beguile." Olive Chancellor's smile was like a "thin ray of moonlight resting upon the wall of a prison."[27]

Miss Chancellor is a philanthropist in the modern sense of someone who contributes financially to a cause she or he wants to succeed. She declines an invitation to speak on behalf of women's rights but welcomes the opportunity to use her money to help end the unhappiness of women. At the moment she decides to give, Miss Birdseye approaches. Overcome with love for "the poor little humanitarian hack," who already seems a martyr, Olive, in one of the few kindly deeds allotted her, tenderly closes one of Miss Birdseye's "battered brooches," which has become unfastened.[28]

Like some other upper- and middle-class young people in the 1880s Lady Aurora Langrish in *The Princess Casamassima* seeks to enrich her life by befriending and helping the poor. "She is like one of the saints of old come to life again," declares Rosie Muniment, a bedridden cripple Lady Aurora cheers with her visits. Lady Aurora has some of the social characteristics of sainthood, having a passion for charity, being by her own admission "a little bit mad," and being driven to the company of the sick and wretched by boredom at home and alienation from her class. As a result of her visits in hospitals and tenements she has a wide acquaintance among the poor and thinks better of them than Hyacinth Robinson, a young bookbinder who is the principal character in the book. He is "for" his class, the working poor, but thinks most of them have "third-rate minds," made stupid by centuries of poverty and bad living conditions. She is impressed by the talent and wit of even the "terribly, hopelessly poor." Robinson replies that he has not yet got as far down as the lowest depth of poverty and doesn't know many paupers. After further conversation he wonders whether Aurora's charity is founded less on love of the poor than hostility to "the squire and the parson and the conservative influence of that upper-class British family [he] had supposed to be the highest fruit of civilization."[29]

Rosie's brother, Paul Muniment, likes Lady Aurora well enough (she loves him), but it is unlikely that in the revolution he looks forward to any member of her class will be spared. He is the leader of an underground group ready to use assassination to hasten the coming of the uprising that will rid the world of its iniquities and establish a just social and political order. Muniment has no more confidence than Carlyle in the ability of charity and rosewater or the mild method of reform to bring about the changes he wants, and he has no qualms about employing drastic methods to obtain them.

Little more than thirty years separate Muniment in *The Princess Casamassima* from Hollingsworth in *The Blithedale Romance*, but how modest Hollingsworth's "grandiose" scheme for reforming criminals by appealing to their better instinct seems when compared to Muniment's plan to create a just society by murder and violence. And how much more leniently Muniment is dealt with than Hollingsworth. One reason is that we see Muniment from the perspective of Robinson, who is more committed to social revolution than Coverdale was to the reform of criminals. The other is that revolutionaries are not held to the same moral standards as philanthropists. Honor and loyalty to friends are not expected of them because revolution demands and justifies deviousness and cruelty.

Coverdale tells us that when Hollingsworth shifted from genial benevolence to hard purpose his smile changed to a frown. Robinson says Muniment masks his care for the misery of the world with the appearance of a virtuous and cheerful workman. He is always good-natured and smiling even when, asked if he supports capital punishment, he replies that he does and would extend it to habitual liars and drunkards.

Robinson's time to flinch and blanch will come; for the moment, fascinated rather than frightened, he knows that Muniment is turning over extraordinary ideas in his mind and will think them through to their logical conclusion; "and that night he should produce them, with the door of the club-room guarded and the company bound by a tremendous oath, the others would look at each other and turn pale."[30]

Notes

1. "The Philanthropists," *Blackwood's Edinburgh Magazine* (1841), 197–98. Fox Maule (1801–74), a Liberal member of Parliament, 1835–52, was one of the few Scottish noblemen to support the Free Church of Scotland. Norris Pope describes Dickens's relationship with the evangelicals in *Dickens and Charity*, (New York: Columbia University Press, 1978), 1–12. Richard D. Altick, in *Victorian People and Ideas* (New York: W.W. Norton and Company, 1973), 140–41, offers a sympathetic account of the "evangelical temper" and the reforms it advanced.
2. Thomas Carlyle, "Model Prisons" (1850), in *Carlyle's Latter-Day Pamphlets*, edited by M.K. Goldberg and S.P. Siegel (Port Credit, Ontario, 1983), 63–65, 83–84.
3. Dickens, "Whole Hogs," *Household Words*, No. 74 (August 23, 1851), 505–7; and "Sucking Pigs," ibid., No. 85 (November 8, 1851).
4. Dickens, *Our Mutual Friend*, 138–41 (book 1, chapter 11).
5. Dickens, *The Mystery of Edwin Drood* (London: Andre Deutsch, 1980), 44–46 (chapter 6).
6. Trollope, *The Warden*, (London: Oxford University Press, 1952), 14–16 (chapter 2); 43–45 (chapter 4).
7. "New England Reformers" (1844), in *Essays: Second Series*, in *The Collected Works of Ralph Waldo Emerson*, 3:149; Nathaniel Hawthorne, *The American Notebooks*, edited by Claude M. Simpson (Columbus, Ohio: Ohio State University Press, 1972), 10.
8. "New England Reformers," 149–52.
9. "Self-Reliance" (1841), in *Essays: First Series*, in *The Collected Works of Ralph Waldo Emerson*, 2:30–31.
10. Lowell, "A Letter from Boston" (December 1846), in *The Poetical Works of James Russell Lowell* Revised and with a new introduction by Marjorie R. Kaufman, Boston: Houghton Mifflin Company, 1978), 111.
11. Lowell, "On the Death of Charles Turner Torrey, ibid., 104.

12. Lowell, "To W. L. Garrison," ibid., 103.

13. Lowell to C.F. Briggs, March 26, 1848, ibid., 103.

14. Thoreau, *Walden*, edited by J. Lyndon Shanley (Princeton, N.J.: Princeton University Press, 1989), 72–79.

15. Roy Harvey Pearce, "Introduction to the Blithedale Romance," in Nathaniel Hawthorne, *The Blithedale Romance* (Centenary Edition, Columbus, Ohio: Ohio State University Press, 1964), XXIV. Hawthorne, "The Procession of Life," in *Mosses from an Old Manse* (Columbus, Ohio: Ohio State University Press, 1972), 217–18.

16. Hawthorne, *The Blithedale Romance*, 21–22 (chapter 3).

17. Ibid., 70–71 (chapter 9).

18. Ibid., 54–57 (chapter 7; 131–32 (chapter 15).

19. Ibid., 70 (chapter 9).

20. Ibid., 131–33 (Chapter 15).

21. William Dean Howells, *Annie Kilbourne* (New York: Harper and Brothers, 1888), 67 (chapter 7); Emerson's words are in "New England Reformers," 151.

22. *Blithedale Romance*, 246, (chapter 29).

23. Henry Wadsworth Longfellow, "Table-talk," *Outre-Mer and Driftwood* (New York: AMS Press, 1966), 405.

24. Henry James, Jr., *Hawthorne* (New York: Harper and Brothers Publishers, 1879), 131–32.

25. Henry James, *The Bostonians* (New York: Random House, 1956), 26–27 (book 1, chapter 4).

26. Leon Edel, ed., *Henry James Letters*, 3 (Cambridge: Harvard University Press, 1980), 68–70.

27. *The Bostonians*, 4 (book 1, chapter 1); 26–27 (book 1, chapter 4).

28. Ibid., 36–38 (book 1, chapter 4).

29. Henry James, *The Princess Casamassima*, in Henry James, *Novels, 1886–1890* (New York: Viking Press, 1989), 96–98 (Book First, chapter 9); 172–77 (Book First, chapter 15).

30. Ibid., 159–60 (book First, chapter 14).

12

Love and Kindness

Toward the end of Samuel Taylor Coleridge's life, when he was more active as a critic than poet, he saluted "Charity in Thought":

> To praise men as good, and to take them for such,
>   Is a grace, which no soul can mete out to a tittle; —
> Of which he who has not a little too much,
>   Will by Charity's gage surely have much too little.[1]

Thinking and speaking well of people costs less than any other form of charity but requires a commitment on the part of the donor. Fear of being naive or, among scholars, of being "uncritical," inhibits charity in thought just as fear of being duped inhibits charity in deed. Trust in others is at the heart of giving; people can make mistakes by being too suspicious as well as by being too credulous. "Dupery for dupery," William James asked in *The Will to Believe* (1897), "what proof is there that dupery through hope is so much worse than dupery through fear?"[2] James was talking about religion, but his words apply as well to charity.

Authors sometimes ask readers to be charitable in their judgment of a character. *The History of Pendennis* (1848–50), Thackeray's second major novel, is subtitled *His Fortunes and Misfortunes, His Friends and His Greatest Enemy*. Arthur Pendennis, the leading character, has much in common with Thackeray. The last paragraph of the book calls on readers to "give a hand of charity to Arthur Pendennis, with all his faults and shortcomings, who does not claim to be a hero, but only a man and a brother."[3] Anthony Trollope does not care for and does not ask charity for John Vavasor in *Can you Forgive Her?*, but he feels

135

obligated to give this weak character his due: "He was a man from whom no very noble deed could be expected; but he was also one who would do no ignoble deed." Dickens used scrupulosity toward a character for comic effect when, in *The Mystery of Edwin Drood*, he described Mr. Durdles, the stonemason, as being "as seldom drunk as sober."[4]

W.S. Gilbert (1836–1911), author of the librettos of the Gilbert and Sullivan operas, offers a picture of an uncharitable man, a self-styled philanthropist, who opens people's eyes "to all their little weaknesses":

> If you give me your attention, I will tell you what I am:
> I'm a genuine philanthropist — all other kinds are sham.
> Each little fault of temper and each social defect
> In my erring fellow creatures, I endeavor to correct.
> A charitable action I can skillfully dissect;
> And interested motives I'm delighted to detect.[5]

A story by Sarah Orne Jewett (1849–1909), "The Spur of the Moment," demonstrates an author's ability to depict an unpleasant character forthrightly while giving her the benefit of the doubt — and a happy ending. Everybody had called her "old Miss Peet" for twenty years, although she was still not seventy.

> She had an unhappy way of telling you more things to other people's disadvantage than to their credit, and when she has told you, and you saw fit to join in with blame, she looked satisfied at first and then grew severe and prim and reminded you that one must endeavor to be charitable. But somehow she never liked to hear others praised; she would say, "Oh, but she has so much money!" or, "Oh, it's very easy to make use of such opportunities as hers," or, "I have heard it said that he is very close about little things and does something large now and then because he likes to have it known!" . . . In short, Miss Peet was one of those sad, unhappy souls who cannot help looking upon the prosperity of others except as some injustice to themselves.

To Jewett, at least, there was something appealing in Miss Peet's appearance. "You felt anew that she was one of those unhappy persons from whom every year has taken something away; whether it was her own fault or other people's, the fact remained that nearly everything pleasant had gone."

The impulsive kindness of a friend enables Miss Peet to go to a funeral. The daughter of the deceased, catching a glimpse of the old woman in a rare moment of remorse, resolves to continue the assistance her father had given Miss Peet because of his friendship with her father. The last lines of the story are: "There is always the hope that 'our unconscious benefactions may outweigh our unconscious cruelties,' but the world moves on, and we seldom really know how much we have to do with other people's lives."[6]

One day in 1842, after responding to a woman who came to his door with a certificate endorsing her need for help, Nathaniel Hawthorne reflected on kindness as a principle of life. "There is so much want and wretchedness in the world," he wrote in his *Notebook*, "that we may safely take the word of any mortal, when they say they need our assistance, and even should we be deceived, still the good to ourselves, resulting from a kind act, is worth more than the trifle by which we purchase it." His visitor, he recalled, had seemed a "homely, decent old matron enough," but "with somewhat of a wild and wandering expression." As she made her way through the sunshine and shade down the long avenue to the Old Manse Hawthorne noted her "singular gait, reeling as it were — and yet not quite reeling — from one side of the path to the other; going onward as if it were not much matter whether she went straight or crooked." Hawthorne, admitting a fondness for vagrants of all sorts, declared, "Such persons should be permitted to roam through our land of plenty, scattering the seeds of tenderness and charity — as birds of passage bear the seeds of precious plants from land to land, without ever dreaming of the office which they perform."[7]

Hawthorne's "The Procession of Life" in *Mosses From an Old Manse* envisages a vast parade of people marching under the banners of their convictions. The Evil are chained together with their crimes. No one answers the call to march under the banner of the Good, since all who might qualify are conscious of their errors and imperfections. The principle of Love, however, has a large and various multitude in its ranks. Here are the men and women "whose impulses have guided them to benevolent actions;" there are the "apostles of humanity" — social reformers — "who have studied all the varieties of misery that human nature can endure" and have tried to lessen the horrors of prison, insane asylum, almshouse, factory, and cotton field. Here, too, are "the benefactors of humanity" who have occupied "their lives in generous and holy contemplation for the human race . . . [and] by a certain heavenliness of spirit have purified the air around them, and thus supplied a medium in which good and high things may be projected and performed."[8]

Hawthorne objects to only one marcher: a rich man who has bequeathed his property to a hospital might better, Hawthorne suggests, be represented by his ghost than by his living body. He notes and calls attention to the "shyness" that exists between those who march under the principle of love: They love humanity but not each other. "Each surrounds its own righteousness with a hedge of thorns. It is difficult for the good Christian to acknowledge the good Pagan; almost impossible for the good Orthodox to grasp the hand of the good Unitarian, leaving to their Creator to settle the matters in dispute."[9]

James Russell Lowell's "The Vision of Sir Launfal" (1848) holds out the hope that those who follow the principle of love may become better as they grow humbler. In the poem the youthful Sir Launfal, at the start of his quest for the Holy Grail, encounters a leper begging at the gate of his castle. Repelled by the sight of the beggar, Launfal scornfully tosses him a coin. Years later, disappointed in his quest, he returns to his castle and once again meets the beggar who asks alms "for Christ's sweet sake." This time Launfal gives him half of his remaining crust of moldly bread and breaks ice on a stream to bring him a bowl of water. In a radiant vision the beggar becomes Christ, saying to the knight

> The Holy Supper is kept, indeed
> In whatso we share with another's need;
> Not what we give, but what we share,
> For the gift without the giver is bare;
> Who give himself with his alms feeds three
> Himself, his hungering neighbor, and me.[10]

Sometimes sharing a figurative crust of bread with a "hungering neighbor" is not enough to win either divine approval or a feeling of fulfillment on the part of the giver. Marius in Victor Hugo's *Les Miserables* (1862), poor himself, pays the rent of his neighbors to keep them from being evicted. He knows they are in difficult straits because he can hear their groans, footsteps, and even their breaths through the thin partition that separates his tenement room from theirs; they seem to be an unpleasant lot, and Marius, although sympathetic with their plight, does not want to get personally involved with them. When he subsequently learns the extent of the family's degradation he berates himself for not having made a greater effort to overcome his distaste or given the family more of his attention and concern. "Is it not when the fall is lowest that charity should be greatest?" he asks himself.[11]

Hugo uses Marius's dissatisfaction with his behavior as a device to advance the plot: Marius finds a hole in the wall to spy on his neighbors and their visitors, keeping readers informed of what he sees. His feeling of guilt for not having become more involved with the family deserves attention because it reflects a growing awareness among thoughtful people on both sides of the Atlantic that helping the poor requires close and persistent care rather than sporadic and impulsive generosity. "Not alms but a friend" was the slogan of charity reformers; their methods — which they called "scientific philanthropy" — included thorough investigation of need and its causes, personal association ("friendly visiting") to teach respectable behavior, and encouragement in obtaining work.[12] It is doubtful whether Marius's neighbors — professional beggars and blackmailers — would have responded any more positively to such efforts than the brickmaker did to Mrs. Pardiggle's friendly visit.

Advocates of scientific philanthropy were convinced that spreading the gospel of self-help to the poor was a more effective way of helping them, and of carrying out the religious obligation to "love thy neighbor as thyself," than casual benevolence. In close-knit communities, however, the older tradition of kindness in giving continued to be honored. Reb Nachum Grodner (1811–79) of Grodno, Lithuania, a scholar so modest that he aspired to no higher position than *shammes* (sexton) in a synagogue, won fame for the consideration he showed in helping the poor. "Reb Nochemka," as he was familiarly known, assumed responsibility for providing for widows, orphans, and the sick, obtaining money to do so by begging from the rich — when there were any to be found — and from card players and tipplers at inns and taverns. "Reb Nochemka," said an admirer, "took great pains not to hurt the sensibilities of the needy whom he aided, for he was poor himself and only too well understood the pride of the poor." Once, learning that a father of an infant son had no money for a post-circumcision celebration, he gave the man enough money to pay for the festivities, asking him to take it to someone in Kovno, whenever he happened to go there, and meanwhile, to use it as he saw fit.[13]

Charity is one way of expressing good will for others; service is another. After a cross-continental railway trip Robert Louis Stevenson, provoked by the railway companies' indifference to the comfort and convenience of passengers and the suffering imposed on passengers by the companies' inefficient operations, came to the conclusion that "kindness is the first of the virtues; and capacity in a man's own business the greatest kindness in his reach." On the same trip Stevenson was impressed by a newsboy on a train who was unfailingly friendly, cheerful, and attentive. "When I think of that lad coming and going, train after train, with his bright face and civil words," Stevenson wrote, "I can see how easily a good man can become the benefactor of his kind."[14]

Father Zossima in Dostoevsky's *The Brothers Karamazov* (1880) probably had both charity and service in mind when he recommended "active love" to a woman made miserable by uncertainty about life after death. By loving her neighbors "actively and tirelessly," he tells her, she will become less concerned with her own problems and surer of the reality of God and the immortality of her soul. The woman says she loves humanity so much that she sometimes dreams of giving up everything in order to tend the afflicted, providing that those she serves are grateful and demonstrative in their appreciation. Father Zossima replies that active love is very different from dream love: it requires labor and fortitude, respect, and absolute honesty with oneself as well as others.[15]

"Neighbors!" objects Ivan, the intellectual and atheistic brother in *The Brothers Karamazov*. "It is precisely one's neighbors that one cannot possibly love."[16] Less fastidious and literal-minded people come to the aid of (that is, show love for) others whether they know them or not. Simon, the poor shoemaker in Tolstoy's story "What Men Live By" (1881), has never set eyes on Michael, a fallen angel, until he discovers him naked and shivering in a roadside shrine. Simon puts a coat on the stranger, takes him home, and allows him to remain as his helper. Michael has been banished from heaven for disobedience: instead of bringing the soul of a sick woman to heaven he tried to prolong her life so that she could care for her newborn twins. His punishment is to remain on earth until he learns the answers to three questions: "what dwells in man; what is not given to man; and what men live by."

The shoemaker's wife's willingness to share the family's few resources with a stranger gives Michael the answer—love dwells in man—to the first question. When a man destined to die before nightfall orders a pair of boots guaranteed to last a year Michael divines the answer to the second question: it is not given to man to know the needs of the future. And when a woman enters the shop with two little girls—the daughters of the mother Michael had tried to keep alive—who she has adopted and looked after as her own, Michael finds the answer to the third question. "Men live not by care for themselves but by love" for others. The answers must have been correct for, before Simon's and his wife's eyes, "wings appeared upon the angel's shoulders and he rose into the heavens."[17]

Which is more likely to rehabilitate someone, sternness or kindness? Anton Chekhov's story "The Beggar" (1886) begins with a woebegone man, who says he was once a schoolmaster, asking a lawyer, Skvortsoff, for money to get to a new job. The latter recognizes the beggar as the same man who had accosted him with a different story a few days earlier. Skvortsoff, a kind and charitable man, is enraged by the deception, which profanes "the charity which he liked to extend to the poor out of the purity of his heart." Instead of turning his back on the beggar he decides to subject him to a work test. "Will you come and chop wood for me?" he asks. The beggar agrees to do so, and Skvortsoff takes him home and tells the cook to take him to the woodshed. The man's strength has been so undermined by drink that he can barely tap a block of wood with the axe. Nevertheless, an hour later the cook reports the wood has been cut. Thereafter Skvortsoff occasionally finds other work for the man, whose name is Lushkoff, and eventually provides him with a recommendation for copy work in the office of a friend.

Two years later the men meet by chance. Lushkoff is now a notary and earning enough to support himself. Skvortsoff, pleased with the news, takes credit for having put him on the road to sobriety and independence. Lushkoff thanks him for his assistance but says it was the cook's worry and tears for him that made him give up drinking and that it was the cook who chopped the wood.[18]

Notes

1. Samuel Taylor Coleridge (1772–1834), "Charity in Thought," in *The Poems of Samuel Taylor Coleridge*, edited by Ernest Hartley Coleridge (London: Oxford

University Press, 1957), 486. First published in 1834.

2. William James (1842–1910), *The Will to Believe and Other Essays in Popular Philosophy* (New York: Longmans, Green and Company, 1897), 27.

3. William Makepeace Thackeray, *The History of Pendennis* (New York: Wm. M. Allison, n.d.), 457 (chapter 75).

4. Anthony Trollope, *Can You Forgive Her?* (London: Oxford University Press, 1948), 1:37 (chapter 4); Dickens, *The Mystery of Edwin Drood* (London: Andre Deutsch, 1980), 30 (chapter 4).

5. W.S. Gilbert, "The Disagreeable Man," in Gilbert, *The Bab Ballads* (London: Macmillan and Company, 1964), 16–17.

6. Sarah Orne Jewett, "The Spur of the Moment," in *The Uncollected Stories of Sarah Orne Jewett*, edited by Richard Carey (Waterville, Maine: Colby College Press, 1971), 165–71.

7. Nathaniel Hawthorne, *The American Notebooks* (Columbus, Ohio: Ohio State University Press, 1972), 352–53 (August 30, 1842).

8. Nathaniel Hawthorne, "The Procession of Life," in *Mosses from an Old Manse*, (Columbus, Ohio: Ohio State University Press, 1972), 215–17.

9. Ibid., 217–18.

10. "The Vision of Sir Launfal," in *The Poetical Works of James Russell Lowell*, (Boston: Houghton Mifflin Company, 1978), 108–11.

11. Victor Hugo, *Les Miserables*, translated by Norman Denny (Harmandsworth, England: Penguin Books, 1987), 638–40 ("Marius," book 8, chapter 5). "Marius" is the third of five major segments of the novel; Book VIII is entitled "The Noxious Poor."

12. Advocates and tenets of "scientific philanthropy" are discussed in Robert H. Bremner, *American Philanthropy* (Chicago: University of Chicago Press, 1988), 85–99.

13. "The Father of the Poor," in Nathan Ausubel, ed., *A Treasury of Jewish Folklore* (New York: Crown Publishers, 1948), 127–30.

14. James D. Hart, ed., *RLS from Scotland to Silverado* (Cambridge: Harvard University Press, 1966), 104, 121. Stevenson (1850–94) made the transcontinental trip in 1879 after having crossed the Atlantic in steerage.

15. Fyodor Dostoevsky (1821–81), *The Brothers Karamazov*, translated and annotated by Richard Pevear and Larissa Volokhovsky (San Francisco: North Point Press, 1990), 55–58 (part 1, book 2, chapter 4).

16. Ibid., 236 (part 2, book 5, chapter 4).

17. Leo Tolstoy (1828–1910), "What Men Live By," in *What Men Live By, Russian Stories and Legends* (New York: Pantheon Books, 1944), 39–44.

18. Anton Chekhov (1860–1904), "The Beggar," in *Stories of Russian Life*, translated by Marian Fell (London: Duckworth, 1914), 139–47.

PART FIVE

1890s to the Present

Prologue: And May Not This Be?

Henry George (1839–97) was one of a number of non-Marxist social philosophers and reformers in the late nineteenth-century United States who disputed the view expressed by Andrew Carnegie and other disciples of Herbert Spencer that great inequality in wealth and living conditions was inevitable, natural, and necessary for the progress of civilization. George, humane and deeply religious, could not bring himself to believe that "the great Architect of the Universe, to whose infinite skill all nature testifies," had made such a botch of the world that even in the most advanced countries "large classes should want the necessaries of human life, and the vast majority should only get a poor and pinched living by the hardest of toil."[1]

George's *Social Problems* (1883), published a few years after *Progress and Poverty* (1879), the work that gained him fame and devoted followers on both sides of the Atlantic, contains a chapter entitled "That We All Might Be Rich." The following is from one of the opening paragraphs of the chapter:

I join issue with those who say that we cannot all be rich; with those who declare that in human society the poor must always exist. I do not, of course, mean that we all might have an array of servants; that we all might outshine each other in dress, in equipage, in the lavishness of our balls or dinners, in the magnificence of our houses. That woud be a contradiction in terms. What I mean is, that we all might have leisure, comfort and abundance, not merely of the necessaries, but even of what are now esteemed the elegancies and luxuries of life. I do not mean to say that absolute equality could be had, or would be desirable. I do not mean to say that we could all have, or would want the same quantity of all the different forms of wealth. But I do mean to say that we might all have enough wealth to satisfy reasonable desires; that we might all have so much of the material things we now struggle for, that no one would want to rob or swindle his neighbor; that no one would worry all day, or lie awake at nights, fearing he might be brought to poverty, or thinking how he might acquire wealth.[2]

In the twentieth century belief in man's ability to create a more or less poverty-free world has animated social and political reformers of many persuasions who, like Conner in John Updike's *The Poorhouse Fair* (1959), may never have heard of Henry George or Edward Bellamy. Conner is the conscientious but unpopular superintendent of the poorhouse. He believes in progress, puts his faith in reason, and is committed to "bring order and beauty out of human substance." Conner confides to some of the old men and women in his charge that he foresees a "heaven placed upon this earth" in which there will be no political or economic oppression, no waste, no poverty, and, presumably, no need for philanthropy. "The state will receive what is made and give what is needed." Conner asserts this heaven on this earth is a certainty, coming soon, although, unfortunately, probably not in the lifetime of his listeners. In that case, they reply, "to hell with it."[3]

How much better to let the listeners or readers have more say about the possibility and sensibility of the dream coming true. Henry George closed the passage quoted above with a one-sentence paragraph:

And may not this be?

Notes

1. Henry George, *Social Problems* (New York: Doubleday, Doran and Company, Inc., 1930), 72. First published in 1883.
2. Ibid., 70–72 (chapter 8). Cf. Edward Bellamy's vision of a poverty-free society established by collectivism in *Looking Backward, 2000–1887* (1888) and *Equality* (1897).
3. John Updike, *The Poorhouse Fair* (New York: Alfred A. Knopf, 1977), 16, 106-08. First published in 1959.

13

Paupers, Tramps, and Beggars

In the heart of Kasrilevke, a Jewish *shtetl* (townlet) in Russia much like the one in which Sholom Aleichem (1859–1915) lived as a boy, there is a large and ornate building with a marble slab over the door bearing golden letters spelling out the Hebrew words for Home for the Aged. Kasrilevke's late rabbi, Reb Yozifl, called attention to the need for the Home and took the lead in raising funds to build it. Since Kasrilevke has no hospital one might ask, Why not a hospital instead of a home for the aged? Aleichem's answer is that if Reb Yozifl had proposed a hospital fault finders would have objected, "Why not a home for the aged?" Reb Yozifl simply believed a sick old man was more to be pitied than a sick young one. As with his other charitable undertakings he had to direct his appeals for money to outsiders because, as a member of his congregation observed, "Kasrilevke is a town of nothing but indigent, poverty-stricken, penniless, impoverished, destitute starvelings."[1]

The rabbi's prime target is a contractor from Moscow, Jewish and apparently very wealthy, who is supervising construction of a railway through Kasrilevke. The contractor, high-strung and easily irritated, is annoyed when Reb Yozifl and his fellow fund raisers enter his hotel room unannounced, and he responds to the rabbi's request for a contribution with a slap in the face. The blow knocks Reb Yozifl's hat and skullcap off his head but does not shake his resolve. Like "Reb Nochema" of Grodno in a similar incident, he tells the contractor he accepts the blow as intended for himself. "Now what are you going to give for the sick old folks?"[2]

Before Reb Yozifl leaves the hotel room the repentant contractor agrees to build the home. He keeps his promise and the yellow brick building stands, just where the mud is deepest in Kasrilevke. It is a monument to the piety and persistence of Reb Yozifl, who has long since left this world. Unfortunately it is just a monument; the home has no occupants. There are many aged poor in Kasrilevke, but the town has no money to run the institution. That's the way it is with the people of Kasrilevke, comments Aleichem: "When they dream of good things to eat — they haven't a spoon, when they have a spoon — they don't dream of good things to eat."[3]

Not want of endowment but strict admission policy is the problem at the old men's home in "The Applicant" (1891) by Ambrose Bierce (1842–1914?). The building is less imposing than The Home for the Aged in Kasrilevke, having been designed in what Bierce called "Early Comatose" style by an architect who did "what he honestly could to insure it against a second look." Nevertheless, it cost a lot of money to build and even more to endow. The donor, following the centuries-old practice of founding a "hospital" or almshouse for select pensioners, robbed his heirs of half a million dollars "flung away in riotous giving."[4]

At the time of the story the donor has been away from the scene of his charity for many years. The twenty occupants of the old men's home are no more grateful and no less given to grumbling and bickering than the bedesmen in Hiram's Hospital; the superintendent has nothing in common with the kindly Mr. Harding in Trollope's *The Warden*; and the trustees who manage the institution in the absence of the donor operate it as if it had been established as "a place of punishment for the sin of unthrift."[5] The donor's intention had been to establish a refuge for victims of misfortune. *His* misfortune is that when he returns, hard up and unrecognizable after his long absence, he is denied admission to the home and dies of exposure.

Both Reb Yozifl and the donor-applicant in Bierce's story assumed that being old, poor, and male was a sorrier state than old, poor, and female. Mary E. Wilkins Freeman's story "A Mistaken Charity" (1887) tells of two sisters, Charlotte and Harriet, both old, one blind and the other deaf and rheumatic, who live in a house so old and broken down that it seems "as much a natural ruin as an old tree stump." The rich man who holds the mortgage on the property allows the sisters to use it rent- and interest-free — a trifling charity on his part, observes Freeman: "he might as well have taken credit to himself for not charging a squirrel for his tenement in some old decaying tree in his woods."[6]

Age and ill health have forced Charlotte and Harriet to give up their work as seamstress and tailoress. They have a small garden, two trees that still bear fruit, a few currant bushes, and some vigorous pumpkin vines. From time to time people on nearby farms bring them gifts of potatoes, apples, eggs, butter, and meat. One day Mrs. Simonds, a neighbor, brings them some doughnuts. Freeman describes Mrs. Simonds as "a smart, energetic person, bent on doing good, and she did a good deal. To be sure, she always did it in her own way."[7] Mrs. Simonds is appalled by the sisters' deplorable housing and haphazard housekeeping. Without consulting them she arranges to have a well-to-do friend pay the fee to admit them to a home for old ladies.

Entering the home against their will, Charlotte and Harriet feel out of place in its refined and genteel atmosphere. They don't like the delicately seasoned food, feel guilty about wearing good dresses every day, and are uncomfortable in the company of the other prim and decorous residents. "Nothing could transform these two unpolished old women into nice old ladies." After a stay of two months they run away and manage to find their way back to their old house. With the currants ripe and the pumpkin vines spreading, the sisters resume their accustomed way of living.

Mrs. Simonds's drastic intervention in the life of the sisters, although well-intentioned, was more an exercise of power than an act of charity. Her arranging to have them admitted to the Old Ladies Home is an example of the kind of inappropriate and inconsiderate giving Seneca warned against.[8] Freeman's emphasis on the sisters' lowly status and rude manners suggests she saw the charity as mistaken, at least in part, because it took them above their proper station; when circumstances make their departure from their decaying home absolutely necessary the rough and ready accommodations of the public poorhouse should be their destination.

Most but not all poorhouses in fiction are forbidding places. The vacationing Peterkin family in Lucretia Hale's *The Peterkin Papers* (1880) spend several days at a prosperous-looking farmhouse in New England before discovering it is the poor farm. Not even the unworldly Peterkins would have made that mistake at an English workhouse of the period, where husbands and wives were separated: an old couple in "The Paupers" by Arthur Quiller-Couch bid each other a stoic farewell at the entrance gate. A happy contrast is the cheerful, comfortable poor farm of the town of Byfleet, Maine, depicted by Sarah Orne

Jewett in "The Flight of Betsey Lane" (1894). Three old women carry on a conversation while shelling beans before a sunny window; calves bawl in the barnyard; and the men working there shout at each other as though they were deaf. Except for a young woman with several children, who resents her lot, the inmates are not distressed or unhappy. "Almost everyone was possessed of a most interesting past, though there was less to be said about the future." Many went home during the summer, supporting themselves by whatever work they could find and do. "Old age had impoverished most of them by limiting their power of endurance; but far from lamenting the fact that they were town charges, they rather liked the change and excitement of a winter's residence on the poor farm."[9]

Betsey Lane is one of the bean shellers; her companions are Peggy Bond, whose "upsightedness" has won her the distinction of being the inmate with the most interesting affliction, and Mrs. Lavinia Dow, the dignified and august social arbiter of the poor farm. For many years Betsey worked for the most prominent family of Byfleet. Her employers left her well provided for, and she had some savings of her own, but generosity, misfortune, and illness reduced her to poverty. She still has friends in the town but has sensibly decided it is easier for the whole town to support her than for part of it. She comes from an adventurous, seafaring family, and her "flight," the subject of the story, is a trip, made possible by a gift from an old friend, to Philadelphia to attend the Centennial Exposition. Having satisfied her desire to see something of the world, Betsey returns to the poor farm.

Adeline, the "Beggar's Nurse" in George Gissing's story of that name, flees for more pressing reasons than Betsey. Down on her luck, she applies for a job as nurse in the infirmary of an English workhouse, and she is accepted although she has no training for or experience in the work. The assumption is that anyone willing to do so can look after paupers. Sensitive and compassionate at the outset of the experience, she welcomes hardships and looks upon helping those in her care as a religious duty. Tending for forty difficult and demanding patients on twelve-hour shifts, however, proves so exhausting that she almost falls asleep at the bedside of the dying. In addition to hard work and long hours she suffers from lack of privacy and the knowledge that the doctor and other nurse are indifferent to the patients. She eventually realizes that it is impossible to give the patients the attention they need, and with this realization her heart begins to harden against them. She finds herself taking pleasure in neglecting or mistreating those who give her trouble. The infirmary becomes more and more like the "lazar house" in Milton's *Paradise Lost*. In a moment when strength is granted her she flees the institution to regain sanity, character, and self-respect.[10]

Contracting for the care of the poor by the lowest bidder — an overlooked instance of the privatization of public welfare services — was once fairly common in parts of the United States. Jesse Stuart's "Mountain Poorhouse" indicates that the practice continued into the 1930s in a rural county of Tennessee. The winning bidder offered to keep the paupers for $2.30 a week per person, five cents less than anyone else seeking the contract. The poorhouse is a "lean to" across the road from the keeper's house; it leans to nothing and is built like a rough cow shed with stalls for the inmates. There are fifteen of them, including two children and their unmarried mother; a bedridden man who is incontinent; an insane woman; Uncle Peg, who has lost a leg in the mines; and other old people with a variety of ailments. The keeper calls them "a bunch of whores, outlaws, and killers"; by feeding them as cheaply as possible he hopes to clear a profit of $678 for the year. Uncle Peg urges Stuart to do what he can to get an old-age pension law passed.[11]

In the 1880s and 1890s American popular fiction abounded in humorous, cruel, sentimental, and, occasionally, realistic portrayals of tramps, bums, and lowlife.[12] In 1894 the young journalist Stephen Crane (1871–1900), whose novel *Maggie, A Girl of the Streets* (1893) had attracted little notice and fewer sales, published three memorable glimpses of tramp life. "The Men in the Storm" looks at homeless men who, in the midst of a blizzard, gather and wait in line on a New York street for the doors of a charity shelter to open. For five cents — half the price charged at for-profit flophouses — they can get a bed and a breakfast of coffee and bread. Some approach the line with "the characteristic hopeless gait of professional strays," others come hesitantly as if this sort of thing is new to them. In the huddled crowd it is hard to distinguish between those who are unemployed laborers and those who are tramps by choice, taking charity as their due. Crane thinks that of the two the laborers are the more patient; instead of looking angry or defiant they wear an expression of meekness, "as if they saw the world's progress marching from them, and were trying to perceive where they had failed, what they had lacked, to be thus vanquished in the race."[13]

Crane leaves the men as the door finally opens and they begin to crowd inside. In another sketch, however, he describes a night he spent in a cheap (seven instead of the usual ten cents) flophouse. Crane was not much better off financially than the tramps, but his middle-class sensibilities and the smell of a hundred men's breath and their unwashed bodies, accompanied by the sounds of their snoring, coughing, and tossing, made the experience a veritable "Experiment in Misery." It may have been on this occasion that he heard Billie Atkins tell about his excursions. After sixteen years as a tramp Billie remained as impulsive and headstrong as a child. One day in Denver it occurred to him that he wanted to be in Omaha, for no particular reason but to be there. Getting there by freight trains, on which he is attacked and repeatedly thrown off by trainmen is an ordeal, but Billie persists and at length arrives in Omaha in a coal car. Once there, he has nothing to do but look for a place to get warm and go to sleep. After wandering for hours he is lucky to find a bunk in the jail. Just before falling asleep he becomes aware of an irresistible urge to start back to Denver in the morning.[14]

At the same time that Crane was observing and writing about bums and drifters in New York, a young Englishman, W.H. Davies (1871–1940), was experiencing the life of a tramp in the American West. He came to America intending to find work but in 1893 jobs were hard to get. Under the tutelage of a "notorious beggar," Brum, he discovers that one can travel widely and live fairly well without toil. Begging was to Brum a fine art and "a delight of which he never seemed to tire." He believed that every street had a Good Samaritan; he or she might live in the very last house on the street, but sooner or later Brum found him—or more often her. Davies was almost as much impressed by Brum's extravagance as by his audacity. Instead of washing a dirty handkerchief or sewing a button on a shirt he would discard them and beg for replacements. Always neat, he would walk up to a house, ask to wash, and request hot water if available.[15]

Davies worked at agreeable jobs like picking fruit, but for the most part he was content to "beat" his way from place to place, live on handouts, and sleep by campfires or in empty houses. His book, *The Autobiography of a Super Tramp* (1908), does not glamorize a tramp's life or gloss over its hardships and dangers. He mentions, but does not devote much space to, the accident in which one of his legs was cut off while he was attempting to board a moving train. "It is nothing unusual in some parts," he writes, to find a man, always a stranger, lying dead on the track, often cut in many pieces. At the inquest they always bring in a verdict of accidental death, but we know different." Davies and his friends rode on the top of freight cars to avoid attacks by brakemen or, if attacked, to lessen their disadvantage; brakemen as well as hoboes can fall off trains.[16]

Davies found a tramp's life interesting and educational enough to satisfy him for five or six years — about as long as some young people of later years spend in graduate school. When about thirty, he returned to England, lived on a small allowance left him by his grandmother, and eventually gained recognition as a poet. George Bernard Shaw's admiring preface to *The Autobiography of a Super Tramp* laments the time he gave to making a living, while Davies lived "like a pet bird fed on tidbits." A pet bird feels no shame for its dependency, and neither did Davies. In America, he recalled, "food was to be had for the asking, . . . often went begging to be received, and people were not likely to suffer for their generosity."[17]

Peasants in late-nineteenth-century Russia were not able to extend tramps the open-handed generosity and hospitality Davies met in the United States and Canada. Maxim Gorky (1868–1936), born in poverty, spent his youth as a vagabond; his writings make plain the trials he and his fellows encountered as well as the troubles they sometimes made for themselves. Most of their tramping had to be made on foot and over long distances; finding a place to spend the night in a harsh climate and unwelcoming environment was not easy. "Give a traveller a night's lodging!" the narrator of "A Rolling Stone" cries at window after window in a village. Some tell him to go to the neighbors; others tell him to go to the devil. "Go away," shouts a woman, adding "My husband is at home."[18]

In Gorky's day, for the sake of protection, Russian tramps often traveled in twos or threes. They were usually linked by need rather than affection and didn't trust each other or say much about their pasts. All the narrator of "In the Steppe" tells us about himself is that he has "always accounted myself better than other people, and have successfully held to the same opinion down to this very day." Nevertheless he paints a self-portrait of a tramp. He and his companion don't care whether a man who joins them is telling the truth or not when he says he has been a student at the University of Moscow. It made no difference to them whether he had been a student or a thief.

> The only matter of any importance to us was that at the moment of our first acquaintance he stood on our level, in other words: he was starving, engaged the particular attention of the police in the towns, was an object of suspicion to the peasants in the villages, hated everyone with the hatred of an impotent, bated, and starving wild beast, and was intent on a universal vengeance — in a word, he was of precisely the same kidney as ourselves.[19]

Gorky's autobiographical story, "My Travelling Companion," takes place in the summer and autumn of 1891. Maxim takes pity on and befriends Shakro, a twenty-year-old self-styled Georgian prince whose passport and belongings have been stolen. The two walk from Odessa in the Ukraine to Tiflis, Georgia, a four months' journey. Maxim picks up odd jobs on the way; Shakro scorns work, takes advantage of Maxim, and feigns a limp to get alms from Tatar (Muslim) villagers. When they reach Tiflis Shakro disappears without showing or expressing appreciation for Maxim's help. Instead of resenting Shakro's behavior Maxim remembers his bluster, vulnerability, and duplicity with amusement and affection.[20]

There is no need for Toussaint — so named because he was found in a ditch on All Souls' Eve — to pretend a limp: both his legs had been crushed by a carriage on the highroad when he was a boy. Brought up on charity without any education and unable to perform physical labor, what else, could he do but hold out his hand and beg? That is the way Guy de Maupassant (1850–93) sets the stage for his merciless tale of a beggar in the French countryside. As long as a local noblewoman lives Toussaint is assured a place to sleep (a hutch beside the henhouse), bread and cider in the kitchen, and an occasional coin thrown to him by the old lady. Things get worse when she dies — he is an annoyance rather than an object of pity to the tight-fisted, hard-hearted peasants. They want him to go somewhere else and bother other people. Toussaint is scarcely aware that there is a world beyond the limits of the four hamlets that compose his beggardom. "In the midst of men, he lived like the beasts of the wood, knowing no one, loving no one" until death by starvation put an end to his miserable life.[21]

As constant in their work as customs collectors at the frontier, a troupe of beggars collect a tax on the consciences of worshippers at the church of San Sebastian in Madrid. They are so strategically placed in the courtyard, at the entrances, and in the corridors and passageways of the church that there is no way of evading them except by entering and leaving through the roof. Some places get more traffic than others; these are occupied by "old timers" who hold them by right of seniority. They also take the largest share of any parishioner's gift for the collective benefit of the beggars.

Benina, the heroine of Benito Perez Galdos *Misericordia* (1897), is not one of the "old timers." She begs to support her mistress, a once wealthy widow who has fallen on hard times. When the widow receives a long-awaited legacy her family banish Benina from the house because her presence is a reminder of their recent poverty. Benina resumes begging to support herself and a blind beggar; the charity of a kindly priest helps them make ends meet.

Galdos (1845–1920) portrays Benina as truly religious in her selfless devotion to the welfare of others. She is not aggressive in seeking alms but gratefully accepts what is given her as God's way of providing for the poor. Benina, the blind beggar, and other characters in the novel are based on people Galdos came to know during his study and observation of life in the poorest quarters of Madrid.[22]

Economic opportunities in the Jewish ghettos of Eastern Europe were so limited that some poor people, *urimeleit*, although not exactly beggars, had to depend on the more fortunate. To reduce the burden on their immediate neighbors *urimeleit* would go to other Jewish communities to fill their knapsacks with food for their wives and children. When they attended a synagogue on Sabbath eve away from home it was customary for a member of the congregation to invite one or another to his home for the *Shabbes* meal. In Yehudah Steinberg's story, "Reb Anshel the Golden," two *urimeleit* compare the advantages of dining with the rich and the poor. One says he hopes to be invited to a poor man's house because he will get more to eat: the rich, well fed all the time, don't know what it is like to be hungry; the servants take away the plates almost as soon as they put them down. The other hopes to be invited to a rich man's house; the rich lead such monotonous lives that they are eager for news; while they are listening to your stories you can eat your fill. God grants each of them his wish—but that is Steinberg's story.[23]

Why do people give to tramps and beggars? In a story by John

Reed an aggressively ungrateful bum, having just been treated to his first meal in three days, attributes the donor's concern to a desire to enhance his self-esteem and sense of superiority. A more generous interpretation would have diminished the recipient's self-respect.[24] John Galsworthy (1867–1933) advances a straightforward explanation of why a busy writer, interrupted at work, gives a man with the smell of whiskey on his breath and an unlikely story on his lips money to get himself, his wife, and his dog to London. He does it to get rid of them.[25]

You can get rid of needy people but you can't always get them out of your mind. The dilemma facing the narrator of a story by I.L. Peretz (1851–1915) is what to do about a boy of seven or eight who asks him for five kopecks (about five cents) for "a nights's flop." The narrator, a volunteer in a soup kitchen in the Jewish quarter of Warsaw, is neither rich nor religious. The first time the boy asks the man hands the money over automatically, without asking his heart if he feels pity or his brain if he can afford the gift. The next night, when the boy again approaches him, he is more deliberate: if he had been religious he would have considered whether the good deed was worth five kopecks of if a display of fervor at the synagogue would be as effective and cheaper. Not being pious, he thinks only of the boy's welfare, resolving not to give in order to discourage him from begging. Despite his good intention he gives the boy five kopecks and feels better.

On the third night he delivers the boy a lecture about the evils of begging, gives him the money, and tells him he must never beg from him again. The following night he ignores the boy's plea and spends a miserable, sleepless night wondering what, if any, shelter the boy has found from the rain and cold. If he had been religious he would have slept soundly knowing that heaven would provide for the boy. In the morning he is so relieved to find the boy alive and well that he gives him ten kopecks. The next day he gives him nothing, doesn't preach or scold, and still feels dissatisfied with himself. As his devout grandfather used to tell him, the life of an unbeliever is full of heartache and uncertainty.[26]

Notes

1. Sholom Aleichem, *Inside Kasrilevke*, translated from the Yiddish by Isidore Goldstick (New York: Schocken Books, 1965), 207–22. Sholom Aleichem (He-

brew for "Peace Be With You") was the pseudonym of Solomon Rabinowitz, author of more than forty volumes of stories, novels, and plays in Yiddish.

2. Reb Nochemka's efforts for the poor are discussed in Part Four, chapter 12, p. 139. Nathan Ausubel, *A Treasury of Jewish Folklore*, 127–30, recounts a story in which Reb Nochemka is slapped by a prospective donor but continues to press for aid for the poor.

3. Aleichem, *Inside Kasrilveke*, 222.

4. Ambrose Bierce, "The Applicant," in *In The Midst of Life, Tales of Soldiers and Civilians* (1891), *The Collected Works of Ambrose Bierce* (New York: Gordian Press, Inc., 1966), 2:281–82.

5. Ibid., 283–84.

6. Mary E. Wilkins Freeman, "A Mistaken Charity," in *A Humble Romance* (New York: Harper and Brothers, 1887), 234–37. Freeman (1852–1930) was a leading member of the "local color" school of writers. *A Humble Romance* was her first collection of stories about rural life in Massachusetts.

7. Ibid., 239.

8. See Part One, chapter 1, p. 9.

9. Sarah Orne Jewett, "The Flight of Betsey Lane," in *A Native of Winby and Other Tales* (Boston: Houghton Mifflin and Company, 1894), 177–78. "The Paupers" is in Arthur Quiller-Couch, "Short Stories" (London: J.M. Dent, 1944), 34–43.

10. George Gissing, "The Beggar's Nurse," in *Human Odds and Ends* (New York and London: Garland Publishers, Inc., 1977), 238–43. First published in 1898. Gissing (1857–1903) was a successful English author whose reputation declined after his death but revived in the 1960s. The passage on the Lazar House in Milton's *Paradise Lost*, Book XI, is quoted in Part Two, chapter 5, p. 46.

11. Jesse Stuart, "Mountain Poorhouse," in *Head O' W-Hollow* (New York: E.P. Dutton and Co., 1936), 118–21. Stuart (1907–84) wrote stories, poems, novels, and essays about his native state, Kentucky.

The Social Security Act of 1935 inaugurated a new era of social welfare in the United States by establishing federal retirement and unemployment insurance and federal grants-in-aid to the states for aid to the aged, the blind, and dependent children. Beginning in 1939, amendments to the act have extended its coverage and improved benefits, making it the nation's major bulwark against poverty in old age.

12. Representative examples include Bret Harte, "My Friend the Tramp" (1885), in Harte's *Complete Works* (New York: P.F. Collier and Son, 1904), 1:229–39; Richard Harding Davis, "The Hungry Man Was Fed" (1892), in *Van Bibber and Others* (Garden City, NY.: Garden City Publishing Company, 1920), 47–53; and W.S. Porter [O. Henry], "The Cop and the Anthem" (1902/3), in *The Four Million* (New York: Doubleday, Page and Company, 1919), 90–100. The vogue of low life in fiction is discussed in Robert H. Bremner, *From the Depths* (New York: New York University Press, 1956), 98–107.

13. Stephen Crane, "The Men in the Storm," in Thomas A. Gullason, ed., *The Complete Short Stories and Sketches of Stephen Crane* (Garden City, N.Y.: Doubleday and Company), 177.

14. "An Experiment in Misery," ibid., 139–47; "Billie Atkins Went to Omaha," ibid., 163–69.

15. William H. Davies, *The Autobiography of a Super Tramp* (London: Jonathan Cape, 1955), 35–36. First published in 1908.

16. Ibid., 37. The implication is that the man was thrown to his death by members of the train crew.

17. Ibid., 35; Shaw's comments are on pages 10–12.

18. Maxim Gorky, "A Rolling Stone," in *Tales From Gorky*, translated by Nisbet Bain (New York: Funk and Wagnalls Company, n.d.), 82. Gorky was the pseudonym of Alexsey Maximovitch Pyeshkov. His first stories were published in the 1890s, and his play, *The Lower Depths*, was produced in 1902. He wrote of his early years in *My Childhood* (1913), *In the World* (1916), and *My Universities* (1923).

19. Gorky, "In the Steppe," ibid., 20–21.

20. Gorky, "My Travelling Companion," in *Selected Stories* (Moscow, U.S.S.R.: Progress Publishers, 1981), 56–106 passim.

21. Guy de Maupassant, "The Beggar," in *The Odd Number* (New York: Harper and Brothers, 1889), 153–63.

22. Benito Perez Galdos, *Compassion*, translated from the Spanish *Misericordia* by Tony Talbot (New York: F. Ungar Publishing Company, 1962). First published in 1897.

23. Yehudah Steinberg (1863–1908), "Reb Anshel the Golden," translated from The Yiddish by Nathan Ausubel in Ausubel, *A Treasury of Jewish Folklore*, 569–70.

24. John Reed, "Another Case of Ingratitude," in *Adventures of a Young Man, Short Stories From Life* (San Francisco: City Lights Books, 1975), 47–50. First published in *The Masses*, 1913). Reed (1887–1920), sympathetic with the underdog and suspicious of the middle class, does not rebut the tramp's assertion.

25. John Galsworthy, "Philanthropy," in *Caravan* (New York: Charles Scribner's Sons, 1925), 219–22. The story is dated 1922.

26. I.L. Peretz, "The Poor Boy," in *Selected Stories*, edited by Irving Howe and Eliezer Greenberg (New York: Schocken Books, 1974), 144–49. Peretz, a Polish poet, novelist, and playwright, wrote in Hebrew and Yiddish. An unabridged version of the story appears in Peretz, *Stories and Pictures*, translated from Yiddish by Helena Frank (Philadelphia: Jewish Publishing Society of America, 1906).

14

Modern Philanthropy and
Organized Charity

Modern philanthropy took shape in the years between about 1885 and 1915 as multimillionaires like Andrew Carnegie, John D. Rockefeller, and other rich men and women sought practical, socially useful ways of disposing of surplus wealth. Because of the immensity of their fortunes they had to think in wholesale terms: simple acts of kindness and generosity to widows and orphans or a traveler found wounded on a highway were not sufficient for their means. Generally speaking, they favored giving to — or as Rockefeller said, investing in — education, research, and cultural institutions deemed likely, in Carnegie's words, "to stimulate the best and most aspiring of the poor . . . to further efforts for their own improvement." They did not follow the advice Jesus gave to the rich young man to sell all he had and give to the poor because they believed that doing so would result in more harm than good and deprive them of the power and responsibility of deciding how their wealth should be used. Both Carnegie and Rockefeller distinguished between philanthropy and charity. "The best philanthropy," declared Rockefeller, "is not what is usually called charity." According to Carnegie the worst thing a millionaire could do with his money was to give it to the "unreclaimably poor."[1]

Traditional charity was no more popular with some of the groups engaged in dispensing aid to the poor than with millionaire philanthropists. During and after the 1880s relief agencies in many American cities banded together in federations patterned after the London Charity Organization Society in order to eliminate duplication of effort and to reduce competition among their members. These "organized" charities attempted to discipline the charitable impulses of ordinary donors by replacing casual giving with systematic and scientific methods of distinguishing between deserving and undeserving applicants: registration, investigation, work tests, and counseling.

To critics like John Boyle O'Reilly (1844–90), an Irish-born poet and editor of the Boston *Pilot*, organized charity was a manifestation of the selfish values and tight-fisted policies of bankers and businessmen. His poem "In Bohemia" (1886) contrasted the kindness and generosity of a community of artists, writers, and scholars with the coldness and caution of a society devoted to thrift and trade. O'Reilly deplored

> The vulgar sham of the pompous feast
> Where the heaviest purse is the highest priest;
> The organized charity, scrimped and iced,
> In the name of a cautious, statistical Christ;
> The smile restrained, the respectable cant,
> When a friend in need is a friend in want;
> Where the only aim is to keep afloat,
> And a brother may drown with a cry in his throat.

O'Reilly's alternative to organized charity in Bohemia was "the glow of a kindly heart and the grasp of a friendly hand."[2]

William Dean Howells's attitude toward charity, both traditional and organized, was equivocal. Charity is a simple problem when looked at from the standpoint of religion, he wrote in 1896, but very complex when viewed from the perspective of citizenship and public policy. We try to reconcile religious and civic obligations as best we can. "We behave as if it would be the wildest folly to give . . . in the measure Christ bade," and we adjust our giving to the varying degrees of need that come to our attention. "To the absolutely destitute it is plain that anything will be better than nothing, and so we give the smallest charity to those who need charity most."[3]

Howells (1837–1920) had worked as a volunteer "friendly visitor" for organized charities in Boston and New York and knew at first hand "how effective they often are, how ineffective." He approved of much of what the societies tried to do, such as inquiring into the facts of a case and providing work whenever possible, but he reserved to himself the privilege of "giving to him that asketh" without proof of need or merit. All his efforts to find jobs for those he visited had been unsuccessful, confirming his suspicion that the assumption work was available to all who really wanted it was unfounded. Basil March, Howells's spokesman in *A Hazard of New Fortunes* (1890), commented that an individual tramp to whom he gave a coin might be a fraud but nevertheless represent the fact of widespread, undeserved misery. "Perhaps," Howells concluded, "it would be a fair division of the work if we let the deserving rich give only to the deserving poor, and kept the undeserving poor for ourselves, who, if we are not rich, are not deserving either."[4]

In considering the relative claims to assistance of the deserving and undeserving poor, George Bernard Shaw (1856–1950) took issue with both millionaire philanthropists and organized charity. The honest, industrious, and "aspiring" poor were, in Shaw's opinion, the least in need of help and the most likely to be demoralized by it. The undeserving, "unreclaimably" poor were a more challenging problem. Shaw cited the case of a copyist he once knew at the British Museum: she was incompetent, and undependable, could not resist the temptation to drink "and was therefore at a miserable disadvantage in this world — a disadvantage exactly similar to that suffered by the blind, the deaf, the maimed, the mad, or any other victim of imperfect or injured faculty." People like her need help, Shaw argued, whether they "deserve" it or not. Prejudice against them leads to "an almost maniacal individualism and an abhorrence of ordinary 'charity' as the worst of social crimes."[5]

Shaw recognized that it was economically impossible for private benevolence to relieve the awesome needs of the undeserving. Helping them, he said, "is a public duty like enforcement of sanitation, and should be undertaken by the public." Charity is no substitute for social responsibility but the attitude of sympathy and concern for the unfortunate that has traditionally animated charity is essential to an extension and humanization of public poor relief.[6]

"You can't pauperise them as hasn't things to begin with. They're bloomin' well pauped" already, declares a slum dweller in Rudyard Kipling's story "The Record of Badalia Herodsfoot" (1890).[7] Fear of pauperizing the poor, however, haunted turn-of-the-century philanthropists and agents of organized charity, just as it continues to trouble policy makers and voters a century later. The pauperization Shaw deplored in "Socialism for Millionaires" (1896) was the tendency of taxpayers to rely on philanthropic grants or subsidies for support of necessary public institutions such as hospitals. "A safe rule for the millionaire is never to do anything for the public, anymore than for an individual, that the public will do (because it must) for itself without his intervention." As a corollary to this rule Shaw advised public benefactors, "Never give to people anything they want: give them something they ought to want and don't." He praised John Ruskin's gift of a museum to the city of Sheffield — an institution he suspected the people of the town would gladly have exchanged for a holiday with beer. Shaw cited Ruskin's example to show what a wealthy lover of art, architecture, and learning could do to create a need for, or at least to stimulate public interest in, beauty and culture.[8]

Modern philanthropy revived questions about the sources of the donor's wealth. "It is impossible to deny the existence of a considerable class of people who have gained great wealth by predatory methods," asserted the liberal clergyman, Washington Gladden. Can religious and educational institutions accept money tainted by fraud, corruption, and unfair competition without condoning such predatory methods? In most instances pragmatic arguments in favor of taking the money usually prevailed over the moralists' objections.[9] *Major Barbara* (produced 1905, published 1907) presents Bernard Shaw's judgment on the problem. In the play a Salvation Army shelter, about to close because of lack of money, is rescued by a challenge grant from the distiller of Bodger's whiskey, whose terms are met by funds provided by Sir Andrew Undershaft, an arms manufacturer. Major Barbara, Undershaft's daughter, opposes acceptance of money tainted by the ruination and death caused by alcohol and war. The matron of the shelter, on the other hand, welcomes the gifts as heaven-sent answers to her prayers. Major Barbara, disillusioned, pins her Salvation Army badge on her father.

Shaw disposes of the tainted money issue in an "all or nothing" manner similar to Carlyle's disdainful attitude toward reform. In the "Preface to Major Barbara" (1906) he states that the notion some funds can be identified as tainted is impractical: all money available for philanthropy is tainted because it comes from rent, interest, and profit, meaning that it is "bound up with crime, drink, prostitution, disease, and all the evil fruits of poverty." There is no salvation through personal righteousness "but only through the redemption of the whole nation from its vicious, lazy, competitive anarchy."[10] Before the end of the play Barbara has come to recognize that her service in the Salvation Army was an escape from the world and that turning her back on the likes of Bodger and Undershaft, whose influence and power extend into every church, hospital, and shelter, was turning her back on life. Merchants of death and destruction have to be confronted not with prayer or denunciation but by militant action.[11]

While showing his family around the model town and factory where his armaments are manufactured, Undershaft recalls his ruthless struggle to move from poverty in youth to wealth and power in maturity. "I was a dangerous man until I had my will: now I am a useful, beneficient, kindly person. That is the history of most self-made millionaires."[12] Like other "successful scoundrels" he is respected and made much of by society; in return he practices philanthropy, endowing educational institutions and supporting other good causes but scorning pity, love, or forgiveness. The self-made millionaire's character has not changed. Shaw warns that if, instead of offering approbation, you lay hand on his property or seek to lessen his power, he will return to his robber-baron ways.[13]

The questions of where the money comes from and whether or not it is tainted do not arise in a discussion of "How ought I to dispose of my money?" in E.M. Forster's *Howards End* (1910). The discussants are a group of women who offer advice to a member of the group who pretends to be on the point of making her will. The latter says she is leaning toward establishment of local art galleries but is willing to allow various claimants representing different points of view to state their cases. The women assume different roles such as advocates of historic preservation or civic adornments and offer arguments for their causes. In the end the fortune holder, ignoring the advice and arguments offered her as well as the pleas of her son and a loyal servant, announces she is leaving her estate to the Chancellor of the Exchequer.

The decision is an intended anticlimax which, like the discussion leading up to it, allows Forster to examine and comment on philanthropic beliefs and practices current around 1910. His heroine, Margaret Schlegel, who takes a leading part in the discussion, challenges the value of making gifts for such lofty purposes as advancing civilization or elevating mankind. She believes that in the present state of the world doing good to one or, at most, a few persons is the most a philanthropist can hope to do. Margaret succeeds in focusing the group's attention on what should be done for an ambitious young man struggling to escape the shackles of poverty and lower-class status. The women favor efforts to improve his condition without impairing his self-reliance: access to libraries, museums, and debating and physical fitness clubs; opportunities for foreign travel; instruction in deportment and dress; and encouragement in personal endeavor. "In short," writes Forster, summarizing the discussion, "he might be given anything and everything so long as it was not the money itself." Margaret's proposal is to give the young man and a few others like him a grant of money substantial enough to make a difference in his life. "Give them a chance," she urges. "Give them money. Don't dole them out poetry books and railway tickets like babies. Give them the wherewithal to buy these things."[14] Margaret's suggestion finds little approval at the meeting but within a few years would become an accepted practice in philanthropic support for scholarship and the arts.

One of the purposes of organized charity was to take some of the guesswork out of giving by using paid or volunteer almoners to make charitable decisions on the basis of information not available to the average donor. This sounds reasonable enough but, like other aspects of charitable giving, is open to criticism and debate. Ambrose Bierce called the "professional almoners" of organized charity "philanthropists who deem it more blessed to allot than to bestow." Misanthrope though he was, Bierce believed the professional almoner had some uses. "He is a tapper of tills that do not open automatically. He is almoner to the uncompassionate, who but for him would give no alms." Maimonides might have found such services commendable, but to Bierce organized charity lacked savor: "its place among moral agencies is no higher than root beer."[15]

Radicals like John Reed (1887–1920) saw organized charity not as a plan to rationalize charitable giving but as one of the devices capitalists (like Bodger and Undershaft) used to keep labor in a servile condition. Reed's denunciation of organized charity with its "army of officers, investigators, clerks, and collectors" came in the Introduction to *Crimes of Charity* (1917), a muckraking attack on "one of the biggest industries in America" by a journalist, Konrad Bercovici (1881–1961).[16] The narrator of the book is an investigator for a charitable agency whose report on a mother's struggle to support her children (she works to get money to supplement the small amount the agency allows her) causes the agency to cut off aid to her. Guilt-ridden, and convinced that the managers of the charity are not interested in the welfare of the poor but only in running their business as economically as possible, the investigator resolves "to take note of all the evil that organized charity was doing and at the first opportunity give them out for the benefit of the world."[17] The crimes reported in the book include harsh tests to ascertain whether assistance is necessary, humiliating invasion of recipients' privacy, forcing recipients to work as strike breakers, and interfering with their efforts to help strikers.[18]

The stories of immigrant life' by Anzia Yezierska (1885–1970), who came to New York City from Russia in 1901, abound in examples of snooping, prying, and arbitrary decisions by friendly visitors who call on clients to check on their use of the assistance granted them. In "My Own People" in *Hungry Hearts* (1920) a visitor from the Social Betterment Society interrupts an impromptu party given by a poor old man who shares a gift of cake, wine, raisins, and nuts received from a friend with his equally poor tenement neighbors. The visitor reports the incident to her supervisors, who accuse the old man of deceiving the society and imposing on its charity. Yezierska contrasts the genuine charity of the old man, who gives what little he has to his neighbors, with the heartlessness of the Social Betterment Society.[19] The hostility toward friendly visitors displayed by Yezierska in this and other stories in *Hungry Hearts* and *The Open Cage* (1979) reflect the antagonism between the "new" Jewish immigrants from Eastern Europe and the more well-to-do and longer established German Jewish groups that financed and staffed the charity society.[20]

By the time Bercovici's and Yezierska's books were published, the suspicious attitude toward the poor the authors attributed to charity agents was no longer typical of social workers. In the general population, however, disparaging attitudes toward the poor on welfare persist, overshadowing sympathy for the unfortunate and making humanization of public poor relief difficult to achieve.

Notes

1. John D. Rockefeller, *Random Reminiscences of Men and Events* (New York: Doubleday, Page & Company, 1909), 141–42, 145–47, 155–60. Andrew Carnegie, "Wealth," *The North American Review* 148 (1889): 653–54 and "The Best Fields of Philanthropy," ibid., 682–98.
2. John Boyle O'Reilly, "Bohemia and Society," in *Watchwords*, edited by Katherine E. Conway (Boston: J.G. Cupples, 1891), 18–19. O'Reilly came to the United States in 1869 after having been deported from Ireland to Australia for support of the Fenian movement.
3. William Dean Howells, "Tribulations of a Cheerful Giver," in *Impressions and Experiences* (New York: Harper and Brothers, 1896), 156.
4. Ibid., 184–86; Howells, *A Hazard of New Fortunes* (New York: Harper and Brothers, 1890), 2:256.
5. George Bernard Shaw, "Socialism for Millionaires," *The Contemporary Review* 69 (1896): 208–09.
6. Ibid., 210–11.
7. Rudyard Kipling, "The Record of Badalia Herodsfoot," in *Many Inventions* (New York: Grosset and Dunlap, 1893), 326–34; first published in Harper's *Weekly* 34 (1890): 894–96, 910–11.
8. Shaw, "Socialism for Millionaires," 210–11, 217.
9. Washington Gladden (1836–1918) wrote and preached about the propriety of accepting "tainted money" on numerous occasions between 1895 and 1910. The quotation is from Gladden, *Recollections* (New York: Houghton Mifflin Company, 1909), 404. Allan Nevins deals with the tainted money controversy as it applied to John D. Rockefeller in *Study in Power: John D. Rockefeller, Industrialist and Philanthropist* (New York: Charles Scribner's Sons, 1953), 2:345–47.
10. Bernard Shaw, *Major Barbara* (New York, Penguin Books, 1960), 26–27.
11. Ibid., 151–52, (Act III). In the play, Barbara, convinced that under capitalism all money is tainted, decides to help manage her father's munitions business with the intention of using its profits for socially useful purposes. Except for radical rhetoric her decision accords with the pragmatic view that in philanthropy the use to which money is put is more important than its source.
12. Ibid., 143 (Act III)
13. Ibid., 34–35.
14. E.M. Forster (1879–1970), *Howard's End* (New York: Alfred A. Knopf, 1946), 144–47 (chapter 15).
15. Ambrose Bierce, "Charity," in The Collected Works of Ambrose Bierce (New York: Gordian Press, Inc., 1966), 11:258–59. For Maimonides' commendation of charity fund collectors, see Chapter 2, p. 18.
16. Konrad Bercovici, *Crimes of Charity* (New York: Alfred A. Knopf, 1917), ii - iii, 271.

17. Ibid., 47–48.

18. Edith Abbott, a social work educator, pointed out errors and misrepresentations in *Crimes of Charity* in a review in *The Dial* (May 31, 1917), 478–80.

19. Anzia Yezierska, "My Own People," in *Hungry Hearts* (New York: Grosset and Dunlap. 1920), 243–48.

20. Eastern European Jews, like many other groups including African Americans, Mexican Americans, and Italian Americans who felt discriminated against by "elite" charities, formed mutual aid associations of their own to help members in time of hardship. Such associations have served as alternatives to private charity and public relief for many poor people whether black or white, immigrant or native born.

15

Philanthropic Foundations and the
Uses of Philanthropy in
Higher Education and the Arts

The Copstock Foundation, whose history unfolds in *The Faithful Servants* (1975) by Margery Sharp, came into being in 1860 as a fund whose income was to be distributed annually among "all good and faithful female servants within the city of Westminster." It was named after the donor's mistress, Emma Copstock, who, like his relatives, had expected to receive his money. "So old Jacob diddled relations and mistress alike," begins Sharp as she follows the fortunes of the fund, its administrators, and its recipients over the span of a century until the income dwindles to nothing and National Insurance and old age pensions assume responsibility for the faithful servants.[1]

The Copstock and other foundations of the past served designated classes in particular locations; modern philanthropy has created general-purpose foundations whose function is to encourage research, discovery of causes and cures, and prevention of ills rather than relief of need, and that operate on a nationwide or worldwide basis. Many modern foundations, of course, are limited in scope and mainly support local charities. Quantitatively, foundation giving is less important than that of individuals. Foundation practices and policies, however, always receive close attention, partly because of public fascination with wealth and the way it is used and because foundation grants may set trends in giving.

In spite of lofty objectives—for example, "improvement in living and social conditions in the United States," "advancement and diffusion of knowledge and understanding," and promotion of "the well-being of mankind throughout the world" — and indisputable contributions to science, education, social welfare, the arts, and culture, foundations have not been well treated by writers.[2] Burton Raffel, an early editor of *Foundation News*, after surveying the depiction of foundations in fiction, found only two novels, *Arrowsmith* (1925) by Sinclair Lewis and *The Search* (1934, revised 1958) by C.P. Snow, that showed any appreciation of what foundations engaged in advancing knowledge were trying to do.[3] One reason for writers' indifference or hostility is belief that foundations reflect business values and represent the business spirit at its most cautious and conservative. John D. Rockefeller, who set the pace and tone for much of modern philanthropy, advocated establishment of foundations as a way of managing "this business of benevolence" properly and effectively. "Let us be as careful with the money we would spend for the benefit of others," Rockefeller urged, "as if we were laying it aside for our own family's future use."[4] Allen Nevins, in assessing Rockefeller as a philanthropist, states that Rockefeller wanted to give to "well-established or establishable causes and institutions; to give in a way that would stimulate other gifts and enlist numerous supporters; to give to undertakings that would persist after his support was removed; and to give for objects not merely sound, but the soundest within the range of his investigations."[5] There is much to be said in favor of such acumen in giving, but it does not kindle the imagination or arouse sympathy in the way that more impulsive, less calculated generosity would.

Authors criticize foundations, like other philanthropic agencies, for what they do as well as for what they don't do. Why do they "fund" certain causes and projects and turn down others that, in the writers' opinion, have a better claim for support?[6] Inevitably rejections greatly outnumber approvals. Winners acknowledge the aid given them but, since it is their own merit that is recognized, are not overly grateful; losers find little consolation from form letters expressing regret at their rejection.[7]

Arrowsmith's McGurk Institute, which bears some resemblance to the Rockefeller Institute for Medical Research (1901), is among the first foundations to figure prominently in fiction. Lewis (1885–1951) describes the Institute's location on the roof and top two stories of a skyscraper, its "forbiddingly polite" reception room, and the laboratories that seem like laboratories everywhere. Although public relations and press releases would seem less necessary in the operations of a well-endowed research foundation than in organizations dependent on contributions from well-wishers, Lewis contrasts the patience of the Institute's scientists in the conduct of their research with the eagerness of the director to announce results and breakthroughs to the world. Max Gottlieb, Martin Arrowsmith's former teacher, now a senior scientist at the Institute, welcomes Martin to McGurk with a lecture on "the religion of a scientist." "The only real revolutionary," Gottlieb tells Martin, "is the authentic scientist, because he alone knows how liddle" he knows. The real scientist wants everything to be subject to inexorable laws: he works and searches for absolute truth "and never goes about howling how he loves everybody."[8]

Expounding Gottlieb's version of the religion of a scientist gives Lewis a chance to voice his own misanthropic attitude toward society. Beginning with the arch-villains, Professional Optimists and Philanthropists (who have always ruled the world), he lists the people he hates and believes have made the world a mess. The list is a long one: money-grabbing capitalists, self-deceiving liberals, American boosters and European aristocrats, patriots, preachers, doctors, professors of history and anthropology (which they have the "nerf" to call science), faith healers, chiropractors, psychoanalysts, manufacturers who pretend to be concerned about their workers, eloquent statesmen, and soft-hearted authors.[9]

Among the reasons Gottlieb dislikes doctors is that they "want to snatch our science before it is tested and rush around hoping to heal people, and spoiling all the clues." Later in the book Arrowsmith does just that. For humanitarian reasons he makes a serum he is testing available to all victims of a plague instead of only to a select control group, thus nullifying the experiment.

The leading character in Lewis's *Gideon Planish* is more directly involved in "this business of benevolence" than Arrowsmith. The lifework of Planish, managing secretary (but not director) of The Heskett Rural School Foundation, is "skilled encouragement of the virtue of generosity."[10] He is also an "organizator," a person who makes his living by starting an organization and then looking for a purpose for which it can beg money. People who give to the organization are "philanthrobbers." They give to ease their consciences, to gain social acceptance or recognition, or, occasionally, because they believe in the organization's stated purpose.

The foundation for which Planish works is a taxdodge, a Philanthropic Institution, to which the immensely rich Mr. Heskett has assigned, in trust, a portion of his stock in various corporations in order to retain control of them without paying taxes on their earnings. The director orders Planish to advertise the founder's name and enhance his public image by making lavish grants to rural education. He denies Planish's request for a higher salary on the grounds that paying him more would do nothing for Heskett's reputation.[11] Planish's next job is with the Blessed to Give Brotherhood, whose motto is "Don't wait for the widow to bring in her mite. Get right after her at the washtub."[12]

Like Lewis, Kurt Vonnegut, author of *God Bless You Mr. Rosewater; or, Pearls Before Swine* (1965), saw foundations in general as instruments for the concentration of wealth and power and evasion of taxes. In the 1950s and 1960s this view was shared by journalists, bureaucrats, politicians, and lawyers. Persons favorably disposed to foundations in principle admitted that in practice many of the foundations established in the 1950s and early 1960s sought to take advantage of tax laws to benefit donors, their families, and businesses. In these intricate legal creations it was too often true that "sweet charity began at home by first locking the door to the Internal Revenue Service and then considering a remote, intangible, delayed benefit to society at large."[13]

The Rosewater Foundation is a charitable and cultural trust established in 1947 to protect the fourteenth-largest family fortune in the United States from tax collectors and other enemies. Its assets and the income they produce are what attracts a ruthless young lawyer to the foundation. He schemes to get control of the income by having the reigning Rosewater, an idealistic alcoholic who holds the position of president by virtue of being the founder's eldest living descendant, declared mentally incompetent. The lawyer is not interested in the program of the Rosewater Foundation except to the extent that the causes it backs — cancer research, civil rights, civil liberties, disinterested scholarship, and encouragement of the arts — can be used to cast doubt on the sanity of the president.[14]

Recurring criticism of foundations for being stodgy and avoiding controversial issues declined during a period in the 1950s when right-wing pundits and politicians charged that major, well-respected foundations, like leading educational and cultural institutions, were infested with communists and supported subversive, anti-American activities. Two Congressional investigations found little, if any, evidence to support the allegations against foundations but gave witch hunters a chance to air their fears and suspicions. Shortly after the furor died down David Karp (b. 1922) published *All Honorable Men* (1956) in which a liberal foundation executive, Milo Burney, accepts the challenge of heading a foundation to promote "enlightened conservatism." At the time it was necessary to add qualifying adjectives such as "enlightened," "intelligent," or "responsible" to the word conservative to make it intellectually respectable. Burney is liberal enough to recognize that principled conservatism is a legitimate point of view and a useful counterpoise to liberalism. Unfortunately, the multimillionaire who proposes to establish the foundation, his family, and his advisers are more opinionated than principled, and their insistence on investigating the "loyalty" of staff members puts an end to the foundation even before it begins operation.[15] Unlike this fictional failure, many real-life foundations have been set up since 1956 to promote conservative doctrines in education and to influence public opinion on economic and social policy (for example, taxation, government regulation, and welfare) along conservative lines. These foundations, centers, and institutes have played an influential role in the rehabilitation of conservatism and denigration of liberalism.

The target of Nathaniel Benchley's satire in *Lassiter's Folly* (1971) is a philanthropic organization "interested in giving a hand to backward areas" of the United States. Lassiter, the young millionaire who heads the organization, aims to end poverty in a rural community by using his inherited wealth to promote economic development. The project looks dubious from the start. The people of the area are satisfied with things as they are, don't believe in altruism, and distrust outsiders; Lassiter lacks the intelligence, experience, and character to match his good intentions; his chief assistant is dishonest and disloyal. It comes as no surprise to readers that the venture is an ignominious failure. The undertaking may have been ill-conceived and poorly executed, but it seems unfair of the author to have stacked the cards to ensure its defeat.[16]

Why would a self-made millionaire like Sam Baines, who gained his fortune by "bluster, graft, and putting people down," dispose of it by founding a university? Shaw's Sir Andrew Undershaft would answer that the once desperate man, having won his pile, became a kindly beneficent citizen. In "A Tribute to the Founder" (1967) Kingsley

Amis (b. 1922) says that Baines regretted the evils of his past and hoped the university would lead youth to a better path than he had chosen. The opening of the university made Baines happy; death spared him the sorrow of seeing the university refine and practice the arts of bluster, graft, and putting people down.[17]

The benefactor of Kloone University in *Ancestral Vices* (1980) by Tom Sharpe (b. 1928) is not moved by a bad conscience, belief in the moral value of higher education, or a persuasive appeal from the university development office. Lord Petrofact's gift is unsolicited. He hates his children and relatives so much that he has his lawyers draw up a will leaving his entire estate to Kloone. He also gives the university an advanced computer system, saving his company the cost of maintaining it and providing certain tax advantages. Unlike some large donors, he does not ask the university to change its name to his. He hates his ancestors and hires a radical historian to blacken the family name.

Nobody profits in this tale of loveless giving. Sharpe is evenhanded in exposing the donor as venal, the recipients — Kloone's indifferent and incompetent faculty, students, and staff — as undeserving, and the result — a monstrously inefficient library — as inane. In the course of the story the author, as uncharitable and "conscientiously unpleasant" as his characters, manages to disparage radical intellectuals, the Labor party, British autoworkers, architects, librarians, and social workers. Only Doris, a computer, comes out more or less unscathed.[18]

Charles W. Eliot (1834–1926), late in his tenure (1869–1909) as president of Harvard University, wrote that at the "older and richer universities" it was not necessary for the president to engage in personal solicitations for gifts to the institution; grateful alumni contributed generously and voluntarily.[19] At less fortunate colleges and universities fund raising has long been an important part of the responsibilities of the president and his aides. They have to devise methods and stimulate motives for giving to aid poor scholars, add to endowments, improve facilities for teaching and research, and adorn campuses with chapels, memorial windows, gymnasiums, and swimming pools. Who knows what considerations may induce donors to respond favorably to a college's or university's appeal for funds — love, loyalty, hate, fear, pride, prudence, religious convictions, political orientation, self-interest? An extreme example, provided in a story by Richard Stern, is the apparently successful use of the development officers' knowledge of an unsavory episode in a rich alumnus's past to persuade him to contribute to a university campaign.[20]

In *The Philadelphia Negro, a Social Study* (1899), W.E.B. DuBois (1868–1963) observed that the attitude of white Philadelphians to the Negro was contradictory: "Prejudice and apparent dislike conjoined with widespread and deep sympathy. . . . The same Philadelphian who would not let a Negro work in his store or mill will contribute handsomely to relieve Negroes in poverty and distress."[21] DuBois might have added support of Negro education in the South to the list of causes Philadelphians – and Northerners in general – were willing to support. In the late nineteenth and early twentieth centuries institutions like Tuskegee and Hampton (both called Institute rather than college), which emphasized manual, domestic, mechanical, and moral education of Negroes, were popular objects of philanthropy among Northern millionaires, some of whom believed training in practical trades was preferable to liberal-arts education for most youth, white as well as black. As a general rule the philanthropists took "white surpremacy" for granted and opposed "mingling of the races" in education, work, or recreation.

Langston Hughes's story "Professor," in a collection the author (1902–67) entitled *Laughing to Keep From Crying* (1952), shows the forces of prejudice and sympathy manifesting themselves in the Chandlers, a family known for "well-planned generosity on a large and highly publicized scale." The Chandlers, whose philanthropies have made them a significant force in Negro education, are interested in upgrading a small Negro college in the South by endowing a research chair in sociology. The most likely candidate for the chair is Dr. T. Walton Brown, an alumnus of and professor at the college and author of *The Sociology of Prejudice*, "a restrained and conservative" examination of race relations. At a dinner interview Professor Brown impresses the Chandlers as sound and moderate on racial, economic, and social issues and eminently qualified to conduct sociological studies and develop a distinguished department of sociology. The municipal college in the city in which Mr. and Mrs. Chandler live does not admit Negro students; there had been thought of establishing a junior college for them, but perhaps that won't be necessary if the little college where Brown teaches receives further assistance.[22]

Hughes tells the story from the viewpoint of Dr. Brown. Through his eyes we are able to see the miserable Booker T. Washington Hotel, the best accommodation the city offers Negro travelers; the mean and tawdry streets and run-down buildings in the colored section of town; the gradually improving buildings and landscape on the white side of the city, culminating in the park-like grounds and luxury of the Chandler mansion; and the shallow benevolence of Brown's hosts. They are willing to do anything for Negroes except accept them as equals, and are anxious to help as long as their giving does not alter the status quo in race relations. Brown's seven years as a waiter while working on his Ph.D. have taught him how to get along with people like them. He knows what a miserable parody of higher education his college provides its students. He gives the Chandlers the right answers and looks forward to receiving the salary that goes with the endowed chair so that he can take his wife and children on vacations to South America where they won't be treated or feel like Negroes.

"It was a beautiful college," Ralph Ellison (b. 1914) writes of the state college for Negroes to which the narrator of *The Invisible Man* (1952) wins a scholarship. Ellison's description of the buildings and grounds makes the college resemble Tuskegee, which he attended from 1933 to 1936. The narrator earns the enmity of Dr. Bledsoe, the imperious Negro president of the school, by driving a millionaire donor and trustee who is visiting the college on Founder's Day, at the trustee's request through the rural slum surrounding the campus. To make matters worse, the student narrator, again at the visiting trustee's request, stops at the farm of a Negro notorious for having fathered a child by his daughter, at the insane asylum, and at a bawdy roadhouse. Bledsoe accuses the student of undoing the work of half a century and expels him for stupidity. Anyone with any sense would have confined the drive to decent areas and found excuses not to go to or stop at places trustees don't need to know about.[23]

Bledsoe takes pride in his ability to manipulate the college's rich white supporters by showing them what he wants them to see and telling them what they want to hear. He is fiercely devoted to the school because it is the source of the power he wields over both blacks and whites, in the South and North alike. He is not interested in the education of Negroes except as a means of maintaining and enhancing his own authority, prestige, and rewards.[24]

Mr. Norton, the white philanthropist who gets the obedient student into trouble by insisting on being taken where he wants to go, exemplifies Ellison's belief, stated in a review of *An American Dilemma*, that

"philanthropy on the psychological level is often guilt motivated—
even when most unconscious."[25] In *The Invisible Man* Ellison implies
that Norton's philanthropic interest in Negro education is a result of
his admiration of Negro sexual potency and of his incestuous love for
his deceased daughter.[26]

"The Coxon Fund" (1894) by Henry James tells of an early effort to
use philanthropy to reward literary excellence. Lady Coxon, a trans-
planted transcendentalist born in New England circa 1820, gives her
titled English husband the idea of setting apart in his will the sum of
thirteen thousand pounds to be called the Coxon Fund. The widow is
to enjoy the interest for life; if she chooses, she may award it to a
person of genius whose penury has previously rendered it impossible
for him to bestow the fruits of his learning on society but who, with
the aid of the Coxon Fund, will be able to do so. Lady Coxon becomes
terminally ill before she has had a chance to select a candidate, or
"catch her hare," as one character puts it. She bequeaths the Coxon
Fund and the opportunity to choose the recipient to her niece.

"Fancy the idea of constituting an endowment without establishing
a tribunal—a bunch of competent people, of judges," exclaims an
Englishman who thinks the Coxon Fund is ridiculous. The niece, who
might have had the money herself if she had not conscientiously supported the endowment, awards the prize to Frank Saltram, a man who
knows everything about everything and who is more than willing to
share his knowledge with others in brilliant talk. Unfortunately the
magnificence of the award "quite quenches him. . . . The very day he
found himself able to publish he wholly ceased to produce."[27]

Selection procedures developed by modern foundations making
grants to writers, artists, and scholars lessen, but cannot entirely eliminate, the likelihood that latter-day Frank Saltrams will receive awards.
On the other hand, jurors and foundation officers may overlook or find
reason to reject applicants of promise, talent, and achievement. In
"Lines on Being Refused a Guggenheim Fellowship" the poet Reed
Whittemore tells, with suitable venom, how it feels to be passed over
by "Guggy," "Hank," "John," or "Andy."[28]

Ralph Ellison and Langston Hughes, at crucial points in their ca-
reers, obtained aid from private patrons and foundations. While working
on *The Invisible Man* Ellison received a grant from the Rosenwald Fund
and stipends from Mrs. J. Caesar Guggenheimer.[29] In Hughes's case
private patronage seems to have imposed more restrictions on his

artistic and personal freedom than foundation support. From 1927 to 1931 Hughes's patroness was Charlotte (Mrs. Rufus Osgood) Mason, a New York philanthropist who also assisted Zora Neale Hurston and Alain Locke. Mrs. Mason, described by a student of Hurston's life and work as "an extremely controlling woman," subjected her proteges to close control.[30] She appears under a different name in "A Woman With a Mission," a story by Arná Bontemps, a close friend of Hughes. Her mission is to nourish the primitive vitality of a Negro artist and to protect it, against his will, from what she considers the debasing influence of Harlem and Broadway.[31]

In "My Adventures as a Social Poet" (1947) Hughes referred to Mrs. Mason as a "kind and generous woman" and attributed the end of her patronage of him to the increasingly social content of his verse. It is possible that tension in their relationship and its rupture early in 1931 sharpened Hughes's sense of social injustice and intensified the hostility to the rich expressed in his poems "Park Bench" and "Advertisement for the Waldorf-Astoria" (1931).[32]

In 1931, after Mrs. Mason withdrew her patronage, Hughes received an award from the Harmon Foundation and a grant of one thousand dollars from the Julius Rosenwald Fund. The Harmon Foundation, established in 1922 by a New York realtor, made grants for playgrounds and student loans and sponsored annual awards to Negroes making distinguished contributions to American civilization. During a poetry-reading tour of black schools and colleges in the South sponsored by the Rosenwald grant, students at Hampton Institute asked Hughes to speak at a meeting to protest the murder of a fellow student by a white mob in Alabama (he had made the mistake of parking in a "white-only" lot), and the death of Fiske University's dean of women, denied admission to a white hospital after being seriously injured in an automobile accident. Hampton's administrators forbade the meeting. "This is not Hampton's way," they said. "We educate, not protest."[33] Hughes continued to protest against social and racial injustice in his writings and, in 1935, the John Simon Guggenheim Foundation awarded him a fellowship.

The subject of art patronage, not from the viewpoint of the artist but from that of interested bystanders and a prospective donor, comes up in J.I.M. Stewart's *Vanderlyn's Kingdom* (1967). The discussants are Oxford dons in various disciplines and a visiting American millionaire, Vanderlyn. Most of the speakers agree that for the sake of civilization it is essential that "the poet's purse" should be attended to, but they differ on how much (enough for a square meal or "a high protein diet with tolerable claret"), what if any strings should be attached, and whether, in addition to competence, the poet/artist must have a unique "self" to express. "Self-expression is bosh," asserts a Marxist: "an artist who's any good focusses the consciousness of his society." A philosopher advises patrons to be firm. "Make it plain that the artist is your servant, and that he must do what you want. You decide what's wanted." The consensus is that the age of individual patronage is over. Vanderlyn says that in America the money is still there "but confidence, or active interest, has been draining away from the people with the sort of means . . . we tend to set up expert bodies to administer what we are calling patronage." In the absence of patronage in the grand manner — as in the Renaissance or the heyday of finance capitalism — the art public accepts what reasonably honest professionals supply.[34]

Philanthropy and art patronage occasionally figure in mystery novels because money and valuable works of art are frequently involved in crime and murder. David Williams's *Treasure in Oxford* uses a conversation between a husband-and-wife team of amateur detectives to weigh motives and result in architectural patronage. The patron, a nineteenth-century American banker, built model tenements for the poor and hospitals, schools, and churches in England and the United States. The wife dismisses the banker's philanthropies as "salving his conscience and improving his image by giving away the profits of usury." Her comment is an example of a facile interpretation of philanthropic motivation as often met with in life as in literature. It is not based on knowledge of the donor's character but on "casual observation, complacent ignorance, simple prejudice, [and] that lazy judgment that comes more easily than sympathy." The husband points out that Moneybuckle's projects required the services of many architects; when it came to his attention that Oxford had no chair in architecture he offered to put up the money for one. At the time — circa 1860 — the University was not ready to have such a utilitarian subject as architecture taught in its precincts. Moneybuckle therefore established an architectural endowment, housed in a gothic building, with a magnificent library and collection of drawings and enough money to support it in perpetuity.[35]

Another novel by Williams, *Murder in Advent* (1986), examines the problem of priorities in charity. The question that divides the chapter at an English cathedral is whether to use the insurance money received for the loss of an early copy of Magna Carta for badly needed repairs to the cathedral or for relief of hunger and misery in developing countries. The dean's wife, a supporter of restoration of the cathedral, quotes lines she says were written by John Betjeman: "Let no one try to say that flesh is more important than old stones . . . Like saying St. Paul's is less valuable than a cure for cancer."[36]

Assuming that restoration of a historic, architecturally important building and feeding the hungry are equally deserving objects of charity, which one should get the nod? The advice of St. Augustine (not requested in the book) would be to make the decision by "a sort of lot" according to which "happens to be more closely connected with you."[37] Presumably, this would give the money to the cathedral restoration fund, but there might still be difference of opinion, because the close connection could be either bonds of affection and interest or the pull of sympathy and conscience.

To the title character in Garrison Keillor's "Jack Schmidt, Arts Administrator" (1979), art is a commodity and a contract his only connection with his clients. Fortunately the arts are in demand, and in the climate of the times objects and projects that would once have been deemed "impudent absurdities" are viewed as creative innovations. Schmidt is a middleman who helps art groups, the weirder the better, prepare winning applications for submission to government, corporate, and private donors, receiving a percentage of the grant for his efforts. For change of scenery, and to get new ideas, he attends expense-paid conferences held in exotic locations where panels discuss midwestern regionalism, art in rural life, evaluation in arts information, and topics of similar import. The story ends happily — the Highways Department takes Schmidt's faltering Arts Mall for an interchange and gives him a stretch of an unwanted interstate highway to develop — but we know the good times cannot last.[38]

Louis Auchincloss (b. 1917), a lawyer by profession, has been publishing stories and novels about upper-class life in New York City since the late 1940s. *The Golden Calves* (1988) takes readers into the executive offices and board room of The Museum of North America. Sidney Claverack, chairman of the board, believes museums are big business and must be operated accordingly. That is why Mark Adams, with no academic degree beyond a B.A. but an outstanding record as head of the museum's development office, is being named acting head of the institution and is the leading candidate for director. Claverack, a rich and successful lawyer, exemplifies a new breed of trustee, one who is more interested and active in the affairs of the museum than in his own business. His ambition is to quadruple the endowment of the museum and spectacularly increase its attendance. Adams knows that the chairman is well disposed toward him but is aware that his favor could be withdrawn. If that happens Adams doesn't look for much support from the curators and other members of the staff. The difference between profit and nonprofit institutions, as Adams knows, is that in a business employees rally around the boss when he is under attack, even if they don't like him, because their fortune is tied up with his; in a museum or school the staff joins in the attack, taking it for granted the endowment will continue to pay their salaries.[39]

"Charity, Goddess of our Day" in Auchincloss's *False Gods* (1992) has as its hero a socially prominent lawyer, a partner in the firm founded by his grandfather, who has never been very successful in making money for himself. Resigning from the firm after an argument with the managing partner, he accepts the chairmanship of a drive to raise money for a beloved cultural institution. With his connections, knowledge of society, and ingratiating manners, he proves to be a highly successful fund raiser. He takes pride in being able to obtain much larger sums in gifts for the institution than his former partners would have dared to charge as fees. To his and his wife's surprise he also discovers that he is capable of doing for charity what he would not have done in his own behalf: countenancing sharp practices which, although within the law, are ethically dubious. Only his wife's gentle counsel saves him from putting charitable ends above honorable means.[40]

Notes

1. Margery Sharp, *The Faithful Servants* (Boston: Little, Brown, 1975), 12–13. Sharp (b. 1905) is an English novelist, playwright, and author of books for children.
2. The quotations are from the letter of gift and terms of trust of the Russell Sage Foundation (1907), the Carnegie Corporation of New York (1911), and the Rockefeller Foundation (1913).
3. Burton Raffel, "Foundations in Fiction: Philanthropic Folklore," *Foundation News* 3 (1962):7, 10. *Arrowsmith* is discussed below. *The Search* is the story of a young man's effort to find a career that satisfies him intellectually and emotionally; in

the course of his search he works in various institutions for scientific research. The author, C.P. Snow (1905–80), had experience as both a scientist and an administrator. The books Raffel deemed unreliable were Sloan Wilson, *The Man in the Gray Flannel Suit* (1955); David Karp, *All Honorable Men* (discussed below); Theodore Morrison, *To Make a World* (1957); Stringfellow Barr, *Purely Academic* (1958); Stanley Price, *Crusading for Kronk* (1960); and Gwen Davenport, *The Wax Foundation* (1961).

4. John D. Rockefeller, *Random Reminiscences of Men and Events* (Garden City, N.Y.: Doubleday, Doran, 1933), 188. First published in 1909.

5. Allen Nevins, *Study in Power, John D. Rockefeller, Industrialist and Philanthropist* (New York: Charles Scribner's Sons, 1953), 2:157.

6. For example, Ellen Condliffe Lagemann, in her scholarly and objective history of the Carnegie Corporation, faults the foundation trustees' policy in the 1920s of supporting economic research while denying settlement houses aid in conducting social studies. *The Politics of Knowledge, The Carnegie Corporation, Philanthropy, and Public Policy* (Middletown, Conn.: Wesleyan University Press, 1989), 68.

7. See below p. 177 for one author's response to rejection of his application for a fellowship.

8. Sinclair Lewis, *Arrowsmith* (New York: New American Library, 1967), 265–68 (chapter 26). First published in 1925.

9. Ibid.

10. Sinclair Lewis, *Gideon Planish* (New York: Random House, 1943), 230.

11. Ibid., 223–25.

12. Ibid., 311.

13. Julian Levi of the University of Chicago, quoted in Robert H. Bremner, *American Philanthropy* (Chicago: University of Chicago Press, 1988), 181. Provisions of the Tax Reform Act of 1969 relating to foundations are summarized on pages 182–83.

14. Kurt Vonnegut, Jr., *God Bless You Mr. Rosewater; or, Pearls Before Swine* (New York: Henry Holt and Company, 1965), 15–18, 25. Vonnegut (b. 1922) is the author of numerous novels satirizing American attitudes and institutions.

15. David Karp, *All Honorable Men* (New York: Alfred A. Knopf, 1956).

16. Nathaniel Benchley, *Lassiter's Folly* (New York: Atheneum, 1971). Benchley (b. 1915) is the author of numerous works of fiction as well as a biography of his father, the critic and humorist Robert Benchley.

17. Kingsley Amis, "A Tribute to the Founder," in *Collected Poems, 1944–1979* (London: Hutchinson, 1979), 76. The poem appeared earlier in Amis's *A Look Around the Estate* (1967).

18. Tom Sharpe, *Ancestral Vices* (London: Secker and Warburg, 1980). Sharpe is an English novelist and playwright.

19. Charles W. Eliot, *University Administration* (Boston and New York: Houghton Mifflin, 1908), 233–35.

20. Richard Stern, "Idylls of Dugan and Strunk," in *1968* (New York: Holt, Rinehart

and Winston, 1970), 131–67. Stern (b. 1928), novelist and short-story writer, is professor of English at the University of Chicago. In the story Dugan and Strunk are development officers at the University of Chicago.

21. W.E.B. DuBois, *The Philadelphia Negro, A Social Study* (New York: Schocken Books, 1967), 355. First published in 1899.

22. Langston Hughes, "Professor," in *Laughing to Keep from Crying* (New York: Henry Holt & Co., 1952), 97–105.

23. Ralph Ellison, *The Invisible Man* (New York: Random House, 1952), 106–9.

24. Ibid., 109–11.

25. Ralph Ellison, "An American Dilemma: A Review," in *The Shadow and the Act* (New York: Random House, 1964), 306. The review of *An American Dilemma* was written in 1944.

26. Ellison, *Invisible Man*, 29–33. Norton's motivation is discussed in Jonathan Baumbach, "Nightmare of a Native Son," in Harold Bloom, ed., *Ralph Ellison* (New York and Philadelphia: Chelsea House Publishers, 1986), 16–17, and Allen Guttman, "American Nightmare," ibid., 31.

27. Henry James, "The Coxon Fund," in *Henry James Shorter Masterpieces*, edited by Peter Rawlings (Totawa, N.J.: Barnes and Noble Books, 1984), 1:206–9, 233. The "Coxon Fund" originally appeared in *The Yellow Book* 2 (1894): 290–360.

28. Reed Whittemore, "Lines on Being Refused a Guggenheim Fellowship," in *The Self-Made Man and Other Poems* (New York: The MacMillan Company, 1959), 13–14. Whittemore (b. 1919) is author of numerous volumes of poetry and literary criticism and a biography of William Carlos Williams. The John Simon Guggenheim Memorial Foundation, established in 1925, annually awards (and refuses) grants for creative work in the arts and scholarly research in all fields of knowledge.

29. Ellison, *Invisible Man*, xi. The Julius Rosenwald Fund, established in 1917, was active in the field of Negro education and culture.

30. Mary Helen Washington, "A Woman Half in Shadow," in Harold Bloom, ed., *Zora Neal Hurston* (New York and Philadelphia: Chelsea House Publishers, 1986), 128. Mrs. Mason's philanthropy is discussed in Arnold Rampersad, *The Life of Langston Hughes* (New York: Oxford University Press, 1986–88), 1:147, and Robert E. Hemmenway, *Zora Neale Hurston, A Literary Biography* (Urbana, Illinois: University of Ill. Press, 1977), 104–5.

31. Arna Bontemps, "A Woman With a Mission," in *The Old South* (New York: Dodd, Mead and Company, 1973), 71–87. Bontemps (1902–73), librarian at Fisk University, was author of novels, children's stories, and books about black history, including *Chariot in the Sky* (1951), an account of the Fisk Jubilee Singers.

32. Langston Hughes, "My Adventures As A Social Poet," in Faith Berry, ed., *Good Morning Revolution, Uncollected Social Protest Writings by Langston Hughes* (New York: Lawrence Hill and Company, 1973), 135–37. "Park Bench" appears on p. 137 of this volume and "Advertisement for the Waldorf-Astoria" on pages 19–20; the latter was first published in *New Masses*, December 1931.

33. "Tragedy at Hampton," in *The Langston Hughes Reader* (New York: George Braziller, Inc., 1958) 401–4. Reprinted from Hughes, *I Wonder As I Wander* (1956).

34. J.I.M. Stewart, *Vanderlyn's Kingdom* (New York: W.W. Norton and Company, 1967), 52–58. Some of the issues raised in the discussion reappear in the second half of the novel, which deals with Vanderlyn's ill-fated attempt to make his Greek Island kingdom a lighthouse rather than an ivory tower of culture.

35. David Williams, *Treasure in Oxford* (New York: St. Martin's Press, 1989), 26–27. The inspiration for Moneybuckle may have been George Peabody (1795–1869), active in banking and philanthropy in England and the United States. The quotation about prejudice and lazy judgment comes from John McGahern, "The Conversion of William Kirkwood," in *High Ground* (New York: Viking, 1987), 123. After graduating from Oxford, Williams (b. 1926) worked in advertising, before becoming a full-time writer.

36. David Williams, *Murder in Advent* (New York: St. Martin's Press, 1986), 52. John Betjeman (1906–84) was appointed poet laureate of England in 1972. The quotation is attributed to a private letter about Norwich churches.

37. St. Augustine's advice is cited in chapter 2, pp. 14–15.

38. Garrison Keillor, "Jack Schmidt, Arts Administrator," in *Happy to Be Here* (New York: Penguin Books, 1982), 3–14. First published in *The New Yorker* in 1979. The phrase "impudent absurdity" is used in Stewart, *Vanderlyn's Kingdom*, 58.

39. Louis Auchincloss, *The Golden Calves*, (Boston: Houghton Mifflin Company, 1988), 6–7, 43–48.

40. Auchincloss, "Charity, Goddess of Our Day," in *False Gods* (Boston: Houghton Mifflin Company, 1992), 171–91.

16

Giving by and for the Poor

It is one thing for Norman Douglas (1868–1952), author of travel books and the novel *South Wind* (1917), confident of his social, intellectual, and moral superiority, to denounce the practice of charity as a "form of self-indulgence" that has been amply tried and proved "a dismal failure." It is quite another thing for a poor person to be too proud to accept charity. Sometimes the best thing you can say about your family is that it was God-fearing and "we never once took nothing from nobody as help." Such self-reliant people are probably more often met in life and literature than the "god-favored loafer" Douglas deplored.[1] Mr. Perks, the crusty but kindhearted porter in E. Nesbit's *The Railway Children* (1906), is one of them; he refuses to accept the birthday presents the children have collected for him until they convince him the gifts are tokens of friendship and respect rather than an outpouring of charity.[2]

People who feel able to repay kindness are more likely to accept help willingly than those who have little economic or emotional goods to spare. At the time of the story the Railway children — two girls and a boy, ranging in age from about six to twelve — are poor, but they have lived most of their lives in comfortable circumstances and adversity has not yet eroded their confidence and good will. When their mother falls ill while their father is wrongfully imprisoned and needs medicine they haven't the money to buy, the children do not hesitate to ask an old gentleman whose name they don't know to buy the medicine for them. They are as gracious in seeking and receiving help as in extending it, never doubting that in time their father or they will be able to return the favor.[3]

Although the poor may not like to take charity they can be generous in bestowing it. A survey completed in 1990 showed that the poorest American households (income under $10,000 a year) gave 5.5 percent of their 1989 earnings to charity — mainly religion — as opposed to 2.9 percent donated to charity by the wealthiest Americans (those earning $100,000 a year or more).[4] Certainly that is the case in stories dealing with solicitations for good causes in which the poor give more willingly than the rich. Joseph C. Harmon lists and summarizes some of these in a useful survey, *Philanthropy in Short Fiction* (1992). He classifies these stories under the heading "Widow's Mite."[5]

The readiness of poor Negroes to help each other is a familiar theme in black history and literature. At a time when most charities, hospitals, and orphan homes, as well as schools, discriminated against people of color their only resources were relatives, fellow church members, friends, and neighbors. In *Beloved* (1987), a novel by Toni Morrison (b. 1931) set in the outskirts of Cincinnati some years after the Civil War, members of a black church committee "invented so nobody needs to go hungry" take turns in leaving food for the ailing Sethe, her daughter Denver, and the mysterious Beloved. They put their offerings on a stump in the yard with their names or identifying marks on the pans, dishes, or baskets so that these can be returned, with thanks, to the owners. Of course the help they provide does not occur spontaneously. Denver takes the responsibility of telling her former teacher, Lady Jones, of Sethe's sickness and need; Lady Jones alerts the church committee to Sethe's plight; and members of the committee organize the relief effort. Sethe had been at odds with the women who now come to her assistance. Why do they do it? "Maybe," says Morrison, "they were simply nice people who could hold meanness toward each other for just so long and when trouble rode bareback among them, quickly, easily did what they could do to trip him up."[6]

Serving others is one of the ways the poor show charity. Denver serves her mother and Beloved by working and cooking for them, tending to their needs, and finding a job when she decides not to rely on kindness to provide food for them. Janey, housekeeper for a rich white family, loves her employers but can't wait on them day and night, and so she brings Denver in to help at night. Janey, although overworked, is comparatively well off; Gloria, the black nurse in Clyde Edgerton's *In Memory of Junior* (1992), gets paid, but not much and nothing in comparison to the services she renders to two bedfast old people. She wonders why the state names a highway after a young professional basketball player who has never done anything but look after himself and do what he likes to do. "Seem like to me" she grumbles, "the one they name the road after would be somebody who done looked after somebody they *have* to look after—while they love the person but hate all that cleaning up and toting and heaving and lifting. . . . And you doing all this when you ain't feeling so good yourself and ain't got enough money to buy no bed sheets and run plum out of energy but have to keep going anyway. No matter what."[7]

Many parents encourage—or, like Mrs. Pardiggle in Dickens's *Bleak House*, coerce—their children in charitable activities. Through schools, churches, Sunday schools, and youth organizations children and young people have long taken part in fund raising for charitable and civic causes.[8] The charities—often games—children do on their own without parental prodding or guidance are instructive because they are often parodies of adult attempts to do good, revealing without rancor both the presumption and unintended results of some goodhearted, impulsive efforts to help the poor. On the other hand, children's acts of charity often show thoughtfulness and sensitivity in dealing with the unfortunate.

In Nesbit's "The Benevolent Bar" (1901), a simple act of charity leads to a more ambitious project. Oswald Bastable, a boy of about twelve, gives a passing tramp, who complains of thirst, the ginger beer he has been saving for himself. After drinking it the tramp exclaims, "I don't suppose you know what it's like to have a thirst on you. Talk of free schools and free libraries, and free baths and wash-houses and such! Why don't someone start free *drinks*?" The speech inspires the six Bastable children—the oldest fourteen, the youngest eight—to plan a benevolent bar to serve free drinks to weary travelers on the Dover Road. Drinks to them mean lemonade and tea. They pool their money to stock the bar and erect it out of planks and barrels. They go about the work seriously, although they have no illusions about the efficacy of the scheme. "It wouldn't be much," Oswald acknowledges, " — only a drop in the ocean compared with the enormous dryness of all the people in the whole world. Still, every little helps, as the mermaid said as she cried into the sea."[9]

When the bar opens respectable people seem neither thirsty nor weary, passing by, barely acknowledging the children's invitation to free drinks. A few appreciative tramps, including the one who gave the Bastables the idea for the venture, down nineteen tumblers of lemonade. One, calling for beer, scorns lemonade as the slop of charity. As the day wears on the bar attracts a crowd of bullying boys and three adult ruffians. One of the latter demands and receives a drink from a whiskey bottle containing denatured alcohol for the lamp to heat water for tea. He and his companions threaten the children and nearly wreck the bar before the original tramp comes to the rescue of the children. As a result of the experience the Bastables resolve never to try "to be benevolent to the poor and needy again. At any rate not unless we know them very well."[10]

Dorcas societies, found in many Christian churches, take their name from a woman "full of good works and charitable deeds" who was restored to life by the apostle Peter (Acts 9:36–41). Following her example, members of the societies make clothes for the poor. In a story by Kathleen Fitzpatrick the "weans," five children ranging in age from fifteen to six, members of a once wealthy but now impoverished family in Ireland, decide to form a Dorcas society of their own. Using old dresses, coats, and bonnets found in their home they put together garments for their neighbors who are even poorer than they. Since the children's father is dead and their mother confined to bed by chronic illness, they operate without adult supervision except from an indulgent cook and housekeeper. The *haute couture* costumes they create are so extreme in color and design that the recipients, although appreciative of the children's intentions, are embarrassed to wear them. The keeper of the local pub, however, is so amused by the clothes that he gives the wearers free drinks — and not lemonade. The merriment spreads to the whole village; even the police sergeant joins in the impromptu revel.[11]

J.I.M. Stewart (b. 1906) concludes his autobiography with the story "Sweets from a Stranger." As a schoolboy in Edinburgh Stewart, afraid but excited and curious, allows himself to be coaxed into a tenement by an old woman who looks like a witch. Despite her appearance she is a kindly soul seeking only a visitor for her lonely invalid grandson, Jamie. Stewart converses with Jamie and, when it is time to leave, wants to give him a present. All he has in his pockets is a shilling and he knows money would be an inappropriate gift. Fortunately it is an old coin bearing the likeness of Queen Victoria rather than George V. "Jamie," Stewart says, "take this, please take this. It's very old. It would do in a collection. Like a medal."[12]

Regret for selfishness and unkindness in childhood may shape a person's charitable bent in life. In *Grand Opening* (1987) by Jon Hassler (b. 1933) Brendan, twelve or thirteen years old and new in town, welcomes the friendship a poor boy named Dodger offers him. Later, to gain acceptance by boys of greater popularity and better standing in the community, Brendan drops Dodger. After Dodger's death in an accident Brendan considers what he must do to make amends for his shabby treatment of his onetime friend. He must promise "never again to be as unkind to anyone as he had been to Dodger" and "to go through life more openhearted toward others and less concerned with himself."[13]

Peter Maurin (1874–1949) and Dorothy Day (1897–1980), founders of the Catholic Worker movement, preached and practiced the voluntary poverty advocated by Jesus and followed by the early Franciscans. They believed that responsibility for the homeless and hungry should be assumed by individuals, at a personal cost to themselves, rather than delegated to public officials. Maurin's *Easy Essays* (1936) contains his verses originally published in the *Catholic Worker* (1933–) emphasizing the duty of hospitality to God's ambassadors, the poor, condemning tax-supported relief (like Herbert Hoover) as "not coming from the heart," and maintaining that "what we give to the poor is what we carry when we die."[14]

Robert Coles's tribute to Dorothy Day, "The Almoner," says of her that she knew "generosity is not gentility/Nor a ticket to upward mobility;" her generosity was not a response to a sense of plenty but a recognition of her own spiritual need.[15] She revered and wrote a biography of St. Therese of Lisieux (1873–94), a French nun canonized in 1925, who said sanctity is achieved in "the little way," not by performing miracles but by "fidelity and constancy in bringing the love of God into the routine affairs of daily life." Day maintained that "the little way" is the way for everyone to achieve goodness and that without sanctity material means and change in the social order are powerless to end the evils of the world.[16]

St. Therese of Lisieux is a presence in "The Visitation" by Maurice Yves Sandoz (1892–1958). Gabrielle, a rich woman, spends her mornings visiting and trying to help poor people in Rome. Her efforts, although not officious, are not much appreciated. The people she visits rarely receive her with anything but complaints and recriminations. "Things are always getting worse with them," she sighs, "and when they are getting better they find my visits intrusive." After one particularly discouraging morning she returns home and exclaims; "Oh, most gracious Father! Never an affectionate word, never a smile of recognition, or a sign of gratitude! And yet, how much that would help me in my daily task!" While she is speaking her doorbell rings and her maid admits a nun to the drawing room. When Gabrielle goes to meet her caller no one is in the room, but there is a small white rose, a flower associated with St. Therese, on a table. Gabrielle treasures the rose; whenever she fingers its fragrant petals she thinks of how little she has done and all she can still do. "And," she tells herself, "I have been marvelously rewarded."[17]

Thoughts of sanctity and gratitude do not occupy Mrs. Bernstein in Sylvia Townsend Warner's "A Work of Art" (1961). She practices charity "in the disorderly, hole-and-corner style recommended by Jesus," but since she is confined to a wheelchair and not able to climb to attics or descend to basements, where misery is most likely to abide, she employs an almoner, Miss MacTavish. The latter, like her employer, is dead set against "professional do-goodery" and strives only to make people a little better off without attempting to make them better. Mrs. Bernstein recalls how, in earlier days, her uncle used to exact a pound's worth of behavior from her to receive two and sixpence. All goes well until the plight of a sickly old man persuades them to depart from their policy of not trying to help those to whom they give money. He is so obviously unable to take care of himself that they have him moved out of his hovel into a clean and cheerful apartment. He turns out to be as firmly opposed to good deeds — although not above taking money — as his benefactors had previously been. Deliberately fouling the "bright little reformatory" they had designed for him, he creates a masterpiece of dirt, filth, and untidyness.[18]

"Charity saves from death," intoned impressively in Hebrew, is a favorite saying of Jacob's father in Hugh Nissenson's "Charity." Jacob, the narrator, recalls that in 1912 when he was twelve years old his family lived, or tried to, on ten dollars a week, the combined earnings of his parents as pants finishers and his after-school work delivering finished pants to subcontractors. Their home and workshop was one room in a cold-water flat on the fourth floor of a tenement on Ludlow Street on New York's Lower East Side. "I always went to bed hungry," Jacob remembers. The only change from their meager daily diet came on Friday night when his father insisted on a ritual Sabbath eve dinner. At this meal, for which the family skimped and starved itself all week, the father followed the custom of entertaining a guest poorer than he; the guest, often homeless, stayed overnight, sleeping on the table.

One Friday in December 1912 Jacob's mother falls ill and has to be sent to a hospital. Jacob's father, distraught but still devout, sends Jacob shopping for food while he looks for a suitable guest. The man he brings home is a broken-down scholar who barely supports himself by teaching Hebrew at ten cents an hour. During dinner he says the meal is almost the only food he has had for six days. When Jacob asks how his mother is his father says, "In God's hands." The guest says that is true of everyone. If God had not sent him to walk on Ludlow Street where he met Jacob's father he would now be hungry and cold in his dark hole where rats eat his candle.

After dinner the guest stretches out to sleep — and snore and whistle — on the table. Neither Jacob nor his father can sleep, but after a while a happy thought comes to Jacob: Mama will get well because, as his father has often said, "Charity saves from death." When he tells his father the good news the father scolds him for thinking a *mitzvah* (good deed) is a bribe to God. "No, not Mama," he whispers, looking at the guest, "Him."[19]

Every year more than half of American philanthropy consists of giving for religion. All of this is voluntary and much of it is a matter of habit as well as conviction; some, notably the sums sent to television evangelists, is obtained by exhortation and artifice. Clergymen of all denominations have to give attention to raising money for their churches and the charities they support. In *Morte d'Urban* (1962) and *Wheat That Springeth Green* (1988) J.F. Powers deals frankly with the tensions between faith and fund raising in the lives of Roman Catholic priests and parishioners. In one of his stories, "Defection of a Favorite" (1951), the rectory cat contrasts the moderation of old Father Malt, the regular priest, with the aggression of the assistant who takes his place during his illness. The new man does not hesitate to remind parishioners of their duty to give generously for the support of the church; Father Malt had been content to accept whatever they gave — "very little."[20]

Mac, the central character in another of Powers's stories, "The Devil Was a Joker" (1953) is a canvasser for the Clementines, a poor and struggling monastic order. In order to sell the order's magazine and pamphlets he must obtain permission first from the bishop of the diocese and then from the parish priests; permission is not granted automatically by either, and as a layman he is under a handicap. Fortunately the secular clergy, who dislike the well-established religious orders, don't regard the Clementines as a menace, and Mac has developed techniques to deal with both hostility and unwelcome hospitality. He doesn't like people — or work — enough to do house-to-house canvassing. The method Mac prefers is to have the priest endorse *The Clementine* from the pulpit and the ushers distribute the subscription forms while he sits at a card table in the back and accepts the money. In order to obtain the priest's cooperation he may offer to make a contribution for "the upkeep of the church or to the pastor's favorite charity (the latter was often the former)." Mac likes the big, well-to-do city parishes; he seldom calls on country parishes or poor ones in the city where, as he says, little can be accomplished.[21]

Like Mac and solicitors for charitable organizations in general, beggars have to be able to persuade the people they approach of the validity of their cause and the urgent need of a prompt and favorable response. Organized groups utilize professional counsel, brochures, photographs, and celebrity endorsements to make their case. Beggars have to, rely on their own demeanor, meek or threatening, and whatever eloquence they can command; trying too hard may be as self-defeating as not being conscientious enough. In Ray Bradbury's "The Beggar on Dublin Bridge" (1962) a man wearing dark glasses but no hat stands on the bridge over the Liffey singing and playing a concertina, hoping to coax coins from passersby. During the cold and wet winter months rain plasters his hair to his head, runs down his neck, and trickles off the tip of his nose. His bare head, instead of making people feel sorry for him, must make them feel uncomfortable, because they hurry by without putting anything in his cup. One day he gives up, throwing his concertina and then himself into the river. His death attracts as little sympathy as his performance on the bridge, but the narrator of the story, an American visitor, and the manager of the latter's hotel tell each other they are sorry they had never given him anything. Each had thought the man's hatlessness was an overdone effort to win sympathy.[22]

The American visitor has previously wondered about "the people in the street, who somehow become beggars." As he and the manager look down at the entrance to the hotel they discuss some of the familiar characters: the man who wants money to go to Cork (or Galway or Belfast), the woman with the baby, the one who claims to have cancer, an old couple with a piano that makes no music, and the man who greets you with, "There's only a few of us left." The manager, believes "us" refers to the speaker and the person addressed, members of a dwindling company of people who understand each other well enough to ask for and give help when it is needed.

The American asks how you can tell which of the beggars are honest and which frauds. The manager replies that you can't; there is really no difference between them, although some have been begging longer than others. Neither they nor anyone else can tell you what chain of circumstances led them to their stations outside the hotel.

What does it feel like to be a beggar? The visitor goes down the elevator and steps outside the hotel. He gives the money in his pockets to the first people he meets. Then standing alone, shivering in the cold, he puts himself in the place of a beggar looking up at the hotel's lighted windows. What's it like inside, he wonders. Is it warm? Are the people happy? Do they even know he is there?[23]

A young man in Penelope Lively's *City of the Mind* (1991), caught in a crowd in London, experiences "a confusion of feeling: mistrust, distress, incredulity, embarrassment" when he realizes a young woman is asking him for money. Her story is fluent and well-rehearsed as though she has used it many times. Her appearance is dishevelled, but she seems clean and well fed, as does the baby she has with her in a cart. Suspicion and skepticism tell him to deny her request but, like Basil March in Howell's *A Hazard of New Fortunes* in a similar situation, he recognizes that although she may be a fraud, she represents the truth of homelessness and overburdened and underfunded public social services. He gives her all his loose change; she inspects it, puts it in her purse without thanks, and they move on in opposite directions.[24]

In one of the stories in *Childhood and Other Neighborhoods* (1980) by Stuart Dybek, a novice social worker in a slum on the South Side of Chicago says, "People kept hitting me for handouts. Walking around the shabby streets in my white skin and blue suit made me appear wealthy. I *was* relatively rich." He runs the gamut of tough black youths outside a record store who, he comes to realize, are less interested in money than in his response to their demands and taunts. The best way of handling them is to stay cool and joke: "Money, man? I'm paid in food stamps." For a while he gives a quarter to any adult who asks, and dimes to the children who gather round him at an outdoor table at McDonald's. Since a social worker can't afford to be known as a sucker he becomes selective, giving only to those who looked as though they really needed help. Since the people of the neighborhood are all well-acquainted they question his judgment: how come you give to Clyde Jones and not to me? You gave half-a-buck to Lucy Winters. "What's she doin' I ain't?"

On his last day on the job, as a beggar approaches him, he thinks of all the demands on his charity: mental health, cancer drive, Heart Fund, Kidney Foundation, civil rights, peace. At closer range the beggar resembles "a scarecrow assembled at a Goodwill store." Coming up to the social worker, the man says, "Can you give me one cent."[25]

Even if we shut out the pleas of individual beggars we cannot escape the clamor of appeals from charitable organizations—a term which in the United States includes religious groups, relief societies, medical research and preventive agencies, and advocacy organizations of all political complexions.[26] In "Philanthropist," Reed Whittemore records his reaction when, on the top of requests for aid to the poor, the distressed, the homeless, the Native Americans, and whooping cranes, he is asked to do something for the hundreds of millions of people in the world who are illiterate. "He can burn books. . . . He would ask *them* to help *him* if they could read him." In the end he takes two dollars from his wallet "For Christmas Seals." Whittemore's response is more positive than that of a couple in Arthur Guiterman's poem "Charity": The husband gave nothing big, the wife gave nothing small, and so they never gave at all.[27]

One of Langston Hughes's social poems, "How Thin a Blanket," expresses both the sense of futility that sometimes overcomes donors and the despair that engulfs those in need:

> There is so much misery in the world.
> So much poverty and pain,
> So many who have no food
> Nor shelter from the rain,
> So many wandering friendless,
> So many facing cold,
> So many gnawing bitter bread
> And growing old!

What can; I do?
And you?
What can we do alone?
How short a way
The few spare crumbs
We have will go!
How short a reach
The hand stretched out
To those who know
No handshake anywhere.
How little help our love
When they themselves
No longer care.
How thin a blanket ours
For the withered body
Of despair![28]

The word *despair* appears in two significant passages of J.F. Powers's *Wheat That Springeth Green*, first as something to avoid and second as an ingredient, with charity, of wisdom. Joe, a priest, resists pressure to offer prayers in his church for passage of a military spending bill that will provide jobs and stimulate the flagging local economy. Unhappy with himself because he knows he eats and drinks too much and with his materialistic parishioners, he tells his problems to his confessor, Father Day. The latter tells Joe to be on his guard against despair. "Despair's really presumption, you know. Expecting too much. We can't change the world. . . . But we can change ourselves. That's enough. Sometimes it's too much." Father Day's advice is "Prayer, Joe, more prayer" — not for prosperity and defense jobs but for grace and things that lead to salvation.[29]

Fairly late in his pastoral career Joe attends a retreat with fellow priests; to his surprise he abstains from criticizing the retreatmaster and the bishop's office for booking him. After momentary discomfort, "the strange sensation of not speaking his mind to no avail" makes him realize "there was something to be said for whatever it was, charity, or despair, or a blend of both — wisdom? — that moved old men to silence."[30]

Joe's silence reminds readers that sparing others our opinions, when it is not necessary to express them, is a form of charity that can be practiced not just by old men but by everybody, old and young, women and men, rich and poor alike. Self-discipline is the only proper check on expression of opinion because having one's say is an important right even when what is said enlightens or satisfies no one but the speaker.

American courts have ruled that requests for donations by charitable organizations and by individual beggars are protected by constitutional guarantees of freedom of speech.[31] Those addressed can heed or ignore the appeals. The messages of affirmation or protest voiced in the appeals are part of the stories from life, tales not in books that tell us much about charity and philanthropy today.

Notes

1. Norman Douglas, *Old Calabria* (New York: Harcourt Brace and Company, 1956), 327. First published in 1915. The second quote is from Clyde Edgerton, *In Memory of Junior* (Chapel Hill, N.C.: Algonquin Press, 1992), 74.

2. Edith Nesbit, *The Railway Children* (New York: Philomel Press, 1989), 124–29. First published in 1906. Nesbit (1858–1924) remains a popular author of children's literature.

3. Ibid., 50–52.

4. Nathan Weber, ed., *Giving USA 1991, The Annual Report on Philanthropy for the Year 1990* (New York: AAFRC Trust for Philanthropy, Inc., 1991), 45–46. Although the poor who give are generous in their contributions, only 49 percent of households in the lowest income bracket reported giving as compared to 75 percent of all American households.

5. Joseph C. Harmon, comp., *Philanthropy in Short Fiction, An Annotated Bibliography and Subject Index* (Indianapolis: Indiana University Center on Philanthropy, 1992). Among the Widow's Mite stories cited by Harmon are Jacob Adler, "Samples," in *Cheerful Moments* (New York, 1940), and Henry Lawson, "Send Round the Hat," in *Best Stories of Henry Lawson* (London, 1981).

6. Toni Morrison, *Beloved* (New York: Alfred A. Knopf, 1987), 246–49.

7. Edgerton, *In Memory of Junior*, 74.

8. Children's participation in mid-nineteenth-century American charities is discussed in Robert H. Bremner, *The Public Good* (New York, 1980), 21–22.

9. E. Nesbit, "The Benevolent Bar," in *The Bastables, The Story of the Treasure Seekers, The Wouldbegoods* (New York: Franklin Watts, Inc., 1966), 308–11.

10. Ibid., 319.

11. Kathleen Fitzpatrick, "The Dorcas Society," in *The Weans of Rowallan* (New York: Coward-McCann, 1987), 108–21. First published in 1902.

12. J.I.M. Stewart, "Sweets from a Stranger," in *Parlour 4 and Other Stories* (London: Victor Gollancz, 1980), 175–84. The story is reprinted in Stewart's *Myself and*

Michael Innes (1987).

13. Jon Hassler, *Grand Opening* (New York: William Morrow and Company, 1987), 306–7.

14. Peter Maurin, *Easy Essays* (Chicago: Franciscan Herald Press, 1984) 8–10; Maurin, "The Extra Coat in Your Closet Belongs to the Poor," *Catholic Worker* 56 (January-February, 1989): 1. Reprinted from *Easy Essays* (1936).

15. Robert Coles, "The Almoner, To D.D. 1897–1980," in *Rumors of Separate Worlds* (Iowa City: University of Iowa Press, 1989), 14. Coles (b. 1929) is author of the five-volume Children of Crisis series (1967–77) and *Dorothy Day, A Radical Devotion* (1987).

16. William D. Miller, *Dorothy Day, A Biography* (San Francisco: Harper & Row Publishers, 1982), 431. Day's biography of St. Therese of Lisieux was published in 1961.

17. Maurice Yves Sandoz, "The Visitation," in *Fantastic Memories* (Garden City, N.Y.: Doubleday, Doran and Company, Inc., 1945), 113–15. Sandoz was a Swiss scientist, musician, and author.

18. Sylvia Townsend Warner, "A Work of Art," in *The Spirit Rises* (New York: The Viking Press, 1962), 203–10. First published in *The New Yorker* 37 (April 22, 1961): 39–41.

19. Hugh Nissenson, "Charity," in *In the Reign of Peace* (New York: Farrar, Straus and Giroux, 1972), 51–63. Nissenson (b. 1933) is the author of several collections of short stories and a historical novel, *The Tree of Life* (1985).

20. J.F. Powers, "Defection of a Favorite," in *The Presence of Grace* (Garden City, N.Y.: Doubleday and Company, 1956), 113–14. First published in *The New Yorker*, 1951.

21. "The Devil Was a Joker," ibid., 69–75. First published in *The New Yorker*, 1953. Mac has a sideline of religious novelties he sells for his own profit or gives away to win favors; one of the objects is a deck of playing cards with the devil as joker.

22. Ray Bradbury, "The Beggar on Dublin Bridge," in *Saturday Evening Post Stories, 1962* (Garden City, N.Y.: Doubleday and Company, 1962), 206–21. Bradbury (b. 1920) is author of novels, poems, short stories, and film scripts.

23. Ibid., 221–22.

24. Penelope Lively, *City of the Mind* (New York: Harper Collins Publishers, 1991), 142–43. Lively (b. 1933) is an English novelist who has written books for children as well as adults.

25. Stuart Dybek, "Charity," in *Childhood and Other Neighborhoods* (New York: Viking Press, 1980), 139–52. Dybek (b. 1942) is a professor of English at Western Michigan University and author of *The Coast of Chicago* (1990). He grew up in Chicago and in the 1960s was for a time a caseworker for the Cook County Department of Public Aid.

26. The poor benefit from many of these organizations although even human service agencies such as children's day care and family service associations focus their

attention and resources on clients who are above the poverty line. Lester M. Salamon, "Social Services," in Charles T. Clotfelter, ed., *Who Benefits From the Non-Profit Sector?* (Chicago: University of Chicago Press, 1992), 134–38, 149–50.

27. Reed Whittemore, "Philanthropist," in *The Past, The Future, The Present Poems Selected and New* (Fayetteville: University of Arkansas Press, 1990), 94. Arthur Guiterman, "Charity," in *Gaily the Troubador* (New York: E.P. Dutton and Company, 1936), 61.

28 Langston Hughes, "How Thin a Blanket," in *Opportunity Journal of Negro Life*, 17 (December 1939): 361. *USED WITH THE PERMISSION OF THE NATIONAL URBAN LEAGUE, INC.*

29. J.F. Powers, *Wheat That Springeth Green* (New York: Alfred A. Knopf, 1988), 106, 110–11.

30. Ibid., 211.

31. *Village of Schaumburg v. Citizens for Better Environment*, 440 U.S. 620 (1980); and *Loper v. New York Police Department*, decided 30 Sept. 1992 and reported in the national edition of *The New York Times*, 2 October 1992, p. A18. The latter case was initiated by two professional beggars as a class action on behalf of all beggars. James J. Kilpatrick comments on the significance of Federal District Court Judge Robert W. Sweet's decision in his nationally syndicated column appearing in the *Palm Beach Post*, 16 January 1993, p. 23A.

17

Current History: Stories from Life

This chapter is based in large part on news items, feature stories, and obituaries culled from the newspapers I regularly read. It is a sampling of such stories rather than a scientific survey. In some cases I have omitted the names of the characters, partly to avoid causing them or their families embarrassment and partly because, although each is or was a real person, they are also representative figures. I am sure readers, drawing upon their personal knowledge, the newspapers they read, and the solicitations they receive, will be able to add more stories explaining the spirit, method, and, to some extent, the meaning of benevolence in our world and time.

Death stimulates giving in the form of memorial contributions to churches, hospices, colleges, and organizations promoting research and prevention of various diseases. When a popular merchant died of leukemia at the age of forty-four his family invited patrons of his store to contribute to a medical support trust to help pay for his heavy medical expenses. The husband and children of a beloved woman organized a Mother's Day Foundation in her memory. Donations to the foundation will be applied to its long-term goals: offering scholarships to students of opera, recognizing other mothers on Mother's Day, raising funds for diabetes research, and distributing dolls to homeless children during the holidays. The widow and son of a housing developer have established a Memorial Polo Tournament in his honor. Proceeds of the tournament have supported public television, museums, and educational institutions.[1]

An all too familiar story involves a child stricken with illness or injury, the cost of whose care is far beyond the ability of his or her parents to pay. In Okeechobee, Florida, a twelve-year-old boy contracted pneumonia that spread to a blood infection, requiring a month's stay in the hospital. The bills amounted to more than $98,000; his parents do not have medical insurance. The boy is "a well-liked kid." His Little League coach called a public meeting to see what kind of help the community could offer the family. Plans are under way for a softball tournament, a golf tournament, sale of "Friends of J.W." buttons, and a teen dance as benefits for the boy and his family. Another boy, nine years old, paralyzed for a year as a result of an auto accident, has received a Nintendo game he can operate with his mouth. The donor is a businessman who has set up a charitable trust that is raffling a 1993 Jeep to pay for the Nintendo and gifts to two terminally ill children.[2]

Lotteries are an old form of charitable fund raising. At a time when states raise money for education by selling lottery tickets it is not surprising that a YMCA and a hospice for the terminally ill in Florida should support their operations by raffling "dream homes." At the drawing for the hospice 3200 speculative givers who had each donated at least $100 groaned and laughed when the winner — not present and a resident of New Jersey — was announced. "Jeez, another snowbird moves to Florida for good," said the announcer. The hospice expects to raise as much as $140,000 from the raffle. The elderly couple who won the $260,000 house raffled by the Stuart, Florida, YMCA wonder whether they can afford to live in it; the YMCA may make as much as $400,000.[3]

Two professional golfers, Ken Green and Mark Calcavechia, have launched a project to provide group homes for orphans with little chance of being adopted. Since 1990 the Calgreen Foundation they organized has raised $200,000 by selling tickets to two celebrity golf tournaments. The foundation has purchased the first home, hopes to open it "in a couple of months," and is planning a third tournament. Tickets for the latter at $15 apiece are available at a West Palm Beach steak house; the price includes lunch.[4]

Nobody knows how many orphans there are in the United States. At one time the United States Children's Bureau, a federal agency established by Congress in 1912 "to investigate and report upon all matters relating to the welfare of children and child life among all classes of our people," would have been able to provide the information. Since the Nixon administration, however, the Bureau has been downgraded and its functions curtailed. "It is amazing," exclaimed Dr. David Michaels, a medical educator and researcher, "We do not keep track of children in the United States who lose their parents." Dr. Michaels was the chief author of a report published in the *Journal of The American Medical Association* (JAMA) in December 1992 that estimated that at that time there were 18,500 American children and adolescents not infected with the AIDS virus who had been orphaned by AIDS; the report estimated that by the year 2000 the number of AIDS orphans will be 80,000. "Most will be poor and black or Hispanic, living in communities least equipped to care for them," the report states, warning, "Unless increased attention and resources are devoted to this vulnerable population, a social catastrophe is unavoidable."[5]

Clara Hale (1905–92), who died a few days before release of the report on AIDS orphans, demonstrated the ability of a poor person, living in a disadvantaged neighborhood, to help others worse off than herself. Her father was murdered when she was a child and her mother, the inspiration of her work, died when she was sixteen. She and her husband had three children before he died at twenty-seven. She supported the children by cleaning houses by day and theaters by night, and later by caring for other people's children in her Harlem apartment. Eventually she became a licensed foster parent, raising forty foster children, all of whom finished high school and some of whom went to college.

In 1969, when Mother Hale was old enough to retire, her daughter encouraged her to take in one baby — followed by many others — who had become addicted to drugs while in its mother's womb. By the time of Clara Hale's death Hale House, the group home she founded in Harlem and which her daughter now heads, had sheltered 1000 babies, children of addicts and some born infected with the AIDS virus. As a group nursery, Hale House ran counter to the New York State policy of placing infants under five years with individual foster parents; until 1989 shortage of the latter allowed New York City to grant public funds to Hale House. Since the withdrawal of public funds the House has sought private donations.[6]

Business and charity get along better in fact than in fiction. Wilton, Connecticut, like many towns, is fortunate in having a leading citizen who believes civic generosity is good for business. Peter Keating, proprietor of the Village Market, knows the names of his customers, and he and his clerks treat them with consideration and civility. He contributes $20,000 a year to local organizations like Little League and YMCA, matched funds for a school piano and cheerleaders' uniforms, and has coached members of a Brownie troop in how to sell cookies. For similar reasons McDonald's in Salisbury, England, donates a portion of its proceeds to Salisbury Cathedral. The cathedral is the town's chief tourist attraction; McDonald's makes money feeding tourists. Operating expenses of the cathedral are $4,500 a day. Visitors pay no admission but a contribution of the equivalent of three dollars is suggested. They receive a coupon entitling them to two Big Macs for the price of one. One of the newest and most successful recipients of charitable contributions in the United States is Second Harvest, a network of food banks that in 1990 ranked just behind the Salvation Army and American Red Cross in amount of private support. Almost all the contributions it receives are in the form of unsalable but healthy foods, donated by food processors and supermarkets.[7]

Religion is the channel through which many people express good-will — and sometimes ill will — to others. A member who objected to his church's constant demands complained, "As far as I can see this Christian business is just one continuous Give, give, give." His pastor congratulated him on formulating an excellent definition of the Christian life.[8] Islamic or Jewish can be substituted for Christian in the definition because all three faiths emphasize charity as a religious obligation.

The day that follows Ramadan's month of fasting is called Eid-ul-Fur, which means feast of almsgiving; on that day Muslim worshippers make a special contribution for the poor. Members of real-life Dorcas societies, in both Protestant and Catholic churches, meet weekly to sew for the poor and patients in hospitals. Every Tuesday a group of women, all over fifty years of age, in Delray Beach, Florida, divide into groups of cutters, sewers, and "holy rollers" to make clothes for children of unwed mothers in the community and bandages for lepers overseas.[9] A sixty-three-year-old bachelor in Stuart, Florida, retired from work as clerk in the sheriff's office, "leads a secret life of service," visiting and taking clothes and toys to a children's hospital in Haiti and, for fifteen years, sponsoring Mexican orphans as godparent.[10]

On arriving in New York City in 1987 a Dominican immigrant made a "Promessa" to God that if he prospered as a carpet dealer and contractor he would do something for poor people in prison. After five years of success he has kept his vow by providing vocational training for selected inmates of the Riker's Island jail and helping graduates of the program (called M.I.T. for Mateo Institute of Training) find jobs on their release. Keeping faith by loyalty and steadfastness is as exemplary as keeping a vow. For more than forty years Elvin Nichols, a black Baptist, worked as porter and superintendent of maintenance at a synagogue in New York City. During his tenure the fortunes of the synagogue underwent drastic changes. As a result of population shifts the congregation, one of the richest and largest in the city in the 1940s, became in the 1970s one of the poorest and smallest. Through good times and bad Elvin Nichols kept on cleaning, tending the lighting and plumbing, somehow keeping a crumbling building intact, and greeting worshippers with a cheerful "Gut Shabbas." In the 1980s, after decades of decline, an infusion of young Jews with Eastern European backgrounds restored the synagogue to vigorous life. On Mr. Nichols's retirement in 1988 members of the congregation praised him as "the glue that held it all together" and for being the kind of person who showed love just by being himself. When the party was over Mr. Nichols commented, "I didn't realize I was so well-liked."[11]

Much of our benevolence consists not in good deeds or voluntary service but simply in sending a check to some agency or institution. There are a million nonprofit organizations in the United States; half of them are registered as tax-exempt charities supported by soliciting individuals, corporations, and foundations. Many charitable organizations also receive grants from government, earn income from investments, and charge user fees, or in the case of colleges and universities, tuition and money for board and room. Tax-assisted (formerly tax-supported) institutions also seek contributions from private donors; public television and radio stations, museums, libraries, and even parks have "friends" associations that raise funds to supplement public appropriations; at city and state colleges and universities development staffs are expanding while academic programs are being cut back.[12]

Because programs offered by charities are nearly as numerous and diverse as products displayed in a supermarket or drug store, agencies have to compete with one another to catch the attention and sympathy of prospective donors. Whether more inclined to give to health organizations than to social service groups, or vice versa, or well-disposed to both, donors have to pick and choose between agencies which often seem to have similar programs. Rivalries in charity mirror those in business and religion: as in business a well-established and successful service program for poor children at home and overseas attracts competition from a new agency using a similar name and logo; as in religion evangelical and fundamentalist groups insist on doing under their own auspices and in their own way something that is already being done by a secular or mainstream religious agency. In contrast to service agencies, advocacy organizations promoting programs and policies for children, the handicapped, or the environment tend to compete on their respective degree of militancy from moderate to extreme.[13]

It goes without saying that many people give from sentiment, habit, or impulse. Dollar-minded donors can choose between competing service organizations on the basis of the percentage of the agencies' income spent on the program, which should ordinarily be 70 percent or more, as distinct from income devoted to administrative and fund-raising expenses. Using data obtained from a trade journal, *Non Profit Times, Money* ranked the 100 best charities in the United States in order of efficiency, the percentage of income spent on program. The overall average was 80 percent, but figures for individual agencies have to take into account that administrative and fund-raising costs may be kept low by using volunteer and low-paid clerical administrators and by placing too-generous dollar values on "in kind" gifts of old clothes or unsaleable food. On the other hand, fund-raising expenses may be high because the typical donation for name-and-address stickers is small or because the agency assumes new responsibilities requiring additional appeals for help.[14]

Telemarketing firms raising money for police and firefighters' associations, usually by selling bumper stickers or tickets to concerts or sporting events, receive low marks from evaluators on percentage of revenue turned over to the association but earn high profits for themselves. In these campaigns the usual percentages are reversed: about 20 percent goes to the "program" — the police or firefighters' associations and 80 percent to the fund raisers. Of course, as their defenders argue, the promoters do all the work; the drive costs the associations nothing and helps support the causes they are interested in.[15]

In *Coasting* (1987), an account of his circumnavigation of Great Britain in a small boat, Jonathan Raban reports the social life of English retirees and tax exiles on the Isle of Man revolves around charities for arthritis, blindness, kidney and heart disease, and physical and mental handicap. There are so many ailments and afflictions, each with a fund of its own, holding concerts, dances, or dinners that the season from September to March is a dizzy whirl from disease to disease.[16]

Something similar on a grander scale takes place in Palm Beach, Florida, every winter where, almost nightly, society women and their escorts pay large sums to attend balls at the Breakers Hotel for the American Red Cross, the Heart Fund, other medical charities, and The Preservation Society of Palm Beach and to save wildlife in remote areas of the world. Such entertainments are held in other cities, but in Palm Beach, as on the Isle of Man, there isn't much else to do. Holding a successful ball, one that raises money and is such a work of art that it impresses jaded socialites, is such a challenging task that some energetic and able people make a career of organizing and promoting them. Helen B. Rich, who died in 1993 at the age of eighty-nine, helped Marjorie Merriwether Post organize the first American Red Cross Ball and was for many years the leading organizer of such affairs. Mrs. Rich's pet greyhound received invitations from Mrs. Post to visit Mar a Lago with notations: "Bring your Mother;" a widow whose husband died young, Mrs. Rich described her life as "an immensely happy one, but completely by accident." At the time of her death a friend recalled she had "a nun's ability" to make people give to charitable causes.[17]

A common reaction to newspaper reports of charity balls is exasperation. What displays of extravagance and insolent unconcern they seem when—not in Palm Beach itself, but not far away—homeless people are looking for shelter, laid-off aerospace workers are despairing of ever finding well-paying jobs again, and migrant workers huddle in desolate barracks. But the balls have an economic function and serve the needs of society, in both senses of the word; some agencies derive as much as one third of their annual budgets from a single ball. Moreoever, as Samuel Johnson would remind us, the balls provide employment and contribute to the well-being of many people: hotel staff from top to bottom, decorators, caterers, florists, musicians, entertainers, novelty makers, dressmakers, hairdressers, jewelers, wholesale grocers, wine and liquor dealers, limousine rental agencies, insurance agents, off-duty police officers, society reporters and photographers, and parking attendants. Tips to the parking attendants average

$1 a car; after a recent gala one of them told a reporter, "Some people will give you $5 and then some guy with a Rolls-Royce will just get in and drive off."[18]

Both Johnson and Bernard de Mandeville, who Johnson credited with opening his eyes to the real world, would be interested in reports coming out of Somalia early in 1993 that food shipments to that famine-stricken, war-torn country had the potential for harm as well as good. The paradox of famine relief, according to Alison Mitchell in a dispatch to the *New York Times*, is that "the international charity that stopped starvation eventually can be a problem in itself, threatening to destroy what little remains of the local farm economy." In January 1993 there were still hungry and undernourished people in Somalia; representatives of the International Committee of the Red Cross estimated two million people would remain dependent on free food "for the foreseeable future." The influx of relief food, however, had drasticaly reduced the market price of staples like rice, sugar, and corn. Some (not all) officials of relief agencies expressed fear that superfluity of donated food would cause a new cycle of dependency by discouraging farmers from planting crops. A Somali woman who survived the country's civil war harvested a large crop of corn in September 1992 but four months later had not been able to find a buyer for it. "Nobody is interested," she told Mitchell. "Everybody has his own relief supply."[19]

Matel Dawson, a seventy-one-year-old forklift truck operator at the Ford Motor Company in Detroit, donated $50,000 to the United Negro College Fund. In earlier contributions he has given $30,000 to the fund. Dawson's formal schooling ended with the ninth grade but he believes support for Negro higher education is the best investment he can make. "Other blacks," he states, "should do the same to help invest in their education."[20]

Ella Thompson, a tenant leader in the William Penn Homes, a rundown public housing project in Chester, Pennsylvania, takes a judicious attitude toward the planned renovation of the buildings. "New brick and mortar are fine," she told a reporter. "But you have to mend the families, too." She speaks from firsthand knowledge: she is raising her seven-year-old grandson, Aaron, whose father died about the time he was born and whose mother deserted him when she became addicted to drugs. Aaron and other fortunate children in the William Penn

Homes are the beneficiaries of a new initiative launched by Eugene M. Lang, founder in 1981 of the "I Have a Dream" program. Mr. Lang and other sponsors who are able to contribute or raise $400,000 adopt a group of about fifty elementary-school pupils, promise to pay the college tuition of any who finish high school, and keep in close personal touch with the children throughout their school years. The new plan will take the "I Have a Dream" program into housing projects and enlist the assistance of colleges located near the projects. The program was scheduled to go into effect at projects in Chicago, Denver, and New York City, as well as Chester, in 1993; and in 1994 at housing projects in Los Angeles, Boston, and Delray Beach, Florida. Swarthmore College, the University of Denver, Illinois Institute of Technology in Chicago, and the New School for Social Research in New York City are among the colleges and universities involved in the plan. The sponsor of the program at a New York housing project, Gloria Jaricki, a philanthropist of Rye, New York, realizes she is taking on a difficult assignment. "It is easy to make out a check to your favorite charity once a year," she says, "but it's another to look at kids' faces and help them develop over 10 or 12 years."[21]

DeWitt Wallace (1891–1981), founder of *Reader's Digest*, and his wife Lila Acheson Wallace (1890–1984) were childless. Associates of DeWitt Wallace remember that he called the couple's philanthropies "our babies." Before their deaths they established "support organizations" to provide perpetual assistance to some of their favorite institutions: The Metropolitan Museum of Art, Lincoln Center, and the Sloan-Kettering Cancer Center in New York City, and Macalester College in St. Paul. They also established a number of trusts for specific purposes within the New York Community Foundation. One of these, appropriately enough, is for restoration of the periodical room of the New York Public Library where, in 1922, DeWitt Wallace began condensing articles from magazines he could not afford to buy for publication in the fledgling *Reader's Digest*. In their wills the Wallaces left no instructions regarding the philanthropic purposes to which their fortunes should be directed.

In 1987 four funds established during the Wallaces' lifetime merged into two: the DeWitt Wallace — Reader's Digest Fund and the Lila Wallace — Reader's Digest Fund. The officers and directors of the two funds are identical. A former executive director of the funds, who had previously been the Wallaces' personal lawyer, criticized the addition of Reader's Digest to the funds' names on the grounds that Mrs. Wallace, in particular, would not have wanted her philanthropies "corporatized." The chairman of the funds defends the action, pointing out that increase in the value of the funds' holdings of Readers Digest Association stock has made them among the wealthiest of American foundations.[22]

In 1989 the DeWitt Wallace-Reader's Digest Fund, which supports projects in education and youth leadership, invested $40 million in Library Power, a program intended to reopen and reinvigorate closed, neglected, and inadequately financed school libraries in twenty-five cities. Library Power has been widely praised for making school libraries inviting, encouraging students to read, and updating library collections. Naomi S. Smartt, principal of an elementary school in the East Flatbush section of Brooklyn, is enthusiastic about the impact of the program on faculty and staff and the favorable response of the students. She is troubled, however, by the fact that in the neighborhood where the school is located there is no other library within walking distance. "We have children through fifth grade. Then what happens?" she asks.[23]

At the end of 1990 the fund named after Lila Wallace had assets of $577 million and was a major source of contributions to museums and the performing, visual, and literary arts. The program, although modest in comparison to the federally financed and often embattled National Endowment for the Arts, has symbolic as well as tangible value in stimulating and enhancing the credibility of both philanthropic and public support for the arts.[24]

Tax laws can encourage or discourage giving for the arts as well as for other charitable purposes. Before 1986 the laws encouraged giving by allowing donors to deduct the current market value of paintings, securities, or real estate donated to a museum or educational institution. The Tax Reform Act of 1986 allows donors to claim only the original purchase price, often much lower than current market value, as tax deductible. Since 1990 intermittent efforts have been made to restore market-value deductability in order to persuade donors to donate possessions that have appreciated in value instead of keeping or selling them on the open market. In February 1993 President Clinton announced his support for restoration of the "charitable-gifts tax break." Among those who cheered the announcement was the president of the Metropolitan Museum of Art. "It's superb news," he said. "It means that the Clinton Administration supports investments in our large cultural institutions around the country."[25]

The artist and collector Judith Rothschild, who died in 1993, provided in her will for a substantial investment in modern American art. Her collection of her own paintings and works by major modern artists, some of which her parents bought at her urging, is believed to be worth $40 million. Through the Judith Rothschild Foundation the proceeds of her estate will be used during the next twenty-five years to help public museums and galleries buy works of contemporary American artists.[26]

In 1993 the opening of "Splendid Legacy: the Havemeyer Collection," an exhibit at the Metropolitan Museum of Art, prompted art critic Michael Kimmelman to call attention to the role women have played in the past century as patrons, collectors, advisers, and founders of museums. Louisine (Mrs. Henry Osborne) Havemeyer and her friend and adviser Mary Cassatt were mainly responsible for assembling the group of nineteenth-century French paintings that are the core of the immense Havemeyer collection. The 2,000 paintings and objects Mrs. Havemeyer began giving to the Metropolitan in 1929 in the name of her husband remains, in the words of Kimmelman, "perhaps the single greatest gift ever given to the museum, not least because it was made with no strings attached, no galleries to be named after them, no rules about how the collection could be displayed. Mrs. Havemeyer explained the lack of stipulations about the placements and care of the collection with grace and courtesy: "I believe there are those who are as intelligent and as interested as I in the care and conservation of a valuable gift."[27]

A donor may acknowledge the value of a gift, as Mrs. Havemeyer did, without extolling the generosity that impelled it. The Spartans set an example for later givers by minimizing the sacrifice involved in their gift of grain to Smyrna (chapter 1, p. 9). The present tendency, as we have seen, is to replace the element of sacrifice in charitable giving with fun, profit, investment, and tax saving. When the snowbirds leave Florida in the late spring year-round residents, in return for $25 donations to the Cancer and Lung Societies or $15 to the Arthritis Foundation, receive golf privilege cards good for free or reduced greens fees at participating golf courses ("Golf carts required but not included").[28]

In the sense of giving and feeling love, charity continues to show itself in ways that have nothing to do with personal advantage. Many years after becoming a paraplegic as a result of injuries suffered in 1958 in an automobile accident, the former baseball player Roy Campanella said, "I know that breaking your neck is a tough way to learn a lesson. But lying in bed, paralyzed, I learned two things: tolerance and patience, toward myself and everybody else. That's love, isn't it?"[29]

Notes

1. The first item is based on personal experience; the second and third are from obituaries in *The New York Times* (hereafter cited as *NYT*), 12 Oct. 1992, p. A16, and 3 Mar. 1993, p. C17; except where otherwise noted all citations are to the National edition.
2. Helen Gieser, "Names and Faces," *Palm Beach Post* (hereafter cited as *PBP*), 4 Feb. 1993, p. 12D; Michael Lasandra, "Medical Matters," ibid., 19 Feb. 1993, p. 16A.
3. Mitch McKenney, "Visitor is Winner of $225,000 Home," ibid., 29 Mar. 1993, p. 1B; Jeff Houch, "Stuart Couple Wins $260,000 Home," ibid. , 9 April 1993, p. 1B.
4. Thom Smith, "Pro Golfers Raise Money for Orphans," ibid., 19 Feb. 1993, p. 1D.
5. Ibid., 23 Dec. 1992, pp. 1A, 5A. David Michaels and Carol Levine, "Estimates of Motherless Youth Orphaned by AIDS in the United States," *JAMA* 268 (23 Dec. 1992), p. 3456. The report did not consider the possible presence of male parents because such men would probably have potentially fatal AIDS infections.
6. Bruce Lambert, "Clara Hale, 87, Who Aided Addicts' Babies, Dies," *NYT*, 20 Dec. 1992, p. 50 (Metropolitan edition).
7. Andrew H. Malcolm, "Connecticut Grocer Thrives With His Personal Touches," ibid., 29 January 1993, p. A14. "Give to This Day . . . ," *World Press Review*, Jan. 1993, p. 4; Felicity Barringer, "In the Worst of Times American Keeps Giving," *NYT*, 15 Mar. 1992, p. 6E.
8. W.F.A. Stride in *The (Old) Farmer's Almanac, 1939* (Brookline, Mass.: Mabel M. Swan, 1938), 51.
9. Mitch McKenney, "500 Gather for Muslim Holy Day, *PBP*, 26 March 1993, p. 2B; Shana Gruskin, "Delray Group Helps Clothe the Needy," ibid., 4 Feb. 1993, p. 5B.
10. Sally Schwartz, "Stuart Bachelor Leads Secret Life Helping Children," ibid., 25 Jan. 1993, p. 1B.
11. Michael T. Kaufman, "A Promise to Inmates Comes Due," *NYT*, 19 Dec. 1992, p. 16; Douglas Martin, "Keeping Faith: A Loyal Porter and A Synagogue," *NYT*, 19 Oct. 1988, p. 24.
12. Barringer, "In the Worst of Times America Keeps Giving," p. 6E; Maria Newman, "As States Cut Aid, Public Colleges Work Harder for Private Money," *NYT*, 29 Mar. 1993, pp. A1, B12.

13. Andrew L. Yarrow, "2 Charities for Poor Children Battle for a Name and a Turf," ibid., 2 Jan. 1992, p. A12; Jason De Parle, "Advocates Sell Antipoverty Policies Beneath Faces of America's Children," ibid., 29 Mar. 1993, p. A8.

14. Marguerite T. Smith, "Giving Wisely When the Need is Great," *Money*, Dec. 1992, pp. 113–23. The agencies referred to in the last sentence are Disabled Veterans of America, which spent about 29 percent of the receipts of its mail solicitation on fund raising; and the United Negro College Fund, which, after the Los Angeles riots, began a campaign to raise money to help send minority youth in that city to college.

15. Charles Elmore, "Telemarketers Get Rich Off Donors to Police, Firefighters," *PBP*, 28 Mar. 1992, pp. 1A, 4A.

16. Jonathan Raban, *Coasting* (New York: Simon and Schuster, 1987), 76–77. Raban (b. 1942) is an English critic, novelist, and travel writer.

17. Mitch McKenney, "Helen B. Rich, Charity Organizer, Ex-Society Writer, Dies," *PBP*, 1 April 1993, p. 3B.

18. Loretta Grantham, "Putting It Together: The Heart Ball, Feb. 14," ibid., 25 Feb. 1993, p. 1D. Renate Yates, *Social Death, An Entertainment in Three Months* (London: Century, 1986) is a fictional account of preparations for a gala organized by the Crutches for Cripples Society (Mental Health Branch) in Sydney, Australia.

19. Alison Mitchell, "A New Question in Somalia: When Does Free Food Hurt?," *NYT*, 13 Jan. 1993, pp.A1, A3. For Johnson's statement of his debt to Mandeville see chapter 6, p. 59.

20. *NYT*, 19 Dec. 1992, p. 13.

21. Michael de Courcey Hinds, "Fishing for College Prospects in the Projects," ibid., 20 Jan. 1993, pp. 1A, 5B.

22. Kathleen Teltsch, "Digest Founder's Legacy Gives $150 Million a Year to Various Institutions," ibid., 26 Oct. 1992, p. B4.

23. Kathleen Teltsch, "$40 Million Gift to Help School Libraries in 25 Cities," ibid., 29 Oct. 1992, pp. B1, B4.

24. In the year ending January 31, 1990, the Lila Wallace- Reader's Digest Fund awarded $32.2 million in 88 grants. In 1990–91 the National Endowment for the Arts dispensed approximately $170 million. James P. Pinkerton, a columnist for *Newsday*, advocates as a first step in federal budget cuts "eliminating the National Endowment for the Arts, not because it finances pornographic art but because it finances art, period, and that's a luxury we can't afford right now." "A Call for the Loyal Opposition," *PBP*, 26 Feb. 1993, p. 16A.

25. William Grimes, "Clinton Proposes to Restore Charitable-Gifts Tax Break," *NYT*, 19 Feb. 1993, pp. 1A, B9.

26. Bruce Lambert, "Judith Rothschild, 71, a Painter; Began Foundation to Help Artists," ibid., 16 Mar. 1993, p. B9.

27. Michael Kimmelman, "The Havemeyer Legacy Spotlighted at the Met," ibid., 26 Mar. 1993, pp. B1, B8. Mrs. Havemeyer's statement is quoted in the article. Neil

Harris comments on the significance of the Havemeyer Collection for the Metropolitan Museum in his biographical sketch of Louisine Havemeyer (1855–1929) in Edward T. James, ed., *Notable American Women* 2 (1971): 156–58.

28. Advertisements in *PBP*, 11 April 1993, PGA Seniors Championship Tournament Supplement.

29. Dave Anderson, "Campy Has Never Stopped Smiling During His Long Ordeal," *NYT*, 22 Feb. 1990, p. B10. Anderson repeated Campanella's statement in an article published after the latter's death. "In Campanella, The Heart of a Hero." *NYT*, 28 June 1993, p. B5.

Afterword

For a short book *Giving* covers a lot of ground and a long span of time. Another author might have produced a lengthier volume, heavier in detail, and more profound in analysis. I chose to write a book of modest dimension with no attempt at definitiveness because my purpose was to share with others the pleasure I have found in discovering what writers, past and present, have had to say—or have had their characters say—about charity and philanthropy, and in considering the circumstances and significance of their observations. Strength of opinion, whether favorable or unfavorable, and eloquence of expression were my criteria for inclusion; I did not include or exclude persons solely on the grounds of gender. Because selection was based on one person's reading and research numerous authors whose works might or should have been included escaped notice. Publication of the paperback edition provides a welcome opportunity to call attention to writers, characters, and opinions not mentioned in the earlier edition.

Inducing others to give, depending on the actors, can be an important and valuable service (see page 18) or a subterfuge for evading the burden of helping others. Mrs. Norris, the close-fisted wife of a poor clergyman in Jane Austen's *Mansfield Park* (1814) chooses the latter course of charity by remote control. Austen (1775-1817) says of her: "As far as walking, talking, and contriving reached, she was thoroughly benevolent, and nobody knew better how to dictate benevolence to others: but her love of money was equal to her love of directing, and she knew quite well how to save her own as to spend that of her friends."[1] Mrs. Norris persuades her good-natured but indolent sister and rich brother-in-law to undertake the care and education of a poorer sister's daughter, an expensive charity to which she has no intention of contributing anything but advice. Her intervention is inspired by a meddlesome, domineering disposition rather than by sympathy for her impoverished sister or affection for her niece. Nevertheless, when the matter is arranged she returns to the parsonage "in the happy belief of being the most liberal-minded sister and aunt in the world."[2]

213

Selfishness and too easily satisfied self-esteem make Mrs. Norris an unsympathetic character. A kinder and more generous person, or Mrs. Norris seen and portrayed in a different light, might win the reader's approval for stirring the conscience of a well-to-do relative to care for a less fortunate member of the family. When sympathy reaches out to disadvantaged groups outside the immediate family and the public rather than siblings are called on to help, the appeal is called advocacy and recognized, by most, as a legitimate function of philanthropy.

An unmarried woman, without money of her own, living in the country in the home of her parents does not seem a likely subject for philanthropic study. Aunt Lois is a character in *Old Town Folks* (1869), a novel by Harriet Beecher Stowe (1811-96) published a half-century after *Mansfield Park* and taking place for the most part, in the 1790s in rural New England. There are several reasons for paying attention to her. In the first place, although her area of operations and scale of giving are small, she is alert to need and effective in dealing with it. "No person," says Stowe, "rendered more deeds of kindness in the family and the neighborhood than Aunt Lois," and these deeds enhanced her standing and authority among relatives and neighbors. Another reason is her intense involvement in her charitable activities and the extraordinary demands she made on the recipients of her assistance:

> She . . . bore the cares of the whole family on her heart; she watched and prayed and scolded for all. Had she cared less, she might perhaps have appeared more amiable. She invested herself, so to speak, in others and it was vital to her happiness, not only that they should be happy, but that they should be happy on her pattern and in her way. She had drawn out the whole family chart, and if she had only had power to make each one walk tractably in the path she foreordained her sharp, thin face might have had a few less wrinkles. It seemed to her so perfectly evident that the ways she fixed upon for each one were ways of pleasantness and paths of peace, that she scarcely could have patience with Providence for allowing things to fall out in a way so entirely different from her designs.[3]

Aunt Lois is not a likeable person; she might have been depicted as an irascible family tyrant. The best reason for studying her is to note the insight and charity Stowe brings to her portrayal. Without ignoring the absurd and unpleasant aspects of Lois's character Stowe penetrates the "outside wrapper of sharp austerity" to reveal her kind and gentle traits.

Aunt Lois is such a lifelike figure that it is tempting to think Stowe modeled her after someone she knew. Edward Gibbon (1737-94) believed his Aunt Hester was the original of Miranda in William Law's devotional book *A Serious Call to a Devout and Holy Life* (1728), but it is more likely that Hester Gibbon (1704-90) patterned her mature life after the character in Law's book. Miranda is the central figure in chapter 8 of *A Serious Call* dealing with the "Wise and Pious Use of an Estate." Miranda divides her fortune "between herself, and several other poor people, . . . and has only her part of relief from it. She thinks it is the same folly to indulge herself in needless, vain expenses as to give to other people to spend in the same way." She would not give a poor person a penny to go to a puppet show, nor would she think of spending the money in the same way herself. In order to support her charities she lives very frugally. "If you were to see her," Law wrote of Miranda, "You would wonder what poor body it was. . . . She has but one rule that she observes in her dress, to be always clean, and in the cheapest of things. . . . She eats only for the sake of living, and with so regular an abstinence that every meal is an exercise in self-denial."[4]

Law (1686-81) was tutor to Hester Gibbon's brother (the father of the historian), was held in esteem and affection by all members of the family, and was living with them when *A Serious Call* was published. Hester Gibbon, after the death of her father, had an income of five or six hundred pounds a year, sufficient to enable her to live independent of her family. In the 1740s she and a woman friend, also well-to-do and a disciple of Law, joined his household in Kings Cliffe, Northamptonshire. There they put into practice the principles Law had set forth in *A Serious Call*: charity, economy in personal and household expenditures, and frequent prayer, bible-reading, and singing of hymns and psalms. The only luxury they permitted themselves was purchase of pious books for a library they shared with others. Their extensive charities included the founding of schools for boys and girls and building alms houses for widows and spinsters. They gave the milk from the four cows they kept to the poor and everyday they distributed soup—after Law had tasted it to approve its quality—to all who asked for it. They persisted in acts of kindness and generosity despite complaints of townspeople and clergy that the help they gave to beggars was swamping the parish in poverty. Law had anticipated and answered objections to indiscriminate charity in *A Serious Call*. Scripture, he wrote "plainly teaches us, that the merit of persons is to be no rule of our charity, but that we are to do acts of kindness to those that least of all deserve it." In Law's opinion the same "thoughtless objection" that giving encourages people to become beggars could be raised against all charities including clothing the naked and tending the sick, since they might lead people to depend on others, neglect themselves, and be careless of their health. "When the love of God dwelleth in you," Law tells his readers, past and present, "when it has enlarged your heart, and filled you with . . . mercy and compassion, you will make no more such objections as these."[5]

Hester Gibbon outlived Law by almost forty years, paid for his tomb, and had her friend and housemate laid to rest at the foot of his grave. Her nephew, the historian, survived her by only a few years and received a small but welcome legacy from her. Edward Gibbon, acknowledging that he was ill-qualified to speak of "the pain and pleasures of a spiritual life," was inclined to believe his aunt in life had not been unhappy. "Her penance was voluntary," Gibbon wrote in *Memories of My Life* (1796) and, in her own eyes, meritorious; and instead of the insignificance of an old maid, she was surrounded by dependents, poor and abject as they were, who implored her bounty, and imbibed her lessons."[6]

Gibbon praised Law as a "worthy and pious man, who believed all that he professed and practiced all that he enjoyned" but observed that *A Serious Call* exposed the contradiction between faith and practice in Christianity. "Hell-fire and eternal damnation are darted from every page of the book: and it is indeed somewhat whimsical that the Fanatics who most vehemently inculcate the love of God should be those who despoil him of every amiable attribute."[7]

Gibbon's "Fanatics" are usually more impressed by the awesome than the amiable attributes of God. That was certainly true of Jonathan Edwards, a younger contemporary of William Law. Edwards (1703-58), in striving to inculcate the love of God in his New England congregation, often found it useful to put the fear of God in them by graphically describing the terrors of Hell. "They stand on the brink of it," he said in explaining the reasonableness of his fiery sermons, "and are just ready to fall into it, and are senseless of their danger. Is it not a reasonable thing to fright a person out of a house on fire?"[8]

Edwards's sermon "Charity and Its Fruits" (1738), preached a decade after Law's *A Serious Call* and taking chapter 13 of the Apostle Paul's letter to the Corinthians as its text, uses the word charity to mean love, especially love of God. Charity in the sense of "a disposition to hope and think the best of persons, and to put a good construction on their words or behavior" or "a disposition to give to the poor" is but a pale shadow of the love of God, the great virtue "so much insisted on in the New Testament."[9] Like Cotton Mather in *Bonafacius or Essays to Do Good* (1710) Edwards lists and discusses ways in which men and women can demonstrate love of God by serving fellow creatures. Both Mather and Edwards regard chiding others for their faults as a valuable service to God. Edwards goes beyond Mather in citing reclamation of the vicious "by putting them in mind of their misery and danger and so being the instruments of their awakening" as a prime example of the good men may do for others. By helping others in their external circumstances, that is by feeding, clothing, or otherwise making them more comfortable, we gain an advantage in the all-important work of saving their souls.[10]

Whether the purpose of charitable and philanthropic giving is personal salvation, as some writers continue to assume, the salvation of others, as Edwards suggests, or simply self-esteem and worldly recognition and reward remains open to question. The views of another thinker not mentioned in the earlier edition of *Giving* deserves brief mention. The humanist Erasmus (1466? - 1536) was as critical as Luther of abuses in the unreformed Church but he remained loyal to the monastic ideal of religious contemplation, study, and charity and adhered to the New Testament conception of society as an organism, the body of Christ. "Whatever happens to one member of the body happens to the entire body" he wrote in *Handbook of the Militant Christian* (1501). "We are all members of one another." Therefore "we will not envy happier members, and will willingly help weaker ones. We will know that we have received a benefit when we help our neighbor, and also know that we have been injured when harm has been done to our brother."[11]

Erasmus, a member of the same mendicant order of monks as Luther, the Augustinians, scoffed at a person who, with one vow, disposes of all his property and, with another, assumes a lifetime of begging. At the same time he also believed that devoting one's life to the pursuit of wealth was unwise because there were better things to do with one's time, and also because "what wealth really brings is a host of evils." It is not wrong to have money, he declared: "It only becomes wrong when money is loved as an end instead of looked upon as a means." Those who become rich should act like the generous steward; those who become poor should feel as though a friend has relieved them of a dangerous burden.[12] He reserved his harshest criticism for the misers of every age who assert that their property, great or small, is theirs alone, to do with as they will, heedless of the travail of others and indifferent to pleas for their help. In his judgment "the worst evil is hardness of heart,"[13] an affliction affecting behavior of people in all walks of life.

The names of other writers will almost certainly occur to students. Since the aim of *Giving* is to stimulate rather than exhaust interest in the subject I shall leave it to them to satisfy curiosity about those writers' views by consulting their works.

Notes

1. Jane Austen, *Mansfield Park* (New York: Everyman's Library, 1992), 8, chapter 1.
2. Ibid., 9.
3. Harriet Beecher Stowe, *Old Town Folks* (New York: Library of America, 1982), 922. This passage is quoted in Robert H. Bremner, "The Blue River of Truth: Literature and Philanthropy," *Nonprofit Management & Leadership*, 6 (Fall 1995): 106-7.
4. William Law, "A Serious Call to a Devout and Holy Life" in Law, *Selected Writings*, ed. by Janet Louth (Manchester, England: Fyfield Books, 1990), 50-53.
5. Ibid., 56-57. Law and his companions's charitable activities in Kings Cliffe, and their neighbors' response to them are discussed in Leslie Stephen, "Law, William (1686-1761)" in *Dictionary of National Biography*, vol 11: 678-79; Arthur Mee, *Northamptonshire, County of Spires and Stately Homes* (London: Hodden and Stoughton, 1945), 187; Tony Iverson, *Northamptonshire* (London: Robert Hale Limited, 1954), 280-81; and John Steane, *The Northamptonshire Landscape* (London: Hodder and Stoughton, 1974), 220-21.
6. Edward Gibbon, *Memories of My Life*, ed. by Georges A. Bonnard (London: Thomas Nelson and Sons Ltd., 1960), 21, 333 n. 15.
7. Ibid., 22-23. At least in the pages devoted to Miranda, *A Serious Call*, contains no mention of hell-fire and damnation.
8. Quoted in Clarence H. Faust and Thomas H. Johnson, eds., *Jonathan Edwards, Representative Selections* (New York: American Book Company, 1935), 22-23.
9. "Charity and Its Fruits" in *Jonathan Edwards Ethical Writings*, ed. by Paul Ramsey (New Haven and London: Yale University Press, 1989), 129. (Volume 8 of Jonathan Edwards *Works*, General Editor Perry Miller, John E. Miller et al., 13 vols. to date. New Haven and London: Yale University Press, 1957-74).
10. Ibid., 207-8.
11. Erasmus, *Handbook of the Militant Christian*, translated with an introductory essay by John P. Dolan (Notre Dame, Ind.: Fides Publishers Inc., 1962), 131, 150. *Enchiridion Militis Christiani*, written by Erasmus in 1501 was published in Antwerp in 1504 and reissued in 1518 "as the manifesto of Erasmianism in the early debates of the Reformation." Brian Pullam, *Rich and Poor in Renaissance Venice* (Oxford, Basil Blackwell, 1971), 224.
12. Erasmus, *Handbook of the Militant Christian*, 151.
13. Ibid., 131, 146.

Bibliography
Principal Works Cited and Consulted

General

Adler, Mortimer J., and Charles Van Doren. *Great Treasury of Western Thought*. New York and London: R.R. Bowker Company, 1977.

Ausubel, Nathan, ed. *A Treasury of Jewish Folklore: Stories, Traditions, Legends, Humor, Wisdom and Folk Songs of the Jewish People*. New York: Crown Publishers, Inc., 1948.

————. *A Treasury of Jewish Humor*. Garden City, N.Y.: Doubleday and Company, 1951.

Blain, Virginia, Patricia Clements, and Isobel Grundy. *The Feminist Companion to Literature in English*. New Haven: Yale University Press, 1990.

Coles, Robert. *The Call of Stories. Teaching and the Moral Imagination*. Boston: Houghton Mifflin Company, 1989.

Curti, Merle. "Philanthropy." In Philip P. Wiener, ed., *Dictionary of the History of Ideas*, 3:486–93. 4 vols. New York: Charles Scribner's Sons, 1973.

Daly, Mary. "Faith, Hope, and Charity." In Philip P. Wiener, ed., *Dictionary of the History of Ideas*. 2:209–16. 4 vols., New York: Charles Scribner's Sons, 1973.

Drabble, Margaret, ed. *The Oxford Companion to English Literature*. Oxford: Oxford University Press, 1985.

Eliade, Mircea, ed. in chief, *The Encyclopedia of Religion*. 16 vols. New York: The Macmillan Publishing Company, 1987.

Gabel, John B., and Charles Wheeler. *The Bible as Literature, An Introduction*. New York: Oxford University Press, 1986.

Hart, James D., ed. *The Oxford Companion to American Literature*. New York: Oxford University Press, 1986.

Joy, Charles R., comp. *A Concordance Of Bible Readings*. Cleveland and New York: The World Publishing Company, 1965.

Loch, Charles Stewart. "Charity and Charities." In *The Encyclopedia Brittanica*, eleventh edition, 2:860–91. 29 vols. New York: The Encyclopedia Brittanica Co., 1910.

McCarthy, Kathleen D. "The Gospel of Wealth: American Giving in Theory and Practice." In Richard Magat, ed., *Philanthropic Giving*. New York: Oxford University Press, 1989.

Mencken, H.L., ed. *A New Dictionary of Quotations on Historical Principles from Ancient and Modern Sources*. New York: Alfred A. Knopf, 1942.

Mitchison, Rosalind. *Coping with Destitution: Poverty and Relief in Western Europe*. Toronto: University of Toronto Press, 1991.

O'Connell, Brian. *America's Voluntary Spirit. A Book of Readings*. New York: The Foundation Center, 1983.

Payton, Robert L. "Philanthropic Values." In Richard Magat, ed., *Philanthropic Giving*, 29–45. New York: Oxford University Press, 1989.

————. *Philanthropy, Voluntary Action for the Public Good*. New York: American Council on Education, 1988.

Pray, Kenneth L.M. "Charity." In *Encyclopedia of the Social Sciences*, 3: 340–45. 15 vols. New York: The Macmillan Company, 1930–34.

Rosten, Leo. *The Joys of Yiddish*. New York: McGraw Hill Book Company, 1968.

————. *Leo Rosten's Treasury of Jewish Quotations*. New York: McGraw Hill Book Company, 1972.

Salzman, Jack, ed. *The Cambridge Handbook of American Literature*. Cambridge: Cambridge University Press, 1986.

Scott, Austin W. "Charitable Trusts." In *Encyclopedia of the Social Sciences*, 3:338–40. 15 vols. New York: The Macmillan Company, 1930–34.

Stapleton, Michael, ed. *The Cambridge Guide to English Literature* Cambridge: Cambridge University Press, 1983.

Woods, Ralph L., comp. & ed. *The World Treasury of Religious Quotations*. New York: Hawthorn Books, Inc., 1966.

Part One   The Ancient World

Alter, Robert, and Frank Kermode. *The Literary Guide to the Bible*. Cambridge, Mass.: Harvard University Press, 1987.

St. Augustine. *On Christian Doctrine*. Translated by D.W. Robertson, Jr. Indianapolis: Bobbs-Merrill Educational Publisher, 1958.

Baron, Salo Wittmayer. *A Social and Religious History of the Jews*. New York: Columbia University Press, 1952.

Deferrari, Roy J. *Saint Basil, The Letters*. 4 vols. Cambridge, Mass.: Harvard University Press, 1962.

Der Meer, F. Van. *Augustine the Bishop, The Life and Work of a Father of the Church*. Translated by Brian Battershaw and G.R. Lamb. London and New York: Sheed and Ward, 1961.

Fox, Sister Margaret Mary. *The Life and Times of St. Basil the Great as*

Revealed in His Works. Washington D.C.: The Catholic University Press, 1939.

Frisch, Ephraim. *An Historical Survey of Jewish Philanthropy From the Earliest Times to the Nineteenth Century.* New York: The Macmillan Company, 1924.

Frye, Northrop. *The Great Code, The Bible and Literature.* New York and London: Harcourt Brace Jovanovich, 1982.

Hesiod, *Works and Days.* Translated by Apostolo Athanassakis. Baltimore: Johns Hopkins University Press, 1983.

The Holy Bible. Revised Standard Version, Containing the Old and New Testaments. New York: Thomas Nelson and Sons, 1953.

Homer. *The Odyssey.* Translated by E.V. Rieu. Baltimore: Penguin Books, 1962.

The Interpreters' Bible. The Holy Scripture in the King James and Revised Standard Versions with General Articles and Introduction, Exegis, Exposition for Each Book of the Bible. 12 vols. New York: Abington Press, 1951–57.

Jones, Alexander, ed. *The New Testament of the Jerusalem Bible.* Garden City, N.Y.: Doubleday and Company, 1969.

McCurdy, Helen. *The Quality of Mercy. The Gentle Virtues in Greek Literature.* New Haven: Yale University Press, 1940.

Maimonides, Moses. *The Guide for the Perplexed.* Translated by M. Friedlander. London: George Routledge and Sons Limited, New York: E.P. Dutton and Company, 1947.

————. *Mishneh Torah: Maimonides' Code of Law and Ethics.* Abridged and translated from the Hebrew by Philip Birnbaum. New York: Hebrew Publishing Company, 1974.

Moe, Henry Allen. "Notes on the Origin of Philanthropy in Christendom." In *Proceedings of the American Philosophical Society,* 105 (1961): 141–44.

Morison, E.F. *St. Basil and His Rule.* London: Oxford University Press, 1912.

Plumptre, E.H. *Aeschylos, Tragedies and Fragments.* Boston: D.C. Heath and Company, 1900.

Plutarch. *Plutarch's Moralia.* With an English translation by Frank Cole Babbitt. 16 vols. Cambridge, Mass.: Harvard University Press, 1969.

Seneca, Lucius Annaeus. *The Epistles of Seneca.* Translated by Richard M. Gummere. 3 vols. Cambridge, Mass.: Harvard University Press, 1962.

Watt, Mary Caroline. *St. Martin of Tours, The Chronicles of Sulpicius Severus Done into English from the French of Paul Monceaux.* London: Sands and Company, 1928.

Part Two   Middle Ages And Early Modern Times

Aland, Kurt, ed. *Martin Luther's 95 Theses.* Saint Louis: Concordia Publishing House, 1967.

Alpert, Michael. *Two Spanish Picaresque Novels. Lazarillo de Tormes (Anon.) and The Swindler (Francisco De Quevado)*. Harmandsworth: England. Penguin Books, 1969.

Ashley, W.J. *An Introduction to English Economic History and Theory*. 2 vols. New York: Putnam, 1898.

Aydelotte, Frank. *Elizabethan Rogues and Vagabonds*. Oxford: Clarendan Press, 1913.

Bacon, Francis. "Essays or Counsels Civil and Moral." In *The Harvard Classics*, 3:7–149. 50 vols. New York: P.F. Collier and Son, 1937.

Barron, Isaac. "The Duty and Reward of Bounty to the Poor." In *The Works of Dr. Isaac Barrow*, edited by Rev. T.S. Hughes, 2:308–80. 7 vols. London: A.J. Valpy, 1830–31.

Barron, Caroline M. "Richard Whittington: The Man Behind the Myth." In A.E.J. Hollaender and William Kellaway, *Studies in London History*, 192–248. London: Hodder and Staughton, 1967.

Blaiklock, E.M., and A.C. Keys, translators, *The Little Flowers of St. Francis and His Followers*. Ann Arbor, Michigan: Servant Books, 1985.

Bunyan, John. *The Annotated Pilgrim's Progress*. Chicago: Moody Press, 1980.

Chambers, C.K., comp. *The Oxford Book of Sixteenth Century Verse*. Oxford: Clarendon Press, 1932.

Chandler, Frank Wadleigh. *The Literature of Roguery*. 2 vols. Boston: Houghton Mifflin and Company, 1907.

Chaucer, Geoffrey. *The Canterbury Tales*. Rendered Into Modern English by J.U. Nicolson. Garden City, N.Y.: Garden City Publishing Company, Inc. 1934.

Clark, Peter. *English Provincial Society from the Reformation to the Revolution, Religion, Politics and Society in Kent, 1500–1640*. Hassocks, Sussex, England: The Harvester Press, 1977.

Cowper, J.M. *The Selected Works of Robert Crowley*. London: N. Trubner and Company for the Early English Text Society, 1872.

Emanuel, Cyprian W. *The Charities of St. Vincent De Paul; An Evaluation of His Ideas, Principles and Methods*. Washington D.C.: Catholic University of America, 1923.

Fuller, Thomas. *Church History of England*. 6 vols. Oxford: Oxford University Press, 1845.

———. *The Worthies of England*. 3 vols. London: Thomas Tegg, 1840.

———. *The Worthies of England*. edited with an introduction and notes by John Freeman. London: George Allen and Unwin, Limited, 1952.

Furlong, Monica. *Puritan's Progress*. New York: Coward, McCann and Geoghegan, 1975.

Giordani, Igino. *St. Vincent De Paul, Servant of the Poor*. Translated by Thomas J. Tobin. Milwaukee: The Bruce Publishing Company, 1961.

Helm, P.J. *England Under Yorkists and Tudors, 1471–1603*. London: C. Bell and Sons, Limited, 1968.

Imray, Jean. *The Charity of Richard Whittington. A History of the Trust*

Administered by the Mercers' Company, 1424–1966. London: Athlone Press, 1968.

Jenner, Michael. *Journeys into Medieval England*. London: Michael Joseph,1991.

Jessopp, Augustus, D.D., comp. *Wise Words and Quaint Counsels of Thomas Fuller*. Oxford: Clarendon Press, 1892.

Johnson, Richard. "The Nine Worthies of London." In *The Harleian Miscellany*, 12: 164–93. 12 vols. London: Robert Dutton, 1811.

Jordan, W.K. *Philanthropy in England, 1480–1660*. New York: Russell Sage Foundation, 1959.

————. *Social Institutions in Kent, 1480–1660, A Study in Changing Patterns of Social Aspirations*. In *Archeologia Cantiana*, 75 (1961).

Lambert, M.D. *Franciscan Poverty*. London: Society for Promoting Christian Knowledge, 1961.

Leach, A.F. *The Schools of Medieval England*. New York: Benjamin Blom, 1968.

Lines, Kathleen. *Dick Whittington*. Illustrated by Edward Ardizzone. New York: Henry Z. Walck, Inc., 1970.

Lysons, Samuel. *Model Merchant of the Middle Ages*. London: Hamilton Adams, and Co., 1860.

Martz, Linda. *Poverty and Welfare in Hapsburg Spain, The Example of Toledo*. Cambridge: Cambridge University Press, 1982.

Mather, Cotton. "Bonafacius." In Perry Miller, ed., *The American Puritans Their Prose and Poetry*. 216–18. Garden City, N.Y.: Anchor Books, 1956.

Matt, Leonard von, and Louis Coget. *St. Vincent De Paul*. Translated from the French by Emma Craufurd. Chicago: Henry Regnery Company, 1960.

Maynard, Theodore. *Apostle of Charity, The Life of St. Vincent De Paul* New York: The Dial Press, 1939.

Milton, John. *Paradise Lost. Paradise Regained, Samson Agonistes*. With a New Introduction by Harold Bloom. New York: Collier Books, 1962.

Mollat, Michel. *The Poor in the Middle Ages. An Essay in Social History* New Haven and London: Yale University Press, 1986.

Moore, Norman, M.D. *The History of St. Bartholomew's Hospital*. 2 vols. London: C. Arthur Pearson Limited, 1918.

Penn, William. *Some Fruits of Solitude*. In *The Harvard Classics* 1:331–416. 50 vols. New York: P.F. Collier and Son, 1937.

Pound, John. *Poverty and Vagrancy in Tudor England*. London: Longman Group Limited. 1971.

Rogers, James Thorold. *A History of Agriculture and Prices in England* Oxford: Oxford University Press, 1866.

Schama, Simon. *The Embarassment of Riches*. New York: Alfred A. Knopf, 1987.

Trevelyan , G.M. *English Social History, A Survey of Six Centuries, Chaucer to Queen Victoria*. London: Longmans, Green and Company, 1942.

Vives, Juan Luis. "On Assistance to the Poor." Translated by Sister Mary

Alice Trobriner. *A Sixteenth Century Urban Report*, 33–57. Chicago: School of Social Service Administration, University of Chicago, 1971.

Walton, Izaak. "The Life of Dr. John Donne." "The Life of Mr. George Herbert." In *Izaak Walton's Lives*. London: Thomas Nelson and Sons, Limited, n.d.

Wheatley, Henry B., ed. *The Diary of Samuel Pepys*. 2 vols. New York: Random House, n.d.

———. *The History of Sir Richard Whittington by T.H.* London: The Villon Society, 1885.

Youings, Joyce. *Sixteenth-Century England*. London: Allen Lane, 1984.

Part Three   The Eighteenth Century

Backscheider, Paula. *Daniel Defoe, His Life*. Baltimore: Johns Hopkins University Press, 1989.

Battestin, Martin C., with Ruthe R. Battestin. *Henry Fielding, A Life*. London and New York: Routledge, 1989.

Bindman, David. *Hogarth*. London: Thames and Hudson, 1981.

Boswell, James. *Life of Johnson*. Edited by R.N. Chapman, revised by J.D. Fleeman. Oxford: Oxford University Press, 1980.

Boyce, Benjamin. *The Benevolent Man, A Life of Ralph Allen of Bath* Cambridge, Mass.: Harvard University Press, 1967.

Brownlow, John. *The History and Objects of the Foundling Hospital, With a Memoir of the Founder*, 3rd ed. London: The Foundling Hospital, 1860.

Burns, Robert. *The Poetical Works of Burns*, Cambridge ed. Edited by Raymond Bentman. Boston: Houghton Mifflin Company, 1974.

Cook, Richard. *Bernard Mandeville*. New York: Twayne Publishers, Inc., 1974.

Cunnington, Phillis, and Catherine Lucas. *Charity Costumes of Children, Scholars, Almsfolk, Pensioners*. New York: Harper and Row Publishers, Inc., Barnes and Noble Import Division, 1978.

Defoe, Daniel. "Giving Alms No Charity." In *Defoe's Writings*, 13:153–88. 14 vols. Boston and New York: Houghton Mifflin Company, 1927.

———. *A Tour Through England and Wales*. 2 vols. London: J.M. Dent and Sons Limited, 1948.

Dobson, Austin, ed. *Steele, Selections from the Tatler, Spectator and Guardian*. Oxford: Clarendon Press, 1886.

———. *Henry Fielding, A Memoir*. New York: Dodd Mead and Company, 1900.

———. *A Paladin of Philanthropy and Other Papers*. London: Chatto and Windus, 1899.

Erskine-Hill, Howard. *The Social Milieu of Alexander Pope, Lives, Example and the Poetic Response*. New Haven: Yale University Press, 1975.

Fielding, Henry. *The Adventures of Joseph Andrews*. Edited by Martin C. Battestin, Middletown, Connecticut: Weslyan University Press, 1967.

———. *An Enquiry into the Causes of the Late Increase of Robbers and*

Related Writings. Edited by Malvin R. Zirker. Middletown: Conn.: Wesleyan University Press, 1988.

————. *Tom Jones. An Authoritative Text.* Edited by Sheridan Baker. New York, London: W.W. Norton and Company, 1973.

Ford, Newell B., ed. *The Poetical Works of Shelley,* Cambridge ed. Boston: Houghton Mifflin Company, 1874.

Franklin, Benjamin. *Writings.* New York: The Library of America, 1987.

Fuller, Thomas. *Gnomologia: Adagies and Proverbs: Wise Sentences and Witty Sayings, Ancient and Modern, Foreign and British.* London: B. Barker, 1732.

Gay, John. "The Beggar's Opera." In *Dramatic Works,* edited by John Fuller, 2: 1–65. 2 vols. Oxford: Clarendon Press, 1983.

Goldsmith, M.M. *Private Vices, Public Benefits, Bernard Mandeville's Social and Political Thought.* Cambridge: Cambridge University Press, 1985.

Goldsmith, Oliver. *The Poetical Works of Oliver Goldsmith.* Edited with Introduction and Notes by Austin Dobson. London: Oxford University Press, 1906.

Hetzenrater, Richard F. *The Elusive Mr. Wesley.* 2 vols. Nashville: Abingdon Press, 1984.

Johnson, E.D.H. *Paintings of the British Social Scene from Hogarth to Sickert.* New York: Rizzoli, 1986.

Lamb, Charles. "A Complaint of the Decay of Beggars." In *Essays of Eliah,* 148–55. London: G. Bell and Son, 1913.

Law, William. *A Serious Call to a Devout and Holy Life: The Spirit of Love.* Edited by Paul G. Stanwood. New York: Paulist Press, 1978.

Lonsdale, Roger, ed. *The New Oxford Book of Eighteenth Century Verse.* Oxford: Oxford University Press, 1984.

Mandeville, Bernard. "An Essay on Charity and Charity Schools." In *The Fable of the Bees, or, Private Vices, Public Benefits.* London: Edmund Parks, 1723.

More, Hannah. "Estimate of the Religion of the Fashionable World." In *The Works of Hannah More,* 1:287–376. 11 vols. London: Henry G. Bohn, 1853.

Nichols. R.H., and F. A. Wray. *The History of the Foundling Hospital.* London: Oxford University Press, 1935.

Pope, Alexander. *Epistles to Several Persons (Moral Essays).* Edited by F.W. Bateson. London: Methuen and Co., Ltd., 1961.

————. *The Complete Poetical Works of Alexander Pope.* Edited by Henry W. Boynton. Boston: Houghton Mifflin Company, 1903.

————. *The Poetical Works of Alexander Pope.* Edited by Sir Adolphus William Ward. New York: St. Martin's Press, 1964.

Porter, Roy and Dorothy Porter. *In Sickness and Health The British Experience 1650–1850.* London: Fourth Estate, Limited. 1988.

Rodgers, Betsy. *Cloak of Charity, Studies in Eighteenth-Century Philanthropy.* London: Methuen and Co., Ltd., 1949.

Scott, Sir Walter. "Advertisement." In *The Antiquary*, 1:9–22. 2 vols. New York: Harper and Brothers, 1901.

Semmel, Bernard. *The Methodist Revolution*. New York: Basic Books, Inc. 1973.

Shepherd, T.B. *Methodism and the Literature of the Eighteenth Century*. London: The Epworth Press, 1940.

Smollet, Tobias. *The Expedition of Humphrey Clinker*. Athens, Georgia: University of Georgia Press, 1990.

Southey, Robert. *The Life of Wesley and the Rise and Progress of Methodism*, with Notes by Samuel Taylor Coleridge. Edited with Introduction by Maurice H. Fitzgerald. 2 vols. London: Oxford University Press, 1925.

Steele, Sir Richard. *The Tatler*. Edited by Louis Gibbs. London: J.M. Dent and Sons, Limited. 1953.

Stephen, Leslie. *History of English Thought in the Eighteenth Century*. 2 vols. London: Smith, Elder and Company, 1876.

Thompson, John D., and Grace Goldin. *The Hospital: A Social and Architectural History*. New Haven: Yale University Press, 1975.

Wheatley, Henry B. *Hogarth's London*. London: Constable and Company, Ltd., 1909.

Part Four   The Nineteenth Century

Alison, William Pulteney. *Observations on the Management of the Poor in Scotland, and its Effects on the Health of Great Towns*. Edinburgh: William Blackwood and Sons, 1840.

Altick, Richard. *Presence of the Present. Topics of the Day in the Victorian Novel*. Columbus: Ohio State University Press, 1991.

―――. *Victorian People and Ideas*. New York: W.W. Norton and Company, Inc. 1973.

Best, G.F.A. "The Road to Hiram's Hospital, A Byway of Early Victorian History." In *Victorian Studies* 5 (1961–62), 135–50.

Beveridge, William Henry. "Charitable Trusts – A Charitable Chamber of Horrors and Other Notes." In *Voluntary Action*, 356–80. New York: The Macmillan Company, 1948.

Briggs, Asa. *The Making of Modern England 1783–1867, The Age of Improvement*. New York: Harper and Row, 1959.

Burton, Richard. *Personal Narrative of a Pilgrimage to El-Medinah and Meccah*. 3 vols. London: Longman, Brown, Green and Longmans, 1855, 1857.

―――. *The Book of the Thousand and One Nights. With an Introduction, Explanatory Notes . . . and a Terminal Essay*. 10 vols. Benares: The Burton Club, 1885.

Butt, John, and Kathleen Tillotson. *Dickens at Work*. London: Methuen and Co., Ltd., 1957.

Carlyle, Thomas. "Model Prisons." In *Carlyle's Latter-Day Pamphlets*, edited by M.K. Goldberg and J.P. Seigel, 60–108. Port Credit, Ontario: Canadian Federation for the Humanities, 1983.

Chalmers, Thomas D.D. *Statement in Regard to the Pauperism of Glasgow, From the Experience of the Last Eight Years.* Glasgow: Chalmers and Collins, 1823.

Coleridge, Ernest Hartley, ed. *The Poems of Samuel Taylor Coleridge.* London: Oxford University Press, 1957.

Cunningham, Valentine. *Everyone Spoke Against Dissent in the Victorian Novel.* Oxford: Clarendon Press, 1975.

Dickens, Charles. *The Adventures of Oliver Twist.* With an Introduction by Humphrey House. Oxford: Oxford University Press, 1987.

———. *Bleak House.* With an Introduction by Sir Osbert Sitwell. Oxford: Oxford University Press, 1987.

———. *Dombey and Son, Wholesale, Retail and for Exportation.* Oxford: Oxford University Press, 1987.

———. *The Letters of Charles Dickens.* 6 vols. to date. Oxford: The Clarendon Press, 1965–1988.

———. *The Life and Adventures of Nicholas Nickleby.* Oxford University Press, 1950.

———. *Martin Chuzzlewit.* New York: Grosset and Dunlap, 1935.

———. *The Mystery of Edwin Drood*, concluded by Leon Garfield, with an Introduction by Edward Blishen. London: Andre Deutsch, 1980.

———. *Our Mutual Friend.* Oxford: Oxford University Press, 1987.

———. *Sketches by Boz Illustrative of Every-Day Life and Every-Day People.* London: Oxford University Press, 1957.

Dostoevsky, Fyodor. *The Brothers Karamazov.* Translated and annotated by Richard Pevear and Larissa Volokhovsky. San Fransisco: North Point Press, 1990.

Edel, Leon, ed. *Henry James Letters, 1883–1895.* Cambridge, Mass.: Harvard University Press, 1980.

Eliot, George. *Adam Bede.* Edited with an Introduction by Stephen Gill. Penguin Books, 1980.

———. *Middlemarch.* Edited by Bert G. Hornbeck. New York: W.W. Norton, Inc., 1977.

Emerson, Ralph Waldo. *Essays: Second Series.* Cambridge, Mass.: Harvard University Press, 1983.

———. *The Journals and Miscellaneous Notebooks of Ralph Waldo Emerson.* 16 vols. Cambridge, Mass.: Harvard University Press, 1960–1982.

———. "Self Reliance." In *The Complete Works of Ralph Waldo Emerson*, 2:43–90. 12 vols. Boston and New York: Houghton Mifflin Company, 1903–04.

Glendenning, Victoria. *Anthony Trollope.* New York: Alfred A. Knopf, 1993.

Hall, N. John. *The Letters of Anthony Trollope.* 2 vols. Stanford, Calif.: Stanford University Press, 1983.

———. *Trollope, A Biography.* Oxford: Clarendon Press, 1991.

Hart, James D., ed. *RLS From Scotland to Silverado*. Cambridge, Mass.: Harvard University Press, 1966.

Hawthorne, Nathaniel. *The American Notebooks*. Edited by Claude Simpson. Columbus: Ohio State University Press, 1972.

———. *The Blithedale Romance and Fanshaw*. Columbus: Ohio State University Press, 1964.

———. *The English Notebooks*. Edited by Randall Stewart. New York: Modern Language Association of America, 1941.

———. *Mosses from an Old Manse*. Columbus: Ohio State University Press, 1974.

———. *Our Old Home: A Series of English Sketches*. Columbus: Ohio State University Press, 1970.

———. *The Complete Short Stories of Nathaniel Hawthorne*. Garden City, New York: Hanover House, 1959.

Himmelfarb, Gertrude. *The Idea of Poverty, England in the Early Industrial Age*. New York: Alfred A. Knopf, 1984.

———. *Poverty and Compassion, The Moral Imagination of the Late Victorians*. New York: Alfred A. Knopf, 1991.

Hobhouse, Sir Arthur. *The Dead Hand, Addresses on the Subject of Endowments and Settlements of Property*. London: Chatto and Windus, 1880.

House, Humphrey. *The Dickens World*. London: Oxford University Press, 1941.

Howells, William Dean. "Tribulations of a Cheerful Giver." In *Impressions and Experiences*, 150–88. New York: Harper and Brothers Publishers, 1896.

Hugo, Victor. *Les Miserables*. Translated by Norman Denny. Harmondsworth, England: Penguin Books, 1987.

James, Henry. *The Bostonians*. New York: Random House, 1956.

———. *Hawthorne*. New York: Harper and Brothers Publishers, 1879.

———. *The Princess Casamassima*. New York: Viking Press, 1989.

James, William. *The Will to Believe and Other Essays in Popular Philanthropy*. New York: Longmans, Green and Company, 1897.

Jewett, Sarah Orne. "The Spur of the Moment." In Richard Cary, ed., *The Uncollected Stories of Sarah Orne Jewett*, 365–71. Waterville, Maine: Colby College Press, 1971.

Johnson, Edgar. *Charles Dickens, His Tragedy and His Triumph*. 2 vols. New York: Simon and Schuster, 1952.

———. *Sir Walter Scott, The Great Unknown*. 2 vols. New York: The Macmillan Company, 1970.

Kaplan, Fred. *Dickens, A Biography*. New York: William Morrow and Co., Inc., 1988.

Keating, P.J., *The Working Classes in Victorian Fiction*. London: Routledge and Kegan Paul, 1971.

Kincaid, James R. *The Novels of Anthony Trollope*. Oxford: Clarendon Press, 1977.

Lascelles, E.C.P. "Charity." In G.M. Young, ed., *Early Victorian England*, 2:317–49. 2 vols. London: Oxford University Press, 1934.

Lowell, James Russell. *The Poetical Works of James Russell Lowell*, Cambridge ed. Revised and with a new Introduction by Marjorie R. Kaufman. Boston: Houghton Mifflin Company, 1978.

Lubove, Roy, ed. *Social Welfare in Transition, Selected English Documents, 1834–1909.* Introductory Essays by John Duffy and Samuel Mencher. Pittsburgh: University of Pittsburgh Press, 1966.

Owen, David. *English Philanthropy, 1600–1960.* Cambridge, Mass.: Harvard University Press, 1964.

Pope, Norris. *Dickens and Charity.* New York: Columbia University Press, 1978.

Prochaska, F.K. *Women and Philanthropy in Nineteenth Century England.* Oxford: Oxford University Press, 1980.

Rice, Edward. *Captain Sir Richard Burton.* New York: Charles Scribner's Sons, 1990.

Scott, Sir Walter. *The Antiquary.* 2 vols. New York and London: Harper and Brothers, 1901.

Smiles, Samuel. *Self-Help, With Illustrations of Conduct and Perserverance.* London: John Murray, 1958.

Stevenson, Lionel. *The Showman of Vanity Fair, The Life of William Makepeace Thackeray.* New York: Charles Scribner's Sons, 1947.

Thackeray, William Makepeace. *The History of Pendennis, His Fortunes and Misfortunes, His Friends and His Greatest Enemy.* New York: Wm. L. Allison, n.d.

———. *The Newcomes.* 2 vols. Cambridge: Cambridge University Press, 1954.

Thoreau, Henry D. *Walden.* Edited by J. Lyndan Shanley. Princeton, N.J.: Princeton University Press, 1989.

Tolstoy, Leo. *What Men Live By, Russian Stories and Legends.* Translated by Louis and Aylmer Maude. New York: Pantheon Books, 1944.

Trollope, Anthony. *An Autobiography.* With an Introduction by Charles Morgan. London: William and Northgate, Limited, 1946.

———. *Barchester Towers.* London: The Zodiac Press, 1975.

———. *Can You Forgive Her?* 2 vols. London: Oxford University Press, 1948.

———. "The Genius of Nathaniel Hawthorne." In *North American Review* 129 (1879), 203–22.

———. *The Warden.* With an Introduction by Ronald Knox. London: Oxford University Press, 1952.

Wordsworth, Jonathan, M.H. Abrams, and Stephen Gill, eds. *William Wordsworth: The Prelude, 1799, 1805, 1850.* New York: W.W. Norton and Company, 1979.

Wordsworth, William. *The Complete Poetical Works of Wordsworth*, edited by A. J. George. Boston: Houghton Mifflin Company, 1904.

———. *Yarrow Revisited and Other Poems.* London: Longman, 1835.

Young, G.M., ed. *Early Victorian England* 2 vols. London: Oxford University Press, 1934.

Part Five   1890s To The Present

Aleichem, Sholom. *Inside Kasrilevke*. Translated from the Yiddish by Isidore Goldstick. New York: Schocken Books, 1965.

Auchincloss, Louis. *False Gods*. Boston: Houghton Mifflin Company, 1992.

———. *The Golden Calves*. Boston: Houghton Mifflin Company, 1988.

Bangs, John Kendrick. *Mrs. Raffles*. New York: Harper and Brothers, 1905.

Bellamy, Edward. *Looking Backward: 2000–1887*. New York: Random House, Inc., 1951.

Benchley, Nathaniel. *Lassiter's Folly*. New York: Atheneum, 1971.

Berry, Faith, ed. *Good Morning Revolution, Uncollected Social Protest Writings by Langston Hughes*. New York: Lawrence Hill and Company, 1973.

Bercovici, Konrad. *Crimes of Charity*. New York: Alfred A. Knopf, 1917.

Bloom, Harold, ed. *Ralph Ellison*. New York and Philadelphia: Chelsea House Publishers, 1986.

———. *Zora Neale Hurston*. New York and Philadelphia: Chelsea House Publishers, 1986.

Bontemps, Arna. "A Woman With A Mission." In *The Old South*, 71–87. New York: Dodd, Mead and Company, 1973.

Bradbury, Ray. "The Beggar on the Dublin Bridge." In *Saturday Evening Post Stories*. Garden City, N.Y.: Doubleday and Company, Inc., 1962.

Chekhov, Anton. *Stories of Russian Life*. Translated by Marcia Fell. London: Duckworth, 1914.

———. *The Unknown Chekhov, Stories and Other Writings Hitherto Untranslated*. Translated by Avrahm Yarmolinsky. New York: The Noonday Press, 1954.

Clotfelter, Charles T., ed. *Who Benefits from the Nonprofit Sector?* Chicago: The University of Chicago Press, 1992.

Gullason, Thomas A., ed. *The Complete Short Stories and Sketches of Stephen Crane*. Garden City, N.Y.: Doubleday and Company, Inc. 1963.

Crossman, R.H.S. *The Role of the Volunteer in Modern Social Service*. Sidney Ball Memorial Lecture, 1973. Oxford: Clarendon Press, 1973.

Curti, Merle, and Roderick Nash. *Philanthropy in the Shaping of American Higher Education*. New Brunswick, N.J.: Rutgers University Press, 1965.

———. *Tradition and Innovation in American Philanthropy. In Proceedings of the American Philosophical Society* 105 (1961): 146–56.

Cutlip, Scott M. *Fund Raising in the United States*. New Brunswick, N.J.: Transaction Publishers, 1990.

Davies, William H. *The Autobiography of a Super Tramp*. Preface by Bernard Shaw. London: Jonathan Cape, 1955.

Du Bois, W.E.B. *The Philadelphia Negro*. New York: Schocken Books, 1967.

Dunne, Finley Peter. "The Carnegie Libraries." In *Dissertations by Mr. Dooley*, 177–82. New York: Harper and Brothers, 1906.

Dybek, Stuart. *Childhood and Other Neighborhoods*. New York: Viking Press, 1980.

Edgerton, Clyde. *In Memory of Junior*. Chapel Hill: Algonquin Books, 1992.

Ellis, Susan J., and Katherine H. Noyes. *By the People, A History of Americans as Volunteers*. San Francisco: Jossey-Bass Publishers, 1990.

Ellison, Ralph. *Invisible Man*. New York: Random House, 1952.

———. *Shadow and Act*. New York: Random House, 1953.

Fitzpatrick, Kathleen. "The Dorcas Society." In *The Weans of Rowallon*, 108–21. New York: Coward - McCann, Inc., 1937.

Forster, E.M. *Howard's End*. New York: Alfred A. Knopf, 1946.

Freeman, Mary E. *A Humble Romance and Other Stories*. New York: Harper and Brothers, 1887.

George, Henry. *Social Problems*. Garden City, N.Y.: Doubleday Doran and Company, Inc., 1930.

Gorky, Maxim. "My Travelling Companion." In *Selected Stories*, 103–6. Moscow: Progress Publishers, 1981.

———. *Tales from Gorky*. Translated by R. Nisbet Bain. New York: Funk and Wagnalls Company, n.d.

Hassler, Jon. *Grand Opening*. New York: William Morrow and Company, Inc., 1987.

Howells, William D. *A Hazard of New Fortunes*. 2 vols. New York: Harper and Brothers, 1890.

Hughes, Langston. *The Langston Hughes Reader*. New York: George Braziller, Inc., 1958.

———. "Professor." In *Laughing to Keep From Crying*, 79–105. Mattituck: New York, Aeonian Press, 1976.

James, Henry. "The Coxon Fund." In *Henry James' Shorter Masterpieces*, edited by Peter Rawlings, 1:169–234. 2 vols. Totawa, N.J.: Barnes and Noble, 1984.

Jewett, Sarah Orne. *A Native of Winby and Other Tales*. Boston and New York: Houghton Mifflin and Company, 1894.

Karp, David. *All Honorable Men*. New York: Alfred A. Knopf, 1956.

Keillor, Garrison. "Jack Schmidt, Arts Administrator." In *Happy to Be Here*, 3–14. New York: Penguin Books, 1983.

Kramer, Ralph H. *Voluntary Agencies in the Welfare State*. Berkeley: University of California Press, 1981.

Lagemann, Ellen C. *The Politics of Knowledge, The Carnegie Corporation, Philanthropy and Public Policy*. Middletown, Conn.: Wesleyan University Press, 1989.

Lerner, Gerda, ed. *Black Women in White America, A Documentary History*. New York: Vintage Books, 1973.

Lewis, Sinclair. *Arrowsmith*. New York: New American Library, 1961.

———. *Gideon Planish*. New York: Random House, 1960.

Lively, Penelope. *City of the Mind*. New York: Harper Collins Publishers, 1991.

Magat, Richard. *Philanthropic Giving*. New York: Oxford University Press, 1989.

Maurin, Peter. *Easy Essays*. Chicago: Franciscan Herald Press, 1984.

McCarthy, Kathleen D., ed. *Lady Bountiful Revisited: Women, Philanthropy, and Power*. New Brunswick, N.J.: Rutgers University Press, 1990.

Miller, William D. *Dorothy Day, A Biography*. San Francisco: Harper and Row Publishers, 1982.

Morrison, Toni. *Beloved*. New York: Alfred A. Knopf, 1987.

Nesbit, E. *The Bastables, The Story of the Treasure Seekers, The Wouldbe-goods*. New York: Franklin Watts, Inc., 1966.

———. *The Railway Children*. New York: Philomel Books, 1989.

Nevins, Allan. *Study in Power, John D. Rockefeller, Industrialist and Philanthropist*. 2 vols. New York: Charles Scribner's Sons, 1953.

Nissenson, Hugh. *In the Reign of Peace*. New York: Farrar, Straus, and Giroux, 1972.

O'Connell, Brian, and Ann O'Connell. *Volunteers in Action*. New York: The Foundation Center, 1989.

Penuel, Arnold M. *Charity in the Novels of Galdos*. Athens: University of Georgia Press, 1972.

Peretz, I.L. *Selected Stories*. Edited by Irving Howe and Eliezer Greenberg. New York: Schocken Books, 1974.

Perez Galdos, Benito. *Compassion*. Translated from the Spanish by Tony Talbot. New York: F. Ungar Publishing Company, 1962.

Piehl, Mel. *Breaking Bread, The Catholic Worker Movement and the Origin of Catholic Radicalism in America*. Philadelphia: Temple University Press, 1982.

Powers, J.F. *Morte D'Urban*. Garden City, N.Y.: Doubleday and Company, Inc., 1961.

———. *The Presence of Grace*. Garden City, N.Y.: Doubleday and Company, Inc., 1956.

———. *Wheat That Springeth Green*. New York: Alfred A. Knopf, 1988.

Raffel, Burton. "Foundations in Fiction: Philanthropic Folklore." In *Foundation News* 3 (May 1962), 7–10.

Rampersad, Arnold. *The Life of Langston Hughes*. 2 vols. New York: Oxford University Press, 1986–88.

Ross, Edyth L., comp. and ed. *Black Heritage in Social Welfare, 1860–1930*. Metuchen, N.J.: The Scarecrow Press, 1978.

Salamon, Lester M. "Social Services." In Charles T. Clotfelter, ed., *Who Benefits From the Nonprofit Sector?* 149–50. Chicago: University of Chicago Press, 1992.

Sharp, Margery. *The Faithful Servants*. Boston: Little, Brown and Company, 1975.

Sharpe, Tom. *Ancestral Vices*. London: Secker and Warburg, 1980.

Shaw, George Bernard. "Major Barbara." In *Bernard Shaw's Plays*, edited by Warren Sylvester Street, 1–73. New York: W.W. Norton Company, 1970.

———. "Socialism for Millionaires." In *Contemporary Review* 69 (1896), 204–17.

Stern, Richard. "Idylls of Dugan and Strunk." In *1968*, 131–71. New York: Holt, Rinehart and Winston, 1970.

Stewart, J.I.M. *Myself and Michael Innes, A Memoir*. London: Victor Gollancz, Limited, 1987.

———. "Sweets from a Stranger." In *Parlour 4 and Other Stories*, 175–84. London: Victor Gollancz, Limited, 1986.

———. *Vanderlyn's Kingdom*. New York: W.W. Norton and Company, 1967.

Strode, Josephine, ed. *Social Insight Through Short Stories, An Anthology*. New York: Harper and Brothers, 1946.

Titmuss, Richard. *The Gift Relationship, From Human Blood to Social Policy*. New York: Pantheon Books, 1971.

Updike, John. *The Poorhouse Fair*. New York: Alfred A. Knopf, 1977.

Van Til, Jon, and Associates. *Critical Issues in American Philanthropy*. San Francisco: Jossey-Bass Publishers, 1990.

Wall, Joseph Frazier. *Andrew Carnegie*. New York: Oxford University Press, 1970.

Whittemore, Reed. *The Self-Made Man and Other Poems*. New York: The Macmillan Company, 1959.

Williams, David. *Treasure in Oxford*. New York: St. Martin's Press, 1989.

Yezierska, Anzia. *Hungry Hearts*. New York: Grosset and Dunlap, 1920.

Index

Nissenson, Hugh, 190–91
Notebook (Hawthorne), 137

O
Odyssey, The (Homer), 5–9
"Of Abbeys" (Crowley), 29–30
"Of Almshouses" (Crowley), 30
"Old Cumberland Beggar, The"
  (Wordsworth), 87–88
Old Testament, 11
Oliver Twist (Dickens), 112–13
On Assistance to the Poor (Vives), 29
On Benefits (Seneca the Younger), 8–9
On Christian Doctrine (Saint Augustine),
  14–15
On Moral Obligations (Cicero), 7–8
"On the Death of Charles Turner Torrey"
  (Lowell), 126–27
Open Cage, The (Yezierska), 165
O'Reilly, John Boyle, 160
Organized charity, 159–65
Orphans, 200–201
Our Mutual Friend (Dickens), 113–14,
  118, 123

P
Palm Beach, Florida, 205
Paradise Lost (Milton), 46
"Paupers, The" (Quiller-Couch), 149
Peabody, Elizabeth Palmer, 131
Peacock, Thomas Love, 101–2
Penn, William, 48–50
Peretz, I.L., 156
Perez Galdos, Benito, 155
Peterkin Papers, The (Hale), 149
Petty, Sir William, 40–41
Philadelphia Negro, a Social Study, The
  (DuBois), 175
"Philanthropists, The," 121–22
"Philanthropist" (Whittemore), 194
Philanthropy
  definition of, 42
  in higher education and the arts, 169–
    81
  modern, 159–65
  motives for in nineteenth century, 107
  and reform, 121–33
Philanthropy in Short Fiction (Harmon),
  186
Pilgrim's Progress (Bunyan), 48

Plutarch, 6, 9
Poorhouse Fair, The (Updike), 146
Poorhouses, 149–51
Poor Law Report, 100–101
Poor laws, 99–101
Pope, Alexander, 71–73
Powers, J.F., 191–92, 195–96
"Prelude, The" (Wordsworth), 88
Princess Casamassima, The (James),
  131–32
Prior, James, 86
"Procession of Life, The" (Hawthorne),
  128
"Professor" (Hughes), 175
Prometheus Unbound, 82
Protestants, 45–50

Q
Quiller-Couch, Arthur, 149

R
Raban, Jonathan, 204–5
Raffel, Burton, 170
Rahere, 23
Railway Children, The (Nesbit), 185
"Reb Anshel the Golden" (Steinberg),
  155
"Record of Badalia Herodsfoot, The"
  (Kipling), 161
Reed, John, 155–56, 164
Religio Medici (Browne), 42–43
Religious charity, 202
Rich, Helen B., 205
Richardson, Samuel, 62
Rockefeller, John D., 159, 170
"Rolling Stone, A." (Gorky), 153
Roman Catholic Church, 28
Royal Hospital (Chelsea), 88
Ruskin, John, 162

S
Saint Augustine, 14–15, 180
Saint Basil the Great, 14
Saint Francis of Assisi, 25–26
Saint John, 13
Saint Louise de Marillac, 45
Saint Martin, 14
Saint Paul, 13
Saint Peter, 13
Saint Therese of Lisieux, 189